PRAYER
PARTNERS

PRAYER PARTNERS

Spiritual Enrichment for Your Marriage

Arnold Prater

ABINGDON PRESS
NASHVILLE

PRAYER PARTNERS:
Spiritual Enrichment for Your Marriage

Copyright © 1987 by Abingdon Press

This book is printed on acid-free paper.

Library of Congress Cataloging-in-Publication Data

PRATER, ARNOLD.
    Prayer partners
    1. Prayer. 2. Marriage—Religious aspects—Christianity.
    I. Title
BV215.P73   1987   248.3'2'0240655   87-11493

ISBN 0-687-33480-2 (alk. paper)

Scripture references marked KJV are from the King James Version of the
Bible.
    Those marked NKJV are from The New King James Version. Copyright
© 1979, 1980, 1982, Thomas Nelson, Inc., Publishers.
    All others are from the Revised Standard Version of the Bible,
copyrighted 1946, 1952, © 1971, 1973 by the Division of Christian
Education of the National Council of Churches of Christ in the U.S.A. and
are used by permission.

MANUFACTURED BY THE PARTHENON PRESS AT
NASHVILLE, TENNESSEE, UNITED STATES OF AMERICA

*T*his is for the staff and membership of Good Shepherd United Methodist Church, West Palm Beach, Florida, and for those of our spiritual family across the country who returned the questionnaires along with their prayers. Without them this book would have been impossible.

Foreword

*S*elf-help books are a dime a dozen, and some of them are worth about that much. Not so with *Prayer Partners*. It is a valuable resource, worth far more than you may have paid for it.

This is a self-help book in the truest sense of the word. Yet it points beyond ourselves. In fact, its theme is prayer, which is a beyond-ourselves business.

I can't think of many subjects that deserve more attention than prayer in the home, especially prayers of wife and husband together. And I doubt if there is anyone who could write such a book better than Arnold Prater.

He has experienced what he is writing about. Also, he has put forth an effort to "test the water," to do research and listen to what others have experienced and what they need. His book has a firm foundation in human reality.

The focus of the book is at the point of a big need: marriage partners who pray together. The first chapters hone in on the core of the issue—"Why Pray Together?"; "What If My Partner Won't Pray with Me?"; "Dos and Don'ts in Getting Started"; and "What Problems Should We

Expect?" The second half of the book addresses principles of prayer applicable to any Christian life, with such questions as "How Can We Release God's Power in Prayer?"; "Are the Prayers of Two Persons More Effective Than Those of One?"; and "Why Are Some Prayers 'Unanswered'?" So while the book has a specific how-to focus on married couples praying together, it confronts tough theological questions in a very helpful way.

Another reason I'm happy Arnold Prater has written this book is that he is such a dynamic communicator. He writes the way he speaks—in down-to-earth, easy-to-understand, convincing language. He says in his Preface that he has "attempted to bring this often profound subject down to the go-to-the-supermarket, pick-up-the-kids, business-meeting level of living we encounter as each day rolls along." He has accomplished his task. There is nothing dull or ponderous in Arnold Prater's writing. It has an almost homespun quality, in the best sense of that image—practical, earthy, honest, unpretentious, warm, personal, even humorous. All this is to say that Arnold Prater is an effective communicator.

One more word. This book throbs with what I call spiritual sensitivity and reality. The writer is not speculating or theorizing. He writes out of the heart and mind of lived experience. An integrity of language and personal account gives this book an authenticity I like.

I'm glad Arnold Prater has written *Prayer Partners,* and I am glad you are reading it.

Maxie D. Dunnam

Contents

Preface

*B*ecause my wife and I have shared a meaningful prayer life together for so many years, it was only gradually that I realized such is not the case with many Christian couples.

When this finally became clear to me I remembered seeing lots of helpful books on communication in marriage, but I had never seen one that zeroed in on *spiritual* communication.

Becoming convinced of the need for such a book, I thought, "Why not ask a significant number of couples to share their own experiences—both the joys and the problems?" And so I sent questionnaires to almost 1,000 people, representing roughly 1,800 couples and 200 singles—all in all, about 3,800 people.

Since prayer is a pretty private thing with most people I was gratified at the response. While many returned questionnaires mirrored the strength and mutual uplift derived from shared prayer, a majority expressed a deep yearning and a need to overcome shyness, reluctance, and other problems.

So this book came to be. In it I have attempted to bring this often profound subject down to the go-to-the-supermarket, pick-up-the-kids, business-meeting level of living we encounter as each day rolls along.

The thing I love about books is that they just lie there and wait. When you're ready, they're ready. My prayer is that the Spirit of God will direct toward this book the steps of many who are ready for it in their lives. Perhaps you are one of those.

Arnold Prater

Chapter I

Why Pray Together?

S ue leaned forward in her chair and, brows drawn together expressing deep sincerity, asked, "Where in the Bible does it say we must pray together in order to have a good marriage?"

She had asked a good question and it deserved an answer. Both Sue and Roger were devout Christians, growing rapidly in their walk with God. Their marriage was a happy one—fourteen years and two fine children, plus their dedicated life-style, bore witness to that. It was an honest question, though a bit defensive.

So I explained that although God's Word does not explicitly say that husband and wife should pray *together*, it certainly implies it and that to do so will please God greatly. (Later I will give the chapter and verse where this may be found.)

God knew I needed to deal with Sue's question at that time. I had been approached by so many partners (mostly women) who had expressed a fervent desire that their mates pray with them, and so many others who had testified to the richness of the experience, that I had become convinced of the great need for a book like this. But I had forgotten to ask the question Sue raised: Why pray *together*? If it is possible to have a happy, fulfilling, fruitful Christian home with each person pursuing a private prayer life, then why pray together? Sue forced me to wrestle with the answer before proceeding further with this book.

I earnestly believe God gave me some answers. But before dealing with them, let's discuss another question, which may help us understand why it is that some share their prayer lives with great rewards, while others who also have seemingly rich marriages do not pray verbally together. How have some couples gotten started on their shared prayer adventure?

Some Couples Pray Together from the Beginning

Miss Martha (my pet name for my wife) and I have been married a long time. We have prayed together, with some few exceptions, every day of our marriage.

I am not speaking now of table graces or "family altars." I am speaking of a regular time of prayer together when each of us prays aloud. The format of our prayers has changed radically from time to time. It has had to, what with two babies and ten thousand committee meetings, to say nothing of three years' separation caused by a war.

Both of us were raised in Christian homes where prayer was the norm rather than the exception. It was as natural for us to begin marriage praying together as it is for a bird to begin to fly.

Some Couples Begin as a Result of a Crisis

Both Jack and Eleanor knew something was wrong when the doctor came into the room. They could tell by the look on his face. In the delivery room, he had frowned as he held up their newborn baby boy.

They had experienced the birth together, had taken training so Jack could be present and lend loving support. It had been an exciting, spiritual time of deep sharing. They were shooting the rapids of ecstatic exhilaration on a raft of high happiness. But now their craft hit a boulder and began to sink rapidly as they heard the dreaded words, Down Syndrome.

When the doctor left they stared at each other in disbelief. Then their tears spilled out as they sought comfort in each other's arms. When the storm finally subsided, Eleanor raised her head and said brokenly, "Jack, let's pray."

So they prayed together for the first time, and as they did, there came upon both of them a peace they had never known before.

That experience was the start of something new and precious. As the years passed, they found in the practice of praying together the daily strength they needed to meet, head-on and triumphantly, the experience of having a Down Syndrome baby in their home to love and nurture for a few years.

Some Pray Together Only Occasionally

Many couples, though they do not pray together daily, have no aversion to it. When a crisis arises, they naturally turn to prayer. One couple prays together every year on their anniversary; another has made it a practice to share their prayers at Thanksgiving; still others find joy in sharing prayer after great mountaintop experiences.

Ben and Janice were members of our church. They had come to the Lord Jesus Christ during the year and were growing rapidly in their faith.

It was the custom of our church to conduct a twenty-four-hour prayer vigil on New Year's Eve, each couple praying for a thirty-minute period. Ben and Janice had signed up for prayer at 2:00 A.M. Janice could hardly wait to share with me the joy they had found.

"Think of it," she said in my office the next day. "One year ago last night we were out on a wild party—I wouldn't even tell you how wild! And last night, for the first time in our lives, we celebrated the New Year on our knees before God!"

She sighed with joy. "Wow! Talk about a different road to travel! I still can't believe it! Ben and I actually prayed together for thirty whole minutes. Thank you, Lord!"

Some Never Do

Allow me to be personal for a moment. My father and mother were a truly happy couple. Although Mother died at the age of forty-eight, she and my father gave us a priceless heritage of Christian love and family togetherness.

I can say in all honesty that not once did we four children ever hear a cross or unkind word from one to the other. This is not to say it never happened. Perhap it did, for my parents were certainly human. But if cross words arose, they never reached our ears.

Since my father was an evangelical minister, one would have expected him to be the head of a Christian household. He certainly was, and I dare to believe that our home was (if I may use the term) super-Christian! Yet, except for table blessings, my father and mother never prayed together with us. There was, as one would expect, silent prayer as they knelt together at the bedside before retiring, but never a shared verbalization.

I would not want to lay a guilt trip on anyone or cause couples to feel they were substandard disciples simply because they do not share their verbal prayers. I know many who do not, and whose love for the Lord I would not question in the least. I am simply making the point that it is never too late to begin.

Two persons may certainly be prayer partners without verbalizing their prayers together; there is no argument about that. But one of the main purposes of this book is to point out the extra blessings God can give two people who lovingly communicate aloud with their heavenly Father. Further, it is still true that "the family that prays together stays together."

So Why Pray *Together?*

Now we are back where we started. Sue's question remains to be answered. I am happy and eager to get to it, now that we have prepared the way and made clear that it is not an absolute for experiencing the far-flung blessings of the Kingdom. Here are some answers.

It Blesses God

There is a praise verse in Psalm 103: "Bless the LORD, O my soul; and all that is within me, bless his holy name!" (Ps. 103:1). That verse bothered me for a long time. How could I bless God? The word *bless* usually means "bestow good things upon," so I certainly understood how Almighty God could bless me, but how could I ever return the favor? It was years before I understood.

But I saw it perfectly illustrated just a few days ago. Our daughter Judy's three-year-old had been playing with his little eighteen-month-old cousin, Stephanie. They were preparing to leave when Jesse Lee went over to Stephanie, put his arms about her, and gave her a kiss.

Judy's eyes glistened as she turned to us and said, "Oh,

how that blesses me!" It was a precious and tender moment (and it zapped their grandparents pretty good, too!).

It is perfectly clear to me now how our heavenly Father is blessed when He observes His earthly children perform loving acts together out of the sincerity of their love.

So when God sees two of His children, joined together in lifelong commitment, place their arms about each other and kneel before Him to pour out their love, adoration, and needs, what kind of God wouldn't be deeply gratified and blessed? Praying together blesses God.

It Helps God Fulfill His Plan

Did you ever ask yourself, Why did God invent marriage? Well, if you did, you can find the answer in the very beginning of the Bible: "The Lord God said, 'It is not good that the man should be alone; I will make him a helper fit for him.' . . . Therefore a man leaves his father and his mother and cleaves to his wife, and they become one flesh" (Gen. 2:18,24).

What do you think it means for a man and woman to "become one flesh"? If you only read something sexual into that, you completely miss the larger and greater meaning. God's ultimate purpose goes far beyond the instruction that they "be fruitful and multiply" (Gen. 1:28). God decreed marriage so that a man and a woman could begin a *lifelong process of loving each other into the fullness of personhood.*

You see, there is a sense in which we are never fulfilled as persons until someone else loves us into that fulfillment. When God created Adam, I imagine He was pleased with His work. Here was the ideal man, with a sharp administrative mind and a strong body crafted to physical perfection. But even for this ideal man something was missing. Adam had certain inadequacies, certain lacks and needs, *simply because he was alone.*

Therefore God created a companion who would be "fit for him"—literally, "corresponding to him." She would fill in the gaps, bring to life's situations those needed qualities he did not have; and he would do the same for her. They would fit together so well, in fact, that in the eyes of the world they would think and act as one person—"one flesh." And in that oneness, each partner would enter into the fullness of personhood.

Let's look at an analogy in God's plan for our salvation. When we are born physically, spiritually we are nonpersons. That is, we are spiritually dead in the eyes of God because of our sin-nature. We are made in the "image of God" but we are lifeless images. We have not yet been brought to life.

But, God's Word tells us, when we receive Jesus Christ as Lord and Savior, "We have passed out of death into life" (I John 3:14)—we are born a second time. This time around, we are filled with the life of God. The Holy Spirit has wooed and won us, and God has loved us into existence as spirit-persons. Doesn't that excite you? Every time I think of it, it sets the glory-bells ringing in my heart!

In a very real way, marriage is a parallel to that new birth. Although the new birth takes place at the *very moment* we, of our own free choice, receive Christ as Lord and Savior, in marriage, loving each other into fullest personhood is a *lifelong* process.

As mutual love within us grows, so our defenses gradually fall away, and more and more we risk making ourselves more vulnerable to each other. Love like God's always makes itself vulnerable, though sometimes it may lead to a cross.

Ideally, then, there comes a time when the trust between two persons, springing out of mature love, brings a couple together until their identities are completely established within each person and within each other. The uniqueness of each is retained but the intertwining of the selfless love each has for the other is completed, so that the "two become one."

This, then, is the greater and deeper meaning of God's purpose in ordaining marriage—that "the two might become one flesh," each completed by and in the other. They have loved each other into completion as persons.

This is why shared prayer aids God in His plan of establishing marriage. For as we shall see a bit later, the beautiful rhythm of continually shared communication with God is like the lapping of the ocean waves upon the beach, making the restless and ever-shifting sand firm and solid.

That is the kind of sand upon which you can build your house, for under the geological miracle of God, it becomes an immovable rock!

Chapter II

What If My Partner
Won't Pray with Me?

W hen we evaluated the results of the questionnaires
we had sent out, we received confirmation of one
fact we had already learned through years of experience:
Far more men won't pray with their wives than the other
way around.

The problems people described in getting their mates to
pray with them were identical, regardless of sex, but since
more men than women were uncooperative, here we will
use men in our examples, bearing in mind that the problem
can apply to either.

Here are a few reasons for the correspondents' refusal to
share prayer.

"I'm Outgoing, and He's Shy"

Understanding some of the reasons your mate is a shy
person not only helps you to understand him, but also
deepens your tenderness toward him, thus robbing the
enemy of the chance to plant resentment in your own heart.
Resentment is a touch of arsenic in the cup of life. If it is

drunk daily over a long period of time, it produces symptoms that are hard to diagnose. Finally, if you do not stop to examine what is in the cup, it can kill any joy in your life. And it can kill your marriage.

People are shy for a reason. It is not a matter of genes, but of jolts. Perhaps your mate had a domineering, authoritative father who did not grant him the privilege of having opinions of his own. His ideas or opinions were scornfully rejected until finally he concluded that they were, in fact, unworthy. So he drew in his antennae and quit transmitting; that was the only way he could keep from being hurt. One could uncover many other reasons, but we should remember that shyness is the darkened window through which we must look to see another's pain.

Your deepest motive in marriage is to love your mate into the fullness of personhood. We will deal with ways to go about this at the conclusion of this chapter.

"I'm a 'Private' Person"

Kathryn is, by her own description, a private person. "I love my husband very dearly," she said, "but he is truly the head of the household. He is a very successful businessman, thoroughly outgoing and self-assured."

Then she described herself (and many other women, according to the survey): "I love flowers and books. Besides my work for the Lord, I enjoy drama and art. . . . And when it comes to God, I enjoy Him most of all. I'm the one the hymn writer might have had in mind when he wrote,

> And He walks with me, and He talks with me,
> And He tells me I am His own;
> And the joy we share as we tarry there,
> None other has ever known.

"My walk with the Lord is so very deep and so very, very personal, as much as I love my husband, I could never bring myself to share that intimacy even with him!"

I respect that and accept it, for there are people whose prayer-lives are utterly their own. Their joy and their lives are their witness to the world of the Savior who lives within.

But again, Christ is in the life-changing business. So you and I cannot judge who are the Kathryns of this world and who are those who don't want to share their spiritual lives simply because of fear. God is the judge of that. Above all, we do not limit Him by saying that our husbands or wives are "just made that way and could never change."

"He's a Christian, But Not as 'Turned on' as I Am"

Among the people of Christ's Church, I suspect this is the most common problem. Much to our shame, women seem to be more deeply excited about Jesus Christ than are we men.

Look about you the next time you go to worship. Count the women present. In the average congregation, they outnumber men about two to one.

There was a time when we could say, "Oh, well, men make the living. They are wrapped up in their work, they must support the family, so it is easy for them to get their priorities misplaced."

But in our rapidly changing culture, this is no longer true. The work force today is approaching equal numbers of men and women. Add to this the number of single persons who, by reason of divorce or death, have been forced to take a job. You can readily see that "making a living" is not really an excuse for lukewarmness. There are *still* far more "turned on for Christ" women than men. We cannot go deeply into the why of it, for here we are concerned with how to overcome it.

Mary Jean made the mistake of getting the cart before the horse. She tried for years, she said, "to get my husband to pray with me, when he was not even excited about Jesus Christ, much less prayer."

Fortunately, she saw the error of her approach and began to concentrate on the chief need—in a loving, understanding way, to help her husband deepen his commitment by her own example and prayers. It worked!

Mistakes to Avoid

All right, so he won't pray with you, and you really yearn for things to be changed. Well, here are a few things you must not do, for they thwart the Holy Spirit, who desires this sharing more than you.

First, don't be pushy. So often in their eagerness for the communion of shared prayer (or even conversion itself!) some mates make the mistake of overaggressiveness. Nagging is still nagging, though it may be for a good cause. The pushy mate invites rejection by bringing up the subject with great regularity.

Most humans do not wish to be pushed into anything, whether it is buying a car or new clothes, emptying the garbage, or praying together. Many a person has alienated a mate from the idea of prayer by trying to *be* the Holy Spirit instead of letting the Holy Spirit work.

Another form of pushiness is to leave books, tracts, or cassette tapes lying around in conspicuous places. This insults the other's intelligence and is sure to accomplish the opposite of the desired result. I guarantee it, and so does Proverbs: "A continual dripping on a rainy day and a contentious woman [or man!] are alike" (Prov. 27:15).
nAnd don't play the martyr. Martyrs are wonderful, provided they never discover they are martyrs. Once they find out, they are the worst pests in the world.

So What Shall I Do?

Well, there are two things you can do. The first is to *pray for your mate.* We've ruled out trying to change your spouse singlehandedly, and rightly so, since this is the kind of change that can be made only by the Holy Spirit, with His power and subtlety. Pray specifically, then, that your mate will be willing to share prayer with you.

And as you pray, *count on God's help.* The improbable and the impossible look the same to God. That is the message we want to post at all four corners of this problem. We are Christians; we keep our eyes focused on the answer, not the problem. We believe in, and expect, victory; we are believers, not doubters. When we pray, we expect answers.

So many people really do not. They just fling their prayers out into the heavens and hope God might just happen to jet by and grab them off with his skyhook.

Then they begin to think, "Oh, well, what's the use? I've been praying for years and nothing has happened. My husband will never change! I guess I should be satisfied that he is a Christian and leave it at that."

When we think in such negative pictures, it not only affects our attitude toward this particular problem, but spills over into many other areas, until it becomes a mindset. We become like Indian work elephants. When they are babies, they are chained to steel stakes set in concrete. The tiny elephants pull and strain for weeks until they finally realize they cannot get loose. Then even after they are grown their handlers can drive a small stake six inches into the ground, tether the elephant to it with a thin rope, and the elephant will not try to escape. It is enslaved by its own mindset.

So it is that when we set limits on God *we* begin to live within those limits, as if our setting them makes them valid. Thus the power we possess in prayer becomes a 6-volt current running along a 110-volt wire, and the result is that we have cheated ourselves.

See Your Mate as You Desire Him to Be

The Lord Jesus Christ promised with his own lips, "Therefore I tell you, whatever you ask in prayer, believe that you have received it, and it will be yours" (Mark 11:24).

While it is true that we cannot violate the free choice of another with our prayers, it is our prayers that sometimes release God to work in the lives of other people. He is set free to bring about things that otherwise He would have left undone because of His own self-limitation. Sometimes He *needs us* to use *our* free choice to pray earnestly! What a fantastic thought! But that is the bedrock source of the power of intercessory prayer.

Here is something *you* can do to add to your own *belief* in your prayers and bring into action the law of faith that Jesus proclaimed in Mark 11:24. Visualize your mate the way you desire him. (Remember, we are using the masculine gender, but it applies to either sex.) See him as perhaps kneeling at your bedside with his arm about you as you pray together, or perhaps seated at a table beside you with his hand in yours.

If he is shy, hear his words as confident and strong. If he is not a "turned on" Christian, see the glow on his face when he becomes an excited disciple. If he is not a Christian at all, see him the day he receives Christ as his Lord and Savior, and sense the joy as you celebrate together.

The visualizing process is, of course, *not the reality*, but it is a *valid vehicle* (for it is God-given) to help bring about the reality, in much the same way the juice or wine and bread in Holy Communion are not the actual body and blood of our Lord, but valid vehicles to make the actual presence of Christ more real.

Maintain a Spirit of Persevering Love

In the final analysis it is *your* loving spirit that will help to bring your mate to fulfillment as a completed person. What is true in converting a non-Christian mate may be true also in a spouse's growth toward shared prayer. As the Holy Spirit wrote through Peter, "Likewise you wives, be submissive to your husbands, so that some, though they do not obey the word, may be won without a word by the behavior of their wives" (I Peter 3:1). Christianity is not as much a *conception* as a *contagion*.

Finally, never give up! Our son was twenty-six years old before he could pray aloud. Until then, other than little childhood prayers, the only prayer we ever heard him utter was, "God bless Mom and Dad, thank you for this food. Amen."

But then one day God did a new thing in his life. His discipleship was upgraded tremendously and now he will pray at the drop of a hat. Many times when we called him long distance he would say, "Well, we'd better have prayer together!" Then he'd pray about $25 or $30 worth! We had waited twenty-six years!

When we give up, we simply forget who God is and tacitly admit our belief—"Oh, well, maybe God is not up to this after all!" We need to remember who God is. We need to remember who God says our mate is. We need to remember Calvary. We need to remember who Jesus is.

After the Civil War, General H. B. Gordon was a candidate for the United States Senate from the state of Georgia. During that time southern Senators were elected by state legislatures.

In the Georgia legislature there was a veteran who had served with the General but, because of personality clashes, was not fond of him. He decided to vote against the General in favor of another man. He got to his feet to cast his ballot

27

when suddenly his eye fell upon the jagged scars that marked the face of General Gordon—the scars that bore silent witness to pain, valor, and suffering.

The old soldier hesitated, then exclaimed quietly, "I cannot vote against him. . . . I had forgotten the scars."

When you pray, you must not forget who Jesus is. You must not sell Him short. Remember His pain and His scars and His power.

Perhaps you too must be willing to pay a price. Remember that your loved one is worth whatever price you must pay. For we know there is no birth without pain. And we know also that the one being born probably is not the one who bears the most pain.

You are asking for a prayer partner. Then pray on!

Chapter III

What Are the Advantages of Praying Together?

A gain it needs to be said that without shared prayer, you may have a beautiful, fulfilling marriage that pleases God. But it also should be pointed out that couples who incorporate this experience into their everyday lives enjoy some blessings and advantages others may miss.

It Adds a New Dimension to Marriage

Francis Forde is a gentle Christian man you would love to have for a close friend. If you don't have a friend like Francis, you should search for one. Sometimes I think he does nothing but go around looking for ways he can be of loving service, usually by just doing what some would call little things for people.

Recently he let me in on one of the intimacies of his marriage. Since the Fordes are so well loved, they quite naturally receive a big stack of Christmas cards each year.

Francis said, "We save the cards, and each morning of the year, as we pray together, we take one of the cards, place it before us and include that person in our prayers for that day!" What a delightful idea!

"Then," he said, "If we receive forty cards, by year's end we have prayed for each person almost ten times!" I could see it in his eyes. This was a deep and growing dimension in their marriage—the joy of intercessory prayer together for dear loved ones.

This is but one dimension of shared prayer which unfolds as time passes, but perhaps this one illustration of shared intercession will make the point. That other new dimensions await the couple who share prayer in marriage may be legitimately inferred, I believe, in one of our favorite Scripture verses: "Eye hath not seen, nor ear heard, neither have entered into the heart of man, the things which God hath prepared for them that love him" (I Cor. 2:9 KJV).

Roughly paraphrased (very roughly!) in my native Ozarkian tongue, this means "Practice it! You ain't seen nothin' yet!"

It Adds a New Dimension to Your Private Prayer-Life

In no way is shared prayer meant to replace your own personal walk with the Lord. But it will add a new dimension to your prayer-life if for no other reason than it allows you to approach God *with someone else.*

The mutually shared experience of approaching God together is totally different from individual prayer-life, because here your words are heard by *another person,* as well as by God.

Joan is one of those gifted persons who can express herself well in a letter. She said, "Since Eric and I have begun to pray together I have had a new sensation. When we pray I feel as if I am not only giving myself away to God, but I am giving part of myself away to Eric."

She added, "To my surprise, I found my own private times with the Lord growing dearer. I am able to relax more in God's presence and be more open and honest with Him!"

What was happening? Joan was simply fulfilling one of God's deepest laws. When you give, you receive more; when you sow, you reap a multiplied harvest; when you die to self, you begin to live. Here is one of the many ways Jesus said it: "Give, and it will be given to you; good measure, pressed down, shaken together, running over, will be put into your lap" (Luke 6:38).

It Allows You to Verbalize Love Feelings

You would be surprised by some of the things I have learned from listening to Miss Martha when we pray together. Some have shocked me, some have amazed me, but most of all, they have blessed me!

Miss Martha is a very outgoing person. People usually fall in love with her instantly—they don't have to build up to it! I really don't believe she has ever had an enemy!

But there is a side of her that I alone know. In many ways she is a very shy person. Although she does well, it terrifies her to appear before an audience. Some folks show off, some "glow off." Miss Martha glows off.

I'm about to let you in on a very intimate and precious thing. After many years of praying together, one night I heard her tell God something she had never said directly to me, although she had *demonstrated* it again and again. She repeatedly tells me of her love, but she had never said it quite like this.

She prayed, "Dear Lord God, I just want to thank you for sending this man into my life. Outside of you, he is the greatest thing that ever happened to me. He is my Rock of

Gibraltar, and when I have one arm in his and one in yours, I can make it just fine!"

You think I wasn't blessed by that? What man wouldn't be? I tell you, the angel band in heaven played a hoedown, and all the Hallelujahs I ever knew joined hands and did a joy-dance around the cockles of my heart!

However, you must understand that when you have been together as long as we have, you become pretty prejudiced about your mate! (Well, if you *must* know, it's been more than forty years!)

It Encourages Mutual Vulnerability

When human beings say or do something that renders them vulnerable to others, there can be no higher expression of trust. If I make myself vulnerable to you, I'm saying, "I trust you completely not to take advantage of this and cause me pain." That is complete trust.

When you made Jesus Christ Lord of your life, you made yourself vulnerable to him. You said in effect, "Lord, I'm trusting you to take my life and guide it along the path that will bring the greatest ultimate reward to both of us. I trust you to bring me to salvation, not destruction."

As you grow in prayer, defenses you had erected will begin to crumble. Perhaps you were not even aware of them, but as they fall they will expose *the real you* to the other person as you expose the real you to God. For remember, ears other than God's are listening.

You make yourself more vulnerable with trust and without fear. And in response, the other person generally begins to do likewise.

What a tremendous aid this is to God, who is teaching us to truly "become one flesh," to love each other into the fullness of personhood.

It Builds on God's Promises

The Word of God contains many promises which relate specifically to shared prayer. Here is perhaps the most familiar and beloved: "Again I say to you, if two of you agree on earth about anything they ask, it will be done for them by my Father in heaven. For where two or three are gathered in my name, there am I in the midst of them" (Matt. 18:19-20).

Does this mean that two of you can generate more power than one? Does it mean that two persons, praying together, can override the free will of another? Is this a blank check from God, on which we are to fill in the results?

These are all very deep, very important, and very fair questions, and I promise to deal with them, as well as with other questions, in a chapter devoted to those very problems.

For now, let's be content that whether we understand all the mysteries of prayer or not, we will believe very firmly two more of God's promises:

I am watching over my word to perform it.
Jeremiah 1:12b

So shall my word be that goes forth from my mouth;
    It shall not return to me empty
but it shall accomplish that which I purpose
    and prosper in the thing for which I sent it.
Isaiah 55:11

On what other foundation as durable and satisfying as that could you build your prayer-life together? No storm can sweep away prayer houses built on the unchanging Word. For "the truth of the LORD endureth forever" (Ps. 117:2b KJV).

It Provides Mutual Encouragement

It was a beautiful day. You started out in the morning with a singing heart. It was good to be alive, and your spirit was bursting with joy as you counted your blessings and reflected on the goodness of God.

Then the roof fell in. Like unwanted creepie-crawlers, here came unforeseen problems. You had a fender-bender, the boss was crabby, the temperature was 90 degrees when the air conditioner broke down, and a call from school brought news that Junior had fallen off the slide and needed X-rays. So on and on stretch the possibilities that lurk within each day.

There went your beautiful mood! As some lovely soap bubble released by a child floats beautifully upward, catching all the lovely colors of the rainbow for a brief moment and then bursts, so your inner joy "poofs" away! We live with the fact that we are creatures of varying mood levels because we inhabit bodies that are subject to all sorts of environmental pressures.

Imogene confided, "Sometimes when Jon comes home in the evening he brings the day's problems with him. After I give him time to relax, I find I can serve as God's channel of encouragement by praying with him."

She added, "That works both ways. More than once when I've been down in the dumps, through his prayers with me Jon has reminded me of God's love, His power, and His Presence, and I've had my joy restored." Shared prayer can sometimes be like the steam valve on a pressure cooker!

It Is a Spiritual 911 Number!

We have already seen how a crisis brought Jack and Eleanor to shared prayer when they were told their baby was a Down Syndrome child. But the couple that has developed a shared-prayer relationship across the years often discover, when the ominous black clouds of crisis envelope them, that unknowingly, they have become possessors of a tremendous power plant.

I well remember the night a phone call brought us the news that our little six-month-old grandson, Jesse Lee, was in intensive care, diagnosed as having spinal meningitis. The outlook, from a human point of view, was pretty hopeless.

I was so overcome with grief and emotion that night, I could not pray verbally at all. But faith rose up like a roaring lion to Miss Martha and, as we said in days past, "she prayed a hole in the sky!" The anointing of God was upon her, and the power spilled over and touched me, and I knew in my deepest heart that this crisis would end in victory.

The story of Jesse Lee's healing by the Lord was told in *How to Be Happy in an Unhappy World* (Nashville: Thomas Nelson, 1983). My point here is that when the crisis came, we had somewhere to turn *together!* And because our "hiding place" had been long established, help came quickly to the scene; we were given spiritual first aid and were heavily saturated with the peace that passes all understanding!

Shared prayer is a 911 number, placed there to meet our needs in great emergencies. And life is so set up that sooner or later the dilemma and the person are always brought together. If not sooner, then later, because of the X-factor of death. But it happens to everybody.

Sometimes only one member of the team is involved, and then shared prayer becomes a treasure chest, opened to spill out its glistening gold and sparkling jewels.

When Miss Martha's mother died, no other immediate relatives were nearby. The sole responsibilities were hers for a grief-filled twenty-four hours. During that time, again she came to my arms so that the Holy Spirit could use me as His vehicle to bring the strength and comfort she needed in shared prayer together.

A little girl and her mother watched as an eagle soared high in the blue sky. It soared upward, sideways, and banked steeply, time and time again. Finally it began a very slow descent, circling widely until it finally settled into its nest on a great jagged cliff.

The little girl pointed and cried, "Look, mother, the eagle got so tired it had to stop flying!"

The mother replied, "No, darling, the eagle hasn't given up flying. It just had to go to its resting place for a while, and then it will fly higher than ever!"

Sometimes the dilemma and the person come together and one can fly no longer. What a blessing to have the nest of shared prayer into which we can settle and rest for a while.

Chapter IV

Dos and Don'ts
in Getting Started

I n the exciting process of getting started on an adventure of shared prayer, it is vital that you get started right. As is true of many things, if you begin with a problem, you will end with a problem, and in the process, you become part of the problem.

So here are some meat-and-potato, down-to-earth suggestions which will, I believe, immeasurably help a couple just beginning this grand new experience.

I would not want to give the impression that every time you pray with your partner you will start shooting out laser beams of glory and snap, crackle, and pop with the ecstasy of experiencing God. No way.

No, you will need to begin in the same world in which you have been living. It's a world of dirty clothes, honking drivers, annoying interruptions, tears, laughter, exhaustion, and exhilaration. A world of bee stings, report cards, and bills. Your world will not change much, but *you will!* That's what it's all about, anyhow, isn't it? So, out of our long experience of shared prayer, and out of the experience of many others who took part in our survey, here are some dos and don'ts in getting started. First, some don'ts.

Don't Require Both to Pray Aloud

It is better if both pray aloud, but if one of you can pray verbally, then don't insist that the other do the same. As we have said, perhaps your mate feels awkward or is shy. If this is the case, then let him read a psalm aloud and then you lead in prayer.

More often than not, there will come a time when your mate will be so familiar with this shared experience that you can quietly suggest, after he has read the Scripture, "Wouldn't you like to say a little prayer this morning and let me read the psalm?" Then bow your head and wait, but not long. if there is no response, just say, "It's O.K., Dear," and resume.

But here it is very, very important to be led by the Holy Spirit. He knows when the ground has been properly plowed and furrowed and is ready to receive the seed. It may take a few months, but wait for God. He is always on time!

This Is a Special Time for the Two of You

Don't, as a rule, include the children in this special time. This is just for you and your spouse. Certainly include the children in other experiences of prayer—at the table and on other occasions. In days gone by many Christian couples had "family altars" at home where they would gather once each day for family prayer.

Sadly, because of this souped-up, break-neck culture in which we live, it is becoming a rarity to find such families. It is a sad thing and has contributed to the decline of our national values, but that's the way it is.

What we are talking about here is a special time for you both, somewhat like having a date, or sharing a sundae, or walking on the beach, but vastly deeper and more precious. So let it be just for the two of you.

Don't Use Prayer to "Get at" Your Partner

Early in our marriage I learned this lesson. One evening when we came together for our prayer, I had had a hard day—but not as hard as Miss Martha's. The children were sick, it rained all day, she had done a big washing and ironing, and on top of that, she had virtually ruined her oven-cooked supper. Her day had been a real bummer.

In my prayer that night, I said, "Lord, help Martha to be a bit more careful in her cooking!"

Don't ever do it, brother, don't ever do it!

Seriously, there will come times when it will be a great temptation to criticize or otherwise voice a dissatisfaction with your partner. *Don't!*

Never try to manipulate, educate, direct, or accuse each other under the guise of prayer. Putting "Dear God" in front of such words does not make them a prayer.

One day Jesus said (my paraphrase of John 13:34): "Fellows, I've been with you three years now, you don't need a revised version of the Ten Commandments flung down from a smoking mountain. You need only one more new one—love one another."

Any time two human beings relate to each other in an unloving manner, especially under the guise of prayer, they are outside the will of God!

Don't Omit Your Prayer-time Because of Anger

Prayer is God's antibiotic. It invades the tissues of anger and drives out the threatening infection. That is why, even though it may be extremely difficult, one partner must give in and insist on the usual prayer-time.

Here is Corrine's one-line testimony: "Any time my husband and I prayed together when there was strife between us, we almost always forgave each other, accepted God's forgiveness, and confessed our individual blame for what had happened."

Anger that is not healed festers and becomes so deeply inflamed it can threaten the entire union. Listen as Cynthia tells of the narrow escape her marriage experienced:

"My husband insisted that I stop nursing our third baby in order to make a 'spiritual pilgrimage' to the Holy Land. With a broken heart I tried to submit to this poorly timed trip. Underneath was hostility, frustration, and resentment at being torn away from my baby at such a critical time. Our journey turned into a nightmare of hard feelings and broken communication.

"The 'Holy Land Nightmare' was later healed as a direct result of prayer together. As we prayed together we finally began to feel a warmth, adoration, and gentleness toward each other that was unparalleled. Our respect for each other was renewed, and we became 'friends' once more."

Nothing can soften the hard clasp of anger like prayer, so never discard your prayer-time because of it. If emotions are completely out of control, it might be omitted, but never for more than twenty-four hours.

One day while he was in prison, Paul took up his pen, and the Holy Spirit wrote for us a decree from the throne of God Himself. It still stands: "Do not let the sun go down on your anger" (Eph. 4:26).

Don't Tolerate False Guilts About Your Prayer-Life

Satan doesn't want you to pray. He'd much rather you would doubt, live in defeat, have a pity-party, or just go on to bed. He knows that when you are in prayer you are a real threat to his operations, so he will do anything he can to cause you to be discouraged about your shared prayer life. Nothing would please the enemy more than for you to decide it just isn't worth the bother.

One weapon he is sure to hit you with is false guilt. If unavoidable circumstances arise and you miss a day in your shared prayer-life, you can be certain he will club you with false guilt. Subtly, he will try to convince you that you have offended God by this action, and you'd better expect big trouble.

Poppycock! God knows our motivations and circumstances, and He doesn't become angry with us because circumstances we can't control have arisen. Further, God's mercy "endures forever," and the psalms repeat this again and again. There may even come days when you are so everlastingly washed out and tired, you give in to your flesh. Well, God isn't going to pick up Saturn and throw it at you. He understands our "thoughts from afar" (Psalm 139:2*b*), and besides, He knows the deepest motivations of our hearts. He knows full well that we love Him.

You may feel guilty because you say the same things over and over again in your prayers. But just apply a little reason here. When I praise God, there are only a certain number of words available to me, so I praise Him with them day after day. It never occurs to me to feel guilty about that! So why should I feel guilty about using some of the same words and phrases every day in prayer?

When you analyze it, you can plainly see this guilt is from the enemy, not from the Holy Spirit.

There are scores of other things about which that enemy loves to try to make us feel guilty. "You're too busy," the voice will whisper. "You have too many things to do." He'll try to cause guilt because you make your partner wait while you finish doing your nails or brushing your hair. You were out too late, or you got up too late and there isn't time—there is no end of things he can find to initiate guilt feelings within you.

But here is a good way to test your feelings. If you feel *condemnation*, it is not from God. He never places His children under condemnation. You can count on it, for His Word says, "There is therefore now no condemnation for those who are in Christ Jesus" (Rom. 8:1).

The Holy Spirit is the author of *conviction*, not condemnation. There is a vast difference.

If a spirit of heaviness persists in you over a period of days, you are probably feeling conviction; it means you need to repent. But if guilt suddenly flames up within you like a fire doused with gasoline because you missed your shared prayer-time last night, and if it erodes through the day and the next day is gone, what you felt was probably false guilt—condemnation from the enemy.

Remember, Satan condemns; the Holy Spirit *convicts.*

Do Have a Place to Pray

Jesus had a place. When Judas went to the chief priests and elders to betray our Lord, he knew precisely where Jesus would be: "Now Judas, who betrayed him, also knew the place; for Jesus often met there with his disciples" (John 18:2). This is not to say that was the only place He prayed. But the Scriptures seem to indicate that wherever Jesus went, He established a spot for prayer.

In your shared prayer-life, you need to do this also. For one thing, it helps establish regularity and fixes a holy habit. It probably will become a hallowed spot in your home. One couple I know had a little table with a cross, candles, and a kneeling pad in their bedroom. What a witness!

But there are ways to beat the problem of establishing a

place. Carolyn was frustrated, for both she and her husband wanted to establish a time and place when they could pray together just as man and wife. But they both worked, they had three children to get ready for school each morning, and she had a household to run. Fortunately, they rode to their jobs together.

Carolyn told how she and Frank solved their problem: "[Now] every morning we pray together on the way to work. After we pray we read one or two chapters from the Bible as we ride. If something speaks to us as we read, we pause and discuss it."

She went on enthusiastically, "It makes the twenty-minute ride to work a pleasure, and it starts us out with God on our mind. Without it, the day doesn't seem to go as smoothly."

Miss Martha and I pray in the car often, and always on Sunday morning as we drive to worship. The car is a wonderful prayer chamber. And besides, you can get pretty loud when you want to rebuke the devil!

Do Be Flexible in Your Prayer-program

Have a place to pray, but don't be bound to it. You can share prayer with your partner in many places and in many circumstances.

Early in our marriage, Miss Martha and I began our shared prayer at the bedside before retiring. Since then the format has changed several times.

She is a night person and I am an early bird. So now that our children are gone from home, we dig into the Word of God at the breakfast table and, like Carolyn and Frank, pause for discussion frequently. Then I offer our prayer. Somtimes we include a devotional reading such as *My Utmost for His Highest* by Oswald Chambers. Then at night after I climb into bed, she sits on the bedside to offer prayer.

As time passes and your "togetherness" develops, other times, methods, and places will suggest themselves. So be ready to change when a seemingly better way arises.

Do Establish a Time

Although Carolyn and Frank had a place that was a bit different, both they and Miss Martha and I have established a time. The Moslems seem to agree that having a time is important for they have established five different times daily for prayer.

An established time does not bind us, for we have emphasized flexibility, but, like having a place, setting a time ties us to the commitment.

You might have a place for a horse to wait for you while you prepare for the ride, but if you don't have it tied to that place, there is a fair chance the horse won't be there when you want it.

Setting a time is the rope that ties us to our place.

Do Begin at the Kindergarten Level

Even though you have a fantastic private prayer-walk with the Lord, when you first begin to pray with your partner there are pretty certain to be awkward moments because of the newness of the experience.

Therefore it is only good logic and wisdom to begin simply. It is probably wise to begin with a short prayer-time, perhaps no more than a few sentences. The length of prayer doesn't necessarily impress God. Jesus made this clear in His criticism of the loud, lengthy prayers of the Pharisees. God looks upon the heart, not upon the volume of words.

To help overcome initial awkwardness or shyness, a list of prayer subjects could be made and agreed upon. Then

44

divide the list. After that, alternate the list between you as time passes.

Donald and Cris keep a prayer-subject list on their refrigerator door. As a prayer is answered, they scratch through the item (adding "Glory!" beside it), and as each develops needs or intercessory concerns, they add to the list.

Do Pray About Your Marriage

Meg gave an example of a blessing she received in a simple shared table grace: "One day my husband prayed, 'Thank you for this great meal and for my beautiful wife who prepared it with love.'"

You think that didn't bless Meg? It started her glory-motor! But then she said, "I felt as if it were more for me than for God." But here Meg was wrong. She had simply tasted one of the sweet fruits of shared prayer. Chris was speaking to God, and Meg was merely listening in. She received an instant added blessing.

Pray positively about your marriage, not just about the problems that arise between you. Thank and praise God for each other and for the blessed qualities your partner possesses.

Melvin has lived in the Word of God for so many years, it is fitting that he should use biblical terms. When he prays, he sometimes says, "I praise You that my wife is a gift from God and that we are of one mind, having compassion toward each other. We are courteous; we do not render evil for evil, but bless each other in Jesus' name" (James 1:17; I Peter 3:7-9).

At other times he will say, "Because of Your Spirit we do not envy, we bear all things. We are patient, we are not rude, we do not take offense, nor do we keep a score of wrongs done us. Thank you for instilling Your love in us" (I Cor. 13).

Do Live by Your Spirit, Not by Your Feelings

We are body, mind, and spirit. The secret of remaining faithful, regular, and consistent in your life as prayer partners lies in listening to your spirit when you are tempted to fall into patterns of neglect.

Feelings arise out of the flesh, the five senses, and everything that is perceived with the senses is subject to change. The eternal God does not change, His Word does not change, and the need of our spirits to commune with Him does not change.

Therefore, battles at times arise between the mind and the spirit. When the time for prayer together rolls around, the mind, speaking out of the fatigue of the flesh, will sometimes say, "You ought not"; the spirit will say, "You ought." Then war erupts on the battlefield of the mind. We "live by the flesh" when we give in, but when we live "by the Spirit," we surrender to the summons of self-discipline.

"If I prayed only when I felt like it," commented Mary Lou, "I'd be cheated out of half the joy of life, and God would be frustrated in his attempt to grow me!"

She was right. So perhaps you will win some and lose some, but the victory is always won by faithfulness and discipline.

Again and again the Bible speaks of the rewards given to those who endure. In one sense, endurance means self-discipline. Nurture of this trait, added to the inner power the Holy Spirit will produce, will make you a winner!

When Napoleon was making preparations for his march on Moscow, he personally supervised the selection of the horses for the cavalry. He ordered that all the horses be denied water for three days.

On the evening of the third day, Napoleon, his staff, and

all the horses assembled at the top of a long hill. At the bottom of the hill, at the end of a long slope, was a beautiful lake of clear, blue water.

The bugler sounded the charge and the horses were released. Wildly they raced down the hill toward the lake, galloping frantically for the blessed water. Suddenly, when they were about half-way down the hill, the bugler sounded the call to halt and regroup. The horses stopped in confusion, whinnying and rearing.

Then many of them continued their headlong dash toward the water, while others obeyed the command. Only those who obeyed the command were selected for the march to Moscow.

So it is for those who desire the blessed rewards of being prayer partners in marriage. There is a price to pay. A lapse here and there does not spell failure. But it is the overall pattern of faithfulness and endurance that forms the end result of success.

"Therefore do not throw away your confidence, which has a great reward. For you have need of endurance, so that you may do the will of God and receive what is promised" (Heb. 10:35-36).

Chapter V

What Problems
Should We Expect?

N o growing Christians seriously doubt the power of
God within. They know it is there and that it is so
magnificently efficient that compared to it, nuclear fission is
a mere dime-store popgun.

But this is a flesh-and-blood, down-to-earth, nuts-and-
bolts world, where stress, feelings, and difficulties as well
as unexpected tragedy and heartbreak are realities with
which we are forced to deal.

We must face up to tight schedules, traffic tie-ups, crabby
bosses, exhausting trips downtown, stopped-up sinks, and
a never ending string of bills. Things *do* happen, obstacles to
our prayer-lives never cease to arise.

Not only that, but God's archenemy and ours ever lurks
in the shadows, waiting to jump feet first into everything
we try to do to the glory of the Father.

On the basis of long experience and out of the hearts of
those who responded to our survey, we want to raise some
of the problems every couple just beginning shared prayer
can normally expect. If you are aware of them in advance,

you will be more likely to recognize them when they arise and will be able to deal with them victoriously.

Fear of Making "Inferior" Prayers

As she sat in my office, her eyes held a quivering rim of tears, and my heart went out to her in a great leap of compassion. She had just made a strange confession.

"When Tom and I pray together," she said, "he usually prays first, and when he finishes it's my turn. But he is such a great pray-er I just feel my little prayers aren't of much value."

She went on, "I know he doesn't want me to feel this way, and I know he loves me, but he is so strong and so beautiful in his prayers, sometimes I almost dread our prayer-time!"

I had never before heard a confession like that. But this dear woman was sincere and obviously very, very upset, so inwardly I asked God's help, and then attempted to explain some things to her. If you have the same problem, perhaps this will help you too.

First of all, in confessing this she had revealed that her idea of God was vastly different from mine, and from the God of the New Testament. Her God is more apt to listen to some than to others, because of the beauty of their words. In other words, He grants some more access to Him than others—which is to say He has His favorites.

If you, as a parent, have two or three children, do you play favorites? Do you stop up your ears to the child who hasn't learned to speak fluently? Those questions are ridiculous. Well, shall we make God less loving than we humans are?

Many times people have said, "Oh, I'll feel so much better, Dr. Prater, if I know you are praying for me!"

Translated, that comes out, "You have an audience with God that He will not grant to me."

To deal with such problems the Holy Spirit wrote such verses as this: "And Peter opened his mouth and said: 'Truly I perceive that God shows no partiality'" (Acts 10:34). And the Lord Jesus Himself set the matter straight: "In praying do not heap up empty phrases as the Gentiles do; for they think that they will be heard for their many words" (Matt. 6:7).

In other words, God always looks upon the heart. He is not distracted by beautiful words and phrases. Now, I love to hear some gifted, sincere disciple pray in beautiful phrases that glorify God, but the Word of God plainly teaches that everyone is equal before God.

If you really believe that and base your whole prayer-life on your faith in *that* kind of God, you can be instantly healed of any inferior feelings about your ability to pray. There are no "good pray-ers" or "bad pray-ers" in His sight. There are only some people who are very good at putting words together.

George wrote, "I well remember my grandfather insisting that we bless the food in a restaurant, and then praying very loudly so that everybody could hear and thus he could 'witness' to them. I am a very private person in my prayer-life. Perhaps that experience had something to do with it."

I certainly believe in quietly blessing one's food in restaurants, but George's letter reminds us that, unfortunately, some of the people Jesus described in the above verse are still around.

In the King James Version of the Bible, Romans 8:26 plainly implies that God hears and understands the heart of a person who simply "groans" before the throne of grace. Sometimes I have done that very thing, haven't you? I assure you, no one has any advantage over you in prayer.

So please, let me say very tenderly that when you signed up for Comparative Praying 101, you did not find it listed in the catalog of the University of the Holy Spirit; the professor in charge of that course is not God the Father, but the archenemy himself. Who else would *want* you to feel inferior about your prayer-life together?

Finding Time

Somewhere around the age of forty or fifty, most people begin to wear glasses. As we get older the eyeballs flatten, and things previously seen clearly begin to seem fuzzy and out of focus. So in the long run, though it's hard to admit we need them, eyeglasses are a real blessing, for they bring things back into focus. We see things as they really are, not as they appeared to be.

A couple that wishes to begin shared prayer will soon discover that finding time for it becomes a problem, and the importance of communication with God can get out of focus. The husband comes home late from a meeting, and the wife gets sleepy and goes to bed. Or she is into a sewing project and doesn't want to stop, and his eyes are too heavy. Or he is in the midst of an exciting football game on TV, and she has had it for the day.

Or if they are childless and their prayer time is in the morning, he is anxious to get to work and she is on the telephone. Or he thinks she is dressing, but actually she has rolled over and gone back to sleep. Or she has an early appointment at the beauty shop, and he doesn't need to report to work until later that morning.

So the question is, Will we surrender to the fuzziness of this one, frantic, rushing moment, or will we pause, put on our spiritual glasses, and bring things back into focus?

I know this instant-breakfast, instant-coffee, instant-news, instant-everything culture of ours dramatically increases the pressure to hurry and "get everything done." That's the way things *are,* not the way we wish they were, and not the way they "used to be." So how do we deal with it?

Well, the analogy of eyeglasses was not lightly chosen. One dark night when Nicodemus was wrestling with the mystery of life, the Lord Jesus said to him, "Truly, truly, I say to you, unless one is born anew, he cannot *see* the kingdom of God" (John 3:3, italics mine).

When you were born into the kingdom of God by freely receiving Jesus Christ as your Savior and Lord, you received a set of spiritual glasses, and now, if you wish, you can see things in focus. You can see things as they are in the light of eternity. You can see the difference between miracles and coincidences, between spirit and the flesh, between an affirmation from God and some merely pleasant little thing that happens during the day.

My own pet phrase for these miracle eyeglasses is *Holy-Spirit eyes.* To solve this problem of "finding time," you must keep your Holy-Spirit eyes handy. Self-discipline and spiritual eyeglasses work every time. When the time has seemingly, because of circumstances (or misplaced priorities), slipped away, just put those glasses on, and the Holy Spirit will put things back into focus in a hurry.

How do you avoid forgetting your prayer-time as you rush about? I have found that if I plant a prayer-seed the first thing after I roll out of bed, it will bear fruit at just the right moment. Simply say, "Blessed Holy Spirit, keep reminding me to keep things in focus today" or "Lord, prompt me if I get my priorities in the wrong place today." Those are prayers the Holy Spirit will store in your unconscious and fire into your conscious mind like skyrockets at just the right time—when the serpent of stress winds its ugly coils around your calendar for the day.

Finally, children of God always should remember that

they do not have time—it is time that has them. Time is a gift from God, and somehow I have always felt we shall be held accountable for our stewardship of this precious gift. But the enemy is a thief, and there are few things he enjoys more than stealing a bit of our time.

You see, the way we use time is mostly up to us. We can blame circumstances, or our schedules, or any one of a thousand things when we fail to find time for our prayers together. There are always plenty of—well, it's a hard word, but I must say it—*excuses*. But ultimately, it is pretty much up to us. We stop being phony the moment we face up to that.

Interruptions

Every praying couple soon discovers that interruptions are like wildcats clawing at our intent with great insistence; they can often destroy a prayer-mood completely. It's very difficult to get back to where we were when the interruption occurred.

In this age there are two kinds of major interruptions— human and mechanical. The human kind occur when Junior comes padding unexpectedly into your bedroom, or the Avon lady knocks at your front door, or your teenage daughter comes home from her date in tears.

The mechanical kind occurs when the telephone rings (doesn't it always?), or your beeper goes off, or your high-schooler turns up the stereo.

Not only prayer, but everyday life itself brings a spiderweb of interruptions. Just since I began to write this morning, Miss Martha came in to kiss me as she left for the supermarket (interruptions are not *always* unpleasant!), the men came to pour concrete for our new patio, others came to install some aluminum storm shutters, the electrician called to bid on some new wiring, the genial young man who mows our lawn came to collect his fee, and—well, that's enough to make a point.

So life itself is a winding river, out of which the many, many rocks of interruption rear their heads. So since we can't eradicate them, how do we deal with them?

In the matter of the telephone, the Lord gave me a surefire method. One day while we were engrossed in prayer the phone rang. In spite of the fact that by now I should surely be a saint, a quick flash of annoyance blazed up within. Annoyance is a blood brother to resentment, and on my way to answer the phone, the Lord said to me, "Hold it! Don't you know that's one of my precious creations waiting to speak with you?"

That did it. Now when the phone rings at the wrong time, He has taught me to say, "Lord, this is one of your children. Thank you for helping me help and bless this person."

That is not easy when it turns out to be someone wanting to sell siding for the house or a recording extolling the virtues of a solar heating panel. But after all, the voice originated from a human being, and hurts and needs are hidden in that person too. Try it. It also works for doorbells, stereos, cement men, aluminum installers, and electricians.

Even time can interrupt. When you or your partner goes on a trip and you are apart for a week or so and miss your shared prayer, there is a temptation to slow down or stop altogether. After any interruption, it is hard to take up where you left off. But again, you must continually answer this question: Will I listen to my feelings, or to His Word?—to my flesh, or to my spirit?

Unrealistic Expectations

The bitter fruits of unrealistic expectations are disillusionment and despair. Neither grow in the kingdom of God.

"We began our prayer-time together on an emotional high," Eloise commented, "and when the glow died down, our flesh began to take over. We would give in to anger or start criticizing each other, and it wasn't long until the newness wore off.

"But," she concluded happily, "we woke up and smelled the roses. One night the Holy Spirit showed us what was happening, and after we realized the cause, we overcame it and resumed on a more lasting basis."

Although we have this enormous power within us, we must never expect prayer to be magic. God does not go around violating His laws just because we pray.

Peter and Earline could not understand why their son was still hooked on drugs after they had, with all the faith they possessed, prayed for more than a year that he be delivered from that terrible bondage.

They began to be disenchanted with prayer. In fact, Earline verbalized it: "Sometimes, I even get to the point where I think we're just fooling ourselves by praying at all!"

The truth is, Earline was a bit angry with God. In her eyes, it was pretty shabby of him to let Mark go on, enslaved by drugs. But God had given Mark free will. You cannot pray your will upon another. Not even God can do that. (We will discuss this in chapter 8.) Unreal expectations had led Peter and Earline into a spiritual trap.

You may find this hard to believe, but one seriously overweight woman said to me, "I even asked God just to let me wake up some morning thin!" Well, that would be nice, and I'm sure many people have wished for such a thing, but that is a dramatic illustration of the dangerous path down which unrealistic expectations can lead us. Prayer is power-packed, but it is not magic.

So never pray, "God, *make* him" do this or that. It doesn't work. You both can know you are maturing when you realize you can't always have your way with another person. And you can *never* have your way with God, unless it's His way, too.

As one character in C. S. Lewis's *Great Divorce* says, "There are only two kinds of people in the end: those who say to God, 'Thy will be done,' and those to whom God says, '*Thy* will be done.' All that are in Hell choose it." All who are in heaven choose it, too—but it's their choice. It can never, ultimately, be ours.

Repeating the Same Things Over and Over

What you believe about prayer reveals the kind of God in whom you believe. Alberta's response on the questionnaire told me she needed a "new" God:

"If there is any one thing that bothers me, it is repeating the same old thing to God in prayer every day." For example, we pray for our parents every day. Not for any specific thing—we just pray, 'Dear God, bless Daddy and Mother.' It's as if I'm insulting God's intelligence, or don't have enough faith, or something."

Alberta needed to learn more about our heavenly Father. We will deal with the matter of faith later, but now she needs to consider that God would never be insulted because of her concern and love for her parents.

But this is not to ignore the problem simply because it doesn't belong to God—it certainly belongs to us. And if I prayed that way for a few months, it would seem quite repetitious to me, too.

The proper way, or at least one way to handle this is to follow the instructions in the Word of God: "In every thing give thanks: for this is the will of God in Christ Jesus concerning you" (I Thess. 5:18 KJV).

In regard to prayer, this surely means that once having petitioned God, we are to continue to "give thanks" concerning the matter.

Let's apply that to the particular example Alberta cited. She and her partner had asked God to "bless" their parents. Since the word *bless* means "bestow all good things upon," the secret of being released from the problem of constant repetition is to give thanks for that blessing, to praise. It also builds one's own inner faith regarding that particular matter. Besides, variations of thanks and praise certainly can raise a request out of the purely routine. Here are a few sample phrases Alberta might use:

"Thank you, Lord, for the way you are watching over my parents."

"Praise you, dear Father, for your watchful care over Daddy and Mother."

"I glorify your name, dear God, for the goodness you are showing them. Your 'lovingkindness is better than life'" (Ps. 63:3 KJV).

"I praise you, Father, that you are the Good Shepherd, watching over my parents."

You will be able to come up with many, many more phrases of praise and thanksgiving.

But what if things are not going too well? Suppose Alberta's father suffers a stroke. What then? Well, then, of course she would need to alter her prayers to apply to that situation. But she would follow the same rule, avoiding repetition and building faith within herself. The Word says, "In everything give thanks." So after asking for healing and standing on God's promises in Isaiah 53:6 and II Peter 2:24, Alberta might pray:

"Thank you, Father, for the glory you will receive from this."

"I praise you, Father, for your answer to my prayers for my earthly father."

"Thank you, blessed Lord, that you hear and answer my prayers for Daddy."

"Father, I'm glad you're not a God of defeat but of victory. Both of us stand on that in this time of crisis."

"Lord, we are believers, not doubters, so we praise you for your answer to our prayer."

Wouldn't you agree that such faith-filled prayer is more satisfying and pleasing? What a victory—to be set free from the enslavement of the universal prayer problem of endless repetition!

Mind Wandering

In our prayer journey together, Miss Martha and I have been plagued by many of the problems mentioned in the survey, but like a glowing thread winding through all the responses, the problem of mind-wandering stands out.

Bert said, "I feel so guilty. Here is Marsha, praying her heart out, and suddenly I'm aware that I'm thinking about something I have to do tomorrow." He asked plaintively, "Is there anything that can be done about this?"

Of course there is, although I suspect there is no putting an absolute stop to it. The first thing we can do is to correct our thinking about it.

Authorities tell us that the attention span of an adult with exceptional powers of concentration is about two and one-half minutes. If this is true, where does it leave the rest of us?

We need to recognize that we did not choose to have our attention spans function in this manner. It is the way God made us. And most people, as they grow older, find even that short span beginning to decrease.

Exercising the mind is helpful. Reading the Scriptures aloud is one useful method. The reading of a psalm before the prayer, for instance, sharpens your attention, helping it to stay fixed on what your partner is saying.

But second, we need to deal with our false feelings of guilt.

Bert admitted his faulty thinking in his opening sentence: "I feel so guilty," he had said. Following this line of reasoning to its conclusion, we discover that Bert (and hundreds of others) are really saying, "I'm afraid God will be fearfully offended if my mind wanders during my partner's prayer (or even during my own)."

What kind of logic would accuse God of being angry because his creation is functioning normally? God's ego is not offended by such mind wandering, because He doesn't have an ego. And I want to stop right now and praise Him for that!

A couple of times while Miss Martha sat on the edge of my bed praying, I have gone to sleep! It is not the greatest way in the world to please your wife, but I assure you it is not a big deal in God's eyes!

I heard Norman Vincent Peale, in a sermon to college students, tell about counseling with a woman who was beset with all kinds of problems. While he was trying to offer some helpful hint about one problem, she would interrupt and begin zeroing in on another.

Finally, he said, "Ma'am, if you will come with me, I can take you to a spot where there are a hundred thousand people who have no problems at all. Would you like that?"

She quickly agreed, so he said, "Get your coat, then. We're going to a cemetery up in the Bronx!" Most of us are not quite ready for that yet!

In this world, and especially in our Christian journey, God's people can expect to have some problems along the way—"tribulations," Jesus called them. But under the marvelous illumination of God, those problems are almost always brilliantly disguised opportunities, if we will only see them.

And that is precisely why we have been given Holy-Spirit eyes!

Chapter VI

How Can We Release God's Power in Prayer?

I'm sure most of us are familiar with some form of Murphy's Law—"If anything can go wrong, it usually does." Frankly, even though designed for humor, that sort of negativism turns me off. However, I think you will agree that almost anything really worthwhile is accompanied by problems.

Speaking to the Lord God of the universe, in the company of one you love, is certainly worthwhile as well as joyful and rewarding. But it can bring many problems that affect your relationship as well as your understanding of the mysteries of prayer itself. This is especially true of newer Christians.

From this point, we will proceed on the assumption that you and your partner now have agreed to share prayer and have established a pattern that is satisfactory to you both.

We have dealt with some of the problems of relationship. Now it is time to go on to deeper things of the Spirit, for people who stay in shallow water will surely never learn to swim.

So, how can we release God's power in prayer?

He Is Always More Willing to Give
Than We Are to Receive

If you do not proceed on this great truth, you are apt to fall into the trap of begging God.

Pat was plainly discouraged. "We wanted a child more than anything in the world. For the first year we asked God to give us one, but by the end of three years we were begging. Then after six years we both got so discouraged we stopped asking."

Her husband, Olan, agreed. "We even began to try to find comfort in the idea that a baby was not God's will for us. We had done everything we were told—we went to doctors and all that—but still no baby. What else could we believe?"

We have said that if you begin with a problem, you end with one and even become a part of the problem yourself. Pat and Olan, in trying to discover why God had seemingly denied them a child, began their quest with a problem. They began with the proposition that God is a reluctant deity. They brushed aside the Scripture in which God had ordained that we should "be fruitful and multiply." They thought of Him as capricious—that He constructed the human anatomy to reproduce in kind, then arbitrarily rebuked His own physiological creation.

We surely open a Pandora's box when we seek the answer to any spiritual problem, unless we begin with trust—the knowledge that *God is good*. He is not a capricious, somewhat senile old gentleman who sits in His big rocking chair in the sky, enjoying His own power and gleefully watching while we beg for the desire of our hearts. He is not an indecisive judge who can be persuaded by some clever argument to change His mind and make a decision in our favor.

His promise is clear and without any limitation: "Ask,

and it will be given you; seek, and you will find; knock, and it will be opened to you" (Matt. 7:7).

Pat and Olan discovered this to their great delight. Their story has a wild and happy ending. After seven years of a barren marriage, they adopted a ten-month-old girl, and about a year later, Pat gave birth to a baby boy.

God is always more willing to give than we are to receive, and it always pays to remember another of his promises: "I am the LORD; those who wait for me shall not be put to shame" (Isa. 49:23).

What Kind of Power Are We Releasing?

It is easy to underestimate the power we are tapping through shared prayer. The world downgrades God's power, calling it puny and undependable, but His children know better, for they have tasted it.

Yet even Christians can lose their sense of God's great power; they can become like electric transformers. We used this analogy earlier, but let's enlarge upon it. A transformer is that big round barrel that sits near the top of your light pole. The main line may be carrying twenty thousand volts, but the transformer reduces that voltage as it flows into your house. So it is that when God's people forget the awesome power available to them, they allow only a limited amount of it to flow into their lives.

When you pray "through Jesus Christ our Lord," you should frequently remind each other just who He is. You are not referring to some plastic image swinging by a string from the rear-view mirror of a sports car. You are addressing the God who plucked a little baby from the waterweeds and "transformed" him into the deliverer of two million of His people.

You are in the presence of the One who "transformed" a dreamy little shepherd boy into a slayer of giants and

Israel's mightiest king; One who raised Daniel, a foreigner, to the vice-presidency of powerful Babylon; One who "transformed" Peter from a fisherman into the rock of His Church; who "transformed" a prejudiced little Jew into a flaming harbinger of the Good News that blew the skylights out of the prison of human hopelessness all around the Mediterranean.

No wonder Paul said, in effect, "Nothing is impossible for the Christ in me, my hope of glory!" (Col. 1:27).

Our God is some kind of a Transformer! You see, there are also transformers, though not commonly used, which increase the voltage instead of reducing it. That stepped-up power is the power that flows from us when we pray.

If you will have faith in this power and constantly be aware of it, your prayer-journey together will take you to some thrilling places! Praise God every time you see a transformer!

How Do We Release It?

In order to release this power, there is a sense in which we must first release God. I do not wish to get into heavy theology here, but in order to at least partially understand what happens when we pray together, we simply must delve into the deeper mysteries of God. We touched on this previously, but now we must enlarge upon it.

You see, when God made us, He gave us another power—the wonderful but terribly awesome power of free choice. In order to do this, He had to place some limitations upon Himself. To put it another way, He had to incorporate some limitations into His own nature. This means that if we are to have perfect free choice, there are some things God cannot do unless we permit it.

In the context of prayer, there are *some* things God cannot do, by His own self-limitation, until He finds people who will, of their own free will, choose or *let* Him do things He otherwise could not do.

In other words, in matters where we have choice, God cannot arbitrarily force us to do His will. If He did, He would violate His own nature, and God cannot violate His own nature any more than we can violate ours. God cannot make a maple leaf with only one side; to do so would violate His nature of orderliness. We cannot commit suicide by holding our breath; it is our human nature to breathe.

So sometimes, in order to release God's power, we must set Him free. What are some ways we pray that seem to set God free? I am certain there are many, but we will mention only three.

1. *Selfless Yielding.* Very seldom are we able to completely, and with no reservtions at all, yield ourselves wholly unto God. Those who have read Catherine Marshall's writings will recall that at one point in her life as a young pastor's wife, she contracted tuberculosis.

She could not believe it was the will of God that she should be bedfast for a year or more. Doctors finally told her they could do no more to help her, and she applied all the prayer-power and every spiritual principle she knew, but to no avail.

Finally one day, in great frustration, despair, and desperation, she lifted her heart to God and cried out, "All right, Lord, I don't understand it at all, but if it is your will that I should have tuberculosis the rest of my life, it's your problem, not mine! I just hand it all over to you!"

She had reached that elusive point at which she truly surrendered *everything* to God, and when she did, she was healed.

Have you noticed that I have been using the words *sometimes* and *seems to*? Well, that is because there is more here than any human can explain. In fact, there is always more to God and His ways than we can explain or understand.

Of course it was not God's intention that Catherine Marshall live with tuberculosis the remainder of her life. But it was that elusive and seldom-reached state of complete, selfless yielding that evoked a response from God, as it sometimes seems to do.

2. *A Heart Broken for Another.* God is indeed unknowable Mystery in His entirety, but this does not mean we know nothing about Him, for Jesus Christ came to reveal what God is like. Indeed, the Bible itself is the inspired record of the revelation of God through Jesus Christ.

So we do indeed know much about Him—we know that "God is love" (I John 4:16*b*). God is not *like* love— He *is* love. And when he sent Jesus, He illustrated the meaning of a heart broken for others.

When the Wycliffe translators were interpreting the Scriptures for a remote Indian tribe in South America, they found that the Indians had no word for *love*. So when the translators came to John 3:16, they wrote: "For God so hurt in His heart for the world that he gave His only Son."

The story is told of a man wracked with disease who went to the famous waters at Lourdes, France. He spent several days there in constant prayer, bathing in the waters, with no indication of improvement in his condition.

One day as he sat in the waters, some people brought to the springs a little child with horribly deformed limbs. As the man watched, he was overcome with compassion and cried out, "Lord, O Lord, if I am not to be healed, then in the name of Jesus, please heal this precious child. Better him than me!"

When that cry came from a heart completely and selflessly hurting for another, two miracles occurred—one for the child, and one for the man who prayed.

So sometimes a heart broken for others evokes a response from God. His Word amply verifies this: "A broken and contrite heart, O God, thou wilt not despise" (Ps. 51:17b).

3. *Faith.* Faith is, without a doubt, the mightiest weapon against the enemy with which God has equipped us. Faith gets God's attention. Jesus taught this again and again. The woman who touched the hem of His garment is one of many examples. When she touched Him, "Jesus turned, and seeing her he said, 'Take heart, daughter; your faith has made you well'" (Matt. 9:22).

The Scripture says, "Without faith it is impossible to please him" (Heb. 11:6). Why is this so? Of course no one knows the answer to that. But let me suggest a concept that has been of immeasurable help to me in attempting to understand this line.

Did you ever ask yourself, Why am I here? Why was I born? What is the purpose and meaning of life? I am certain most of us have asked these things. After being around quite a few years, I found a couple of answers that satisfy me.

First, we are placed here to begin the process of learning to *love as God loves;* second, we are placed here to begin the process of learning what it means to *completely trust God.* I have always known we are to trust God, but only in these later years have I learned that we are *always* to trust Him.

If those two purposes are removed from our existence here on Planet Earth, then life itself is nonsense. That is, no meaning can ultimately be assigned to it. And that is why faith pleases God. At least, in my opinion, it is the fulfillment of one reason for our existence.

So when we pray together in marriage, how can we exercise our faith and put it into action? It is not a matter of "psyching ourselves up" to have "more" faith. God has already given Christians all the faith we will ever need.

We are to "think with sober judgment, each according to

the measure of faith which God has assigned him" (Rom. 12:3). Well, He is a good God, so is He going to "assign to" any of us *less* faith than we need? Is someone going to be shortchanged? I don't think so. No, it is a matter of exercising the faith we already have.

To think otherwise leads to all sorts of agonizing false guilt feelings as well as many other problems, which I wrote about in *How Much Faith Does It Take?* (Nashville: Thomas Nelson, 1982).

So, how do you exercise your faith? There is no way to deal with that question in a paragraph or two. We could almost use John's phrase, "The world itself could not contain the books that would be written" (John 21:25).

Perhaps an illustration would help. You are in an airplane. Its engine has died and it is twisting and turning and falling toward the earth. There is a parachute strapped to your back, so you begin to recite your litany of faith: "I believe in parachutes. They have saved the lives of many other people, and this one will save mine. I believe parachutes are constructed in accordance with God's laws of physics, and the person who packed my chute was highly trained and skilled. I believe my parachute will open and save me!"

But you will never *know* until *after* you have put your belief into action. You can recite your beliefs until you crash into the ground, but you will not know until you jump and pull the ripcord. The exercise of faith is like that.

To be fair, we should say that sometimes miracles happen to people with weak faith or none at all, and that is because of God's *mercy*. But it is about as presumptuous as you can get to ignore faith and hope that God's mercy will bring about the miracle you need.

Let me remind you again how often in these pages I have been using the words *sometimes* and *seems to*, because the only absolutes I have a right to present are found in the

Word of God. But there is more to God than that which is revealed in the Scriptures. There we will find all we need to know in our spiritual journey now, but even in eternity we will never be equal with God and consequently omniscient. Satan made that mistake, and he fell "like lightning" from God's presence.

I'm saying that the Holy Spirit let us know the thoroughness of our humanity once and for all, when He said through the prophet Isaiah, "For my thoughts are not your thoughts, neither are your ways my ways, says the LORD. For as the heavens are higher than the earth, so are my ways higher than your ways and my thoughts than your thoughts" (55:8–9).

We know God has established laws of faith on which we can depend. That is, given certain situations, faith will produce certain results. But this is not like a formula that would attempt to pressure God into courses of action *we* dictate, especially if those courses are outside His perfect will for us. God's laws are *of Him,* and our formulas are *of us.* That's a pretty wide difference!

So before you and your partner come to your time of prayer together, pause for a moment and remember to *Whom* you are coming, and the almost unthinkable power you are about to unleash. Then believe, after you have prayed, that you have unleashed it!

Bring God's Power out of the Deep Freeze!

Speaking of God's highest level of creation, the human being, the Bible asks with awe: "What is man that thou art mindful of him, or the son of man, that thou carest for him? Thou didst make him for a little while lower than the angels" (Heb. 2:6b-7a).

But in some ways God has granted us a potential that no angel can ever possess. The Holy Spirit alive in us is an energy package so fantastic the angels must still be gasping in astonishment at that power-pack with which God has entrusted us.

One day Jesus was confronted with a pitiful scene. Ten men, God's highest level of creation, stood before Him in rags, covered with the rotting flesh of leprosy.

The crowd that had been with Jesus probably drew back and fled in all directions. But the Master, because He was completely aware of the power within Him, and because that power locked out the slightest possibility of doubt, was confidently able to assure the lepers that if they exercised faith by showing themselves to the high priest, their bodies would be healed. They obeyed and were healed, though only one man thanked Him afterward.

And because we are joint heirs with Him, the Christian faith declares that same power resident in us: "Christ in you, the hope of glory" (Col. 1:27). No satanic OPEC group can cut off the supply—Calvary settled all that.

I have shown you some of the keys that will set that power free through your prayers: selfless yielding, heartbrokenness, and faith. So come to your prayer-time together with no doubt about the power within you. Do not be like those of God's children who come to their knees with this tremendous power frozen within them.

Joanna was expressing her frustration with the shared time with her partner. "Sometimes it just seems we are going through the motions," she said, "as if it were some kind of a habit or duty we perform nightly so we won't feel guilty about missing."

Poor Joanna. The power within her, and presumably within her partner, was frozen. She was talking defeat instead of victory.

When I was a small boy, I saw a picture of Niagara Falls in the wintertime. There stood that gigantic power-producing monster frozen into a great wall of glistening white ice. Its awesome rushing waters, able to generate enough power to light up most of New England, stood gaunt and motionless. A helpless giant, bound by the Lilliputians of winter, it was forced to wait for the warming winds of springtime.

Don't let such a thing happen in you. Life is too short, the needs are too great, there are too many hurting people. If you sense the icy winds of listlessness or complacency beginning to blow onto your prayer-experience together, get moving! Try to get away to a retreat for a weekend; go hear an inspiring teacher of prayer; find some motivating cassettes. Seek out every avenue of help available.

Above all, be aware that the enemy wants more than anything that you should judge your prayer-life together by your *feelings* instead of by the Word of the Lord. For faith is the chinook wind that comes stealing from the mountains of discouragement to blow its warming breath on the glaciers of frozen power until the ice is gone and the mighty rivers flow full and fresh again.

It is not for nothing that the Bible pictures the Holy Spirit as coming like the wind.

So let the warm winds blow!

Chapter VII

Are the Prayers of Two Persons More Effective Than Those of One?

*T*his is very similar to the age-old question, Which came first, the chicken or the egg? We really don't know.

But June wants to know. "My Bud and I couldn't be any closer spiritually. We are truly one in the Spirit together, and what a blessing it is. So really, why should we pray together? Will our prayers generate any more power if we do? We both cherish our very own, personal, private times with our Lord. Do you have an answer for me?"

Yes, June, I have an answer for you. First, I doubt that you and Bud couldn't be closer spiritually. To say that sets a limit on God. Second, since God's mighty power is measureless, there is no such thing as "more" or "less" of it. But here we enter the mysteries of God that only the Holy Spirit knows.

When we reach that point, we must always go back to our source book, the holy Word. Jesus *seems* a bit contradictory (not to use the word *seems* would be pretty presumptuous on my part). In the Sermon on the Mount, He said,

> But thou, when thou prayest, enter into thy closet, and when thou hast shut thy door, pray to thy Father

which is in secret; and thy Father which seeth in secret
shall reward thee openly.

Matthew 6:6 KJV

On the other hand, one of the most precious promises ever
to fall from His lips is this:

Again I say unto you, that if two of you shall agree on
earth as touching any thing that they shall ask, it shall be
done for them of my Father which is in heaven. For
where two or three are gathered together in my name,
there am I in the midst of them.

Matthew 18:19-20 KJV

Thus according to the Word of God, our Father honors
both private and corporate prayer. And we find no hint that
one is more effective than the other.

June needs to learn that *sometimes* the prayers of two or
more persons may free God to act in a way that only corporate
prayer could bring about. For example, we know from Psalm
51 that heartbrokenness or selfless yielding sometimes
evokes a response from Him. Therefore, if two or more (or a
thousand) persons join in intercessory prayer, the odds that
someone will yield selflessly would be increased greatly.

If June insists on engaging only in personal prayer, she
may miss the greater blessing from the promise that where
"two of you shall agree . . . it shall be done."

Well then, where is the mystery in all this? It is obvious that
God does not operate by any formula. And we know He is
not capricious, though it seems that *sometimes* He manifests
His answer as a result of corporate prayer; *sometimes* as a
result of the "mustard seed" prayer of one person; *sometimes*
simply out of His mercy and grace; and *sometimes* through
certain persons to whom He has given gifts such as faith or
healing.

So the mystery is, How do we know through which avenue an answer is most likely to be obtained? The answer is, *We don't know*. If we did, there would be no mystery, we would soon trap God in a formula, and then God would no longer be God. And somehow I don't think He is about to give *that* up! We *do* know that "this is the victory that overcomes the world, our faith" (I John 5:4).

So, dear June, in the light of all this, in order that you receive the best of all God has to give through the power of prayer, you *need* at least one partner. If not your husband, then some other dear friend in the Lord. The ideal situation exists when man and wife are one in the Spirit in prayer, but everyone needs somebody.

This may be the reason the Holy Spirit included this admonition for us in the Bible: "And let us consider one another . . . not forsaking the assembling of ourselves together, as the manner of some is, but exhorting one another; and so much the more, as ye see the day approaching" (Heb. 10:24, 25 KJV).

Obviously, "assembling" means for prayer and worship. Might not this apply to prayer partners as well? There seem to be added blessings for those who share their prayer-lives.

I, for one, don't want to miss *any* of God's blessings. Do you?

Chapter VIII

Can We Overcome the Free Choice of Others by Praying Together?

*H*ave you ever heard a person scream out in the sheer agony of pain? I know of few things as chilling as that. I have walked enough hospital halls to be familiar with the sound! Let me assure you, one never becomes hardened to it. It always pierces my soul to the core and momentarily freezes me in my tracks. But worse, I am sure, are the painful cries of a great group of people.

One day God said to Moses, in effect, "All right, I know Pharaoh's heart. Tonight the destroyer will pass through the land, and every family, including that of Pharaoh, will lose its eldest son. Then he will let my people go!"

It happened as God had said, and Exodus 12:30*b* tells us what followed, in one of the most terrible, shattering sentences in the Bible: "And there was a great cry in Egypt, for there was not a house where one was not dead."

In this nation, every night some couples are kneeling by their bedsides, turning their souls toward heaven with agony and longing, and "a great cry" is arising out of America as they pray their hearts out—for sons lost on drugs, runaway daughters who have become prostitutes, loved ones caught in the crushing coils of marital problems. They are praying earnestly, sometimes desperately, for relatives and friends who never have received Jesus Christ as Lord and Savior (which is what being "lost" from God really means).

But is it of any use? Are they wasting their time? God has granted us perfect freedom of choice and has imposed upon Himself the limitation of being unable to violate that freedom. Has He thus, in effect, painted Himself into a corner? Has He tied His own hands? Is He stymied by His own decrees?

Obviously, if God is God and thus omnipotent, He has not left Himself empty-handed. He loves us far too much for that. There are limits beyond which He will not go without our permission, but He is by no means without resources.

However, the enemy is bound by the same restrictions. Satan is helpless until we give him permission to act. But though the enemy is limited, he, like God, also has resources. What are they?

The Holy Spirit is in the world to exalt Jesus Christ, but another task is assigned Him—it is to "convince the world concerning sin and righteousness and judgment" (John 16:8).

In order to do this, He must have access to the human mind. So although God is limited as to our final decisions, He can do many things in order to "convince" us. He can persuade, suggest, initiate thought, argue, affirm, motivate, offer His solutions, introduce His Word, and many, many other things.

Satan also has access to our minds, or there could be no free choice between good and evil. And I really don't need to list all the things he can suggest. It is within his power to imitate most of the things God can do. But again, the final choice is up to us.

Every couple sharing prayer in marriage—indeed, all God's people—should be aware of the awesome responsibility of free choice. With it we can set God free to work His purpose and will in us, or we can set the enemy free to do the same.

Did you ever hear the phrase "The devil made me do it"? That is a spiritually infantile utterance, for the devil cannot "make" us do anything. In his efforts to "convince" us, he is primarily an *initiator*. He initiates a thought and pushes and argues and tells rational lies, but he does not carry out his suggestions in us. *We* do that, and there is no way we can ultimately escape moral responsibility for it.

By the same token, the Holy Spirit is an initiator. But since He has *all* power backing up His resources, He has a huge advantage over His foe.

Thus the human mind is the battleground; the spiritual warfare rages daily. There are no cease-fires, no letups, no truces. The possessor of the superior firepower was decided on the Cross, but the daily struggle continues.

Now that we understand the conditions for battle, we must face up to the question: Can we, as prayer partners in marriage, overcome the free will of another?

The answer, of course, is ultimately no, for the final choice does not belong to us, or to God, or to the enemy. It belongs to the person for whom we are praying.

But *we* have the choice of prayer, and we have learned that intercessory prayer sometimes sets God free to do things He cannot do until we *choose* to pray. We have His promises in His very own Word that this is true.

I heard of a boy who, like so many, went away to college and, once he tasted freedom from parental restraint, threw off all the traces. He blasted out into the giddy spaces of personal freedom and started on a campaign to violate every value his parents had taught him. He drifted into alcohol and a life of carnality and immorality. His grades went down and he lost interest in life. His very body became a filthy thing. He wouldn't bathe, he ate improperly, his health deteriorated, and he entered into long periods of depression.

Then something wonderful happened. The Holy Spirit came roaring into his mind and beat down all his stubborn, rational lies, his proud ego, his strictly intellectual approach. The Holy Spirit simply hounded him until, of his own free will, he finally came weeping to Calvary. When he came home to tell his parents the news, they cried and hugged and celebrated.

Then his father said, "Son, what happened? Your mother and I talked and phoned and went to see you. We got angry, we begged, we did everything, so it certainly wasn't us. Tell us what happened."

The son said, "Yes, it was you, but you didn't know it. It wasn't anything you said. You never could have reached me that way."

He went on, "I was sitting in my room one night, heartsick, depressed, beaten. Then I thought of something. [Remember—the Spirit is an "initiator"!] When I was in high school and came home at night, you wouldn't hear me as I slipped down the hall. But I had to pass your bedroom, and more than once I saw you dressed for bed, on your knees, kneeling and praying—praying for me and sister and the others."

He was overcome for a moment, but continued, "And that night in the dorm, I sat in my room, with no reason for living and no hope for dying. It was about eleven o'clock and suddenly *in my mind* [italics mine] I got a picture of you kneeling at your bedside, and somehow *I knew* [italics again mine] that's what you were doing at that moment. You were praying for me."

He concluded, "I slipped out of my chair, fell on my knees, and called the name of Jesus until finally He came into that room and threw His arms about me. Oh, thank you. Thank you for not giving up on me!"

You could say, "Well, that was all just a wonderful coincidence." But if you were to put on your Holy-Spirit eyeglasses, you could say with me that the Holy Spirit came in for the harvest, knowing that the field, having been plowed and prepared and planted with many prayer-seeds, was ready for the gathering.

I believe the power of love and prayer crumbled the mortar that held up the walls of sin, lostness, and despair until they came crashing down at the Savior's feet! (Do you mind if I say Glory!?)

In the sixteenth chapter of Acts is a verse that has been a source of both comfort and confusion for many. The jail walls had fallen down after Paul and Silas began to sing and praise God, and the frightened Philippian jailer had come running in. Trembling with fear, he asked, " 'Men, what must I do to be saved?' And they said, 'Believe in the Lord Jesus, and you will be saved, you and your household' " (Acts 16:30-31).

Does this mean that when the head of the household comes to Christ, the remainder of the family automatically will be saved? It cannot mean that, if free choice is a reality.

In my opinion, it means that when the head of a household (or the parents) come to Christ, there is born in them such a concern and burden for other members of the family that love will drive them to brokenness and self-yielding in intercessory prayer for their loved ones. Then one day when the field has been planted and plowed and it is time for the ingathering, the Harvester will come.

Do I believe that because it is rational and logical? No—I believe it because it is a promise of God!

It is told that a reporter was standing by Mother Teresa in India one day as she knelt to change the foul-smelling bandages on an old man's limb, rotten with leprosy.

The reporter asked, "Why do you do this? There are others to do this sort of thing. Why don't you just stay in the convent?"

That little woman looked up and, with a smile on her wrinkled face, replied, "Because the love of Christ constrains me!"

It is that sort of burden for loved ones that is born into the heart when one comes into the Kingdom. And that is why I believe the promise the Philippian jailer heard that night. I believe it because the Bible also says, "Love never ends" (I Cor. 13:8).

More often than not, when prayer partners take up the responsibility of prayer for loved ones, the manifestation of the answers is a long time coming. You may not even live to see it. That can happen.

Alben Davis was a minister and a dear friend. He and his wife, Erma, were the parents of seven children. By the time the children were grown, five were Christians. Only two were not. When we met from time to time, inevitably the burden they were carrying for those two sons would surface. It was always in their minds, ready to be voiced.

Then Alben invited me to his church for several speaking engagements. One afternoon we met at the church and knelt at the altar for prayer before going to see some people in the community. When Alben came to the matter of the salvation of the two sons, his prayer etched itself into my mind with such intensity that I shall never forget it:

"O God, whatever it takes for their salvation, let it be. If it takes the sight of their mother and me lying in our caskets, then hasten the day!"

A year later Alben was stricken with a fatal disease which took his life. After the funeral services, I walked over to Luke and Jeremy, who were standing together, and told them of their father's prayer. It seemingly made little, if any, impression on them.

Another year passed and, though I never asked her, I'm certain Erma prayed on. Then there was a family gathering to which I was invited, and as I got out of my car I was met by Luke, his face shining with joy.

I said, "Luke, don't tell me! I know what happened!"

"You're right, I've found the Lord!" he announced, and threw his arms about me. In less than three months, Jeremy also came to the waters and drank from the River of Life.

Today both Luke and Jeremy are radiant Christians, raising families in Christian homes. Alben never saw the fruits of those years he and Erma spent praying together, but the prayer-seeds they planted were nurtured and grew. And finally, when they were ripe, the Harvester came and gathered them in.

Yes, it is possible for a human being to say no to God, and it is true that ultimately the choice belongs to each individual. But those who sell short the power of intercessory prayer built on a foundation of love will rob themselves of far more than they dream.

For the Good Shepherd is constantly out on the wild mountainside—always on the job, always looking for that last beloved lamb, which may belong to you.

So, dear prayer partners, pray on!

Chapter IX

Why Are Some Prayers "Unanswered"?

*T*his question, which springs from discouragement, was on Edwina's heart and obviously was disturbing her.

"My husband is one of the best men who ever lived," she wrote, "and he has been out of work for four months. He has worn himself out looking for a job."

She went on, "He and I have been praying together daily about it, and all my Christian friends at church have been in prayer about it. I don't understand—how could it be God's will that we fail to make our house payment? Or that our children's needs not be met? I just don't understand!"

Situations such as this always touch me deeply. I long to be able to reach out and press some miracle button and make everything all right.

I could see at once that Edwina, with maybe a nudge from the enemy, had allowed her circumstances to turn her thoughts in the wrong direction. But, in her defense and that of many, many couples in similar situations, let me say it is easy to be objective when one is not personally involved. It is not easy to believe in the power of shared prayer and the guidance of the Holy Spirit when your child needs a new pair of shoes or the house payment is due, your savings have dwindled seriously, and there is no visible prospect for any change in your circumstances.

But on the other hand, where did we ever get the idea it was easy to follow and be faithful to Jesus Christ?

He was only a few days old when Herod's CIA agents were sent out to kill Him. His enemies were plotting against Him before He had barely started His adult life. They dogged His steps daily, seeking to trip Him up; even in His own hometown, they took up stones against Him. One of His closest friends sold Him down the river, and finally He was nailed to a crude Roman cross for the world to pass by and mock and spit upon. They tormented Him until the life went out of Him.

Whoever promised anybody anything except trouble if they would follow Jesus Christ here on this earth? He certainly didn't. In fact, one of the last things He ever said to anybody was, "In the world ye shall have tribulation" (John 16:33 KJV).

Edwina's thinking had gotten off track. She was concentrating on the problem rather than on the solution.

She began her plea with the defensive assertion that her husband was "one of the best men who ever lived." We have already established that God is no "respecter of persons"; He shows no partiality. He does not measure our moral performance or our level of spiritual maturity to determine whether He will grant us the answer we desire. If He did, it would give some people an "in" with Him that most of us would not have. So the fact that Edwina's husband is a wonderful Christian has little to do with how much God loves him or the likelihood that he will be led to a job.

Second, Edwina revealed that she doubted the power of prayer—not only her own but that of her friends.

And finally, though she admitted she didn't understand

it, Edwina made the back-door accusation that it *could* be God's will that her family's needs not be met. One could accuse her of slander, especially since His very Word promises that *all* our needs will be supplied (Phil. 4:19).

But our Lord is no stranger to doubt and slander, and our performance has nothing to do with His love for us. I want to pause a moment and praise Him for that, don't you?

I followed Edwina's case and learned that they did not lose their home. And her husband was led to a job in which he not only is much happier than in his former position but is receiving a higher salary!

Now the question, Why did the prayers of Tony and Edwina go unanswered? Well, of course, they did not go unanswered. The answer was delayed, and that is quite a different thing. Most Christians do not have a hold button on their spiritual telephones. They don't want to be kept waiting. One fruit of the Spirit is almost universally lacking in Christians in the United States—patience.

This is true of our citizens in general, whether or not they are Christians. A striking example is the widespread acceptance and patronage of the Concorde supersonic flights. This swift and certainly remarkable aircraft cuts from three to four hours' flight time off that of slower jets in crossing the Atlantic. But the question that boggles my mind is this: Except in very rare instances, what possible advantage could there be in arriving in Europe three or four hours sooner?

After walking most of a lifetime with the Lord, I am amazed that I should need to learn and relearn that God's answers to my prayers may not come exactly at the time I want them, but they will always be *on* time! In many instances I have realized, in retrospect, that the timing of the answer when it did arrive was far better than had it arrived when I desired.

The truth of the matter, as all of us should know, is that

no prayer goes unanswered. God says either Yes, No, or Not yet. But He says Yes on His own timetable, and that frequently may seem like No to us. Sometimes the answer comes precisely when we desire it, but sometimes we must wait and know that He is at work in our best interest, that He is being faithful to His word. For we know He has said, "I am watching over my word to perform it" (Jer. 1:12).

Then again, because we do not use our Holy-Spirit eyes, answers may seem like No when we pray for something we *already have*. One evangelist says such a prayer is like "calling for your dog to come when he's already licking your face"!

There is an old, old tale of a pearl merchant who heard of a pearl much larger, more beautiful, and worth more than any pearl known. So he sold all his other pearls and set out on a journey to find the one. After years of searching, finally reduced to poverty, he returned home only to find the pearl right on his own property!

In almost every complaint against God regarding "unanswered" prayer (in the case of couples, the complaints of one or both partners), one can discover the same three biblically unsound elements we discovered in Edwina's complaints: (a) an expression of their "deserving it"; (b) doubt regarding the power of prayer; and (c) slander against God's will for us. So if some prayer the two of you have been praying seems to go unanswered, why not take a long look at your feelings? Look at your problem in the light of biblical revelation—not your own opinion. If you do, you are likely to find that in trying to answer your "why," once again you began at the wrong place in your thinking, for you implied that God is something less than a "good" God. And inevitably you will be led back to the haven of faith in Him and His Word.

But there is another major cause of "unanswered"

prayer—unbelief. And it may possibly be the greatest cause! In the Scriptures we are plainly told that unbelief blocked the Lord Jesus many, many times.

He came back to His hometown, a small community where many had known Jesus since early childhood. They had watched Him grow up. So out of common courtesy, since they knew He had entered the ministry, He was asked to teach. But when He began to do so, such depth and wisdom came out of Him that they were astonished.

So they must have said, "We know this man. He's one of us. We know his four brothers, and *they* don't have wisdom like this. They are just ordinary citizens. Therefore he *can't* have come by all this knowledge honestly." And the Scriptures say they "took offense" at Him.

So Jesus told them their attitude didn't surprise Him, because everyone knows that a prophet is honored everywhere except in his own hometown. Then is written one of the most chilling observations in the New Testament: "And he did not do many mighty works there, *because of their unbelief*" (Matt. 13:58, italics mine).

Many people, when they pray, are like the man who was shipwrecked on a lonely island. Among the meager supplies he had garnered from the wreckage were a pencil and some paper. He found a bottle that had washed ashore, wrote a message giving his location, placed the note in the bottle, and tossed it into the sea.

In his heart he was earnestly hoping and praying someone would find the message and come to his rescue. But he realized the odds were small that this would happen (another way of saying he didn't really believe it would). So, having set the bottle adrift, he went about the business of trying to survive and very soon forgot about the bottle with the message.

When he threw the bottle into the sea, he did not *believe*—he was only wistfully hoping. And so, after a long period of time, when someone actually did find the bottle and respond to his plea, he was completely amazed.

So it is that sometimes in our discouragement, we listlessly toss out a prayer message to God, who must surely be swooshing around somewhere out there, on the off-chance that He might come across our prayer-bottle and respond. Then, caught up in other efforts, we turn away and forget what we prayed.

And one day when a "ship" comes to rescue us and the "Captain" says, "I found your bottle!" astonishment comes over us. We remember our prayer bottle and realize that the answer has appeared at last! I can tell you that if God were not a God of goodness and mercy, many of our prayer-bottles would have sprung leaks and sunk long ago!

The story of Jesus preaching in His hometown is a clear message to us that God simply will not—indeed, because of His own self-limitation *cannot*—overcome our free choices. The people of Nazareth did not hear Jesus because they chose not to listen.

If we are not open to His answers, they are not likely to be forthcoming. For instance, in churches where the healing power of God is stressed and people expect it to happen and believe it will happen, healings continually occur. On the other hand, where healing is not stressed and the people are not taught to expect it, it just does not happen. This is true also of many other aspects of the Good News.

No one realizes more than I the many questions that surround the subject of faith, and certainly much hurtful, shallow information has been taught.

But one cannot hide from the fact that in the Scriptures there are promises from God that could not possibly have been mistranslated. And these plainly offer possibilities that many earnest disciples never accept. Their own intellectual mountains block the way. Still, the Scriptures tell us in very simple language that "without faith it is impossible to please him" (Heb. 11:6).

So when you pray together, *believe* that God will answer. He will not ignore you. He is a good God. He is like a good father, and a good father answers his children when they speak to him. So *expect* an answer, praise Him both before and after He answers, and ask for Holy-Spirit eyes to see the answer when it is made manifest.

And above all, if you are called upon to wait, wait. It *must* be more than coincidence that this verse is in the *exact center* of the Bible: "It is better to trust in the Lord than to put confidence in man" (Ps. 118:8 KJV). In this sense, *man* means not just one person, but *humanity, humankind.* So according to the Word, it is God alone, not another human, or the world, or the circumstances of your world, that is worthy of your trust.

So when you pray together, take the hammer of faith and nail down all four corners of your lives on that verse. Then you will not fall apart when it *seems* you have been denied an answer.

Chapter X

How Can God Hear Millions of Prayers at the Same Time?

B ev was in her late twenties, petite, with eyes as blue as cornflowers. She had been married only a few months and was a brand-new Christian.

"Sometimes when Will is praying, my mind wanders and I think of all the people in the world who may be praying at the same time," she said, sheer puzzlement wrinkling her brow.

"I can't even listen to him without my thoughts straying," she continued, "so how can God hear all those millions who are praying at the same time, much less Will and me?"

It was a classic question, one every thinking child of God who is new in the Kingdom is prone to ask. When you stop to think about it, it is a fair question, springing naturally from our humanity.

But ah, there is the catch—it does spring out of our humanity. We are very prone to put our own human limitations on God and, in this case, make Him seem like the confused and frustrated wife in the old nursery rhyme —the little old lady who lived in a shoe and had so many children she didn't know what to do! Placing human limitations on God is precisely what causes discouragement when we meet "impossible" situations.

On one occasion, the disciples placed such limits on God's abilities. Jesus had just explained to them that it is very difficult indeed for a person with much wealth to enter the Kingdom. Why, He told them, a camel would find it easier to walk through the eye of a common needle! "When the disciples heard this they were greatly astonished, saying, 'Who then can be saved?' But Jesus looked at them and said to them, 'With men this is impossible, but with God all things are possible'" (Matt. 19:25-26).

If you or I had been a close friend of Saul of Tarsus, we would have known a religious zealot—a fierce devotee of the Law—highly educated, orthodox, rigid, unyielding, known for his extreme intolerance of the slightest threat of deviation from ancient customs and traditions.

And if we had been asked, Could this man ever be a lover of Gentiles? Could he ever know in his heart that love beareth all things? Could he ever forsake the Law's yoke and suffer the loss of all things in order to know Christ? We probably would have assigned to God our limited human knowledge and said, "Impossible!"

But Bev came to learn that she was robbing herself of God's many treasures by making Him human. A quick and eager learner, she soon came to see God as truly without limits in His power, wisdom, and knowledge.

Bev and her huband grew together as prayer partners in their marriage because they learned that *nothing* is impossible with God. It is no problem for Him to hear the prayers of millions simultaneously, for He is not limited to two ears (or eyes), and if it takes four-billion-plus pair, He knows where they are to be had!

It is said that a new arrival in heaven was escorted into a room piled to the ceiling with gift-wrapped parcels.

Drawing closer, the man noticed that every box bore a tag with his name on it.

"What does this mean?" he asked the escorting angel.

And the angel replied, "Those are blessings, every one of which was meant for you. But because you limited God by your unbelief, they never were delivered!"

So when you and you partner pray together, *believe God*. It's so much fun to unwrap packages!

Chapter XI

What Should We Do When We Receive the "Wrong" Answers?

One summer morning in a city in our state, two men walked into a convenience store, splashed gasoline on the clerk and around the room, then ran out and threw a bottle of flaming gasoline inside. In seconds, everything in the room was afire.

The clerk ran outside, where passersby threw him to the ground and smothered the flames. He was rushed to the hospital with severe burns over 80 percent of his body.

The clerk's family gathered in the waiting room and sat huddled together for ten interminable hours in fervent prayer. When the attending physician finally came to them, they scarcely had to ask. The answer was written on his haggard face. Their husband and father was dead. They were devastated, not only by the death but by the sheer senselessness of the crime.

For them, it was the wrong answer.

When I was in school, a little boy, my younger brother's playmate, was stricken with the most virulent kind of pneumonia. His parents were devout followers of the Lord Jesus and strong partners in prayer. My preacher father enlisted the entire church for prayer and the news quickly spread; most of the disciples in our small Midwestern town went to their knees.

That was before the days of wonder drugs and oxygen tents, and one morning when I came downstairs I found my mother sobbing. The little boy had died during the night. We all dressed in our "Sunday clothes" and went up the street to visit the parents. A fourteen-year-old youth, I had never before seen the shattering grief that accompanies the death of a loved one. It impressed me so deeply that even now it brings tears to my eyes.

Not only the parents, faithful prayer partners in marriage, but the entire Christian community had received what, for them, was the wrong answer.

Of course, you must understand that when I use the term *wrong answers*, I do not mean that God's answers are *ever* wrong. I really mean that these dear people did not receive the answer they devoutly desired.

The Bible is full of these kinds of "wrong" answers. Paul and Silas prayed and the walls of the jail fell down. But at another time, the executioner led Paul out, and although the church prayed, Paul was executed.

When Herod threw Simon Peter into jail, he said he personally would relieve Peter of the weight of his head. The church prayed and an angel released Peter from prison. But when he was an old man, although presumably the church prayed again, Peter went to his death.

Indeed, there is a sense in which we might say that our Lord Himself received a "wrong" answer. In Gethsemane's dark garden, with sweat pouring from His body, he prayed out of His *humanity*, "My Father, if it be possible, let this cup pass from me." But he died on the cross, for out of His *divinity*, He prayed, "Nevertheless not as I will, but as thou wilt" (Matt. 26:39 KJV).

Our danger does not lie in the fact that sometimes the

answer we receive is not the one we wanted—our danger lies in our *reaction* to it.

In the case of the man who was burned to death, some of his family became bitter and hate-filled. When a jury found the killers guilty, a newspaper reported the reaction of one member: "It took two men to kill him. I hope they die. And if they don't, I hope they rot in prison!" In the emotion of the moment such a reaction is certainly understandable. Which of us could say we would react differently?

On the other hand, when the parents of the child with pneumonia received their "wrong" answer, it drove them more deeply into their love of God and their faith in their prayer-life together. Now, they said, their ties to heaven were stronger than ever.

Whatever the cause, we know we do not always receive what we want, and many times the reason must lie shrouded in mystery for the moment. When this happens, what should we do?

Dear ones, the answer is as old as the Word of God, and it is very short and very simple: *Trust in God.*

Did you think I had just thought up something new? Did you think I suddenly had stumbled across a better answer to the question that has tormented every generation since Christ? Well, I don't have a better answer because there isn't one. Just *trust in God.*

Let me paint a picture that may help us here. In the second verse of Genesis is the sentence, "The Spirit of God was moving over the face of the waters." Many scholars feel there is a better translation for the Hebrew word than "moving." I agree, and I believe the New King James Version has caught it better than the rest: "And the Spirit of God was *hovering* over the face of the waters (italics mine).

The picture is that of a great eagle hovering high above the turbulent waters—better still, *brooding* over them—as an eagle might hover over a nest filled with little ones.

So if you will, picture the Lord God, as Isaiah said, "high and lifted up" (6:1), looking down upon all the earth spread out beneath Him. As a soaring eagle with its superkeen eyes can spot even a mouse on the ground below, so God, with His eyes of omniscience, sees every person on earth at a glance and is aware of every intimate detail of our lives. He knows all our needs; He knows the consequence of every answer He might give, even years in the future.

Then if, in our bewilderment, we begin with the conviction that God is a good God, has only our very best interests at heart, and will always answer our prayers on that basis, when we trust in Him we will come out ahead every time!

Here is still another picture—right out of modern technology. Some time ago the space shuttle was orbiting the earth hundreds of miles out in space. In a scientific experiment, a laser beam was aimed toward a tiny mirror held out an opening of the orbiting vehicle. The speeding beam of light immediately made a brilliant flashing connection with the mirror. The vast distance was no problem, nor was the timing.

Think then of God, seeing our need, sending the Holy Spirit riding the laser beam of His perfect will, bearing the answer straight down to us. And though it may appear to be a "wrong" answer, we know it ultimately will be the *right* answer. We know that, because *we trust God*. We trust God because we trust His Word, and His Word plainly promises "that all things work together for good to them that love God" (Rom. 8:28 KJV).

* * *

"I'm gonna make it, Arnold. God is going to use this thing as a tremendous witness and testimony for his glory!"

His name was Charles Bardin, and he was speaking from

the hospital bed where he lay struck down by melanoma cancer.

I believed him, and I believed God. His Word is filled with promises that seemed to confirm Charlie's faith, so faith rose up in my heart, too, as we prayed together. I earnestly believed that God's healing would be made manifest in Charlie's body.

Charlie Bardin, in his mid-forties, already was a powerful witness. The lives of Charlie and Wanda, his wife, had been turned around by Christ some years before, and they were aflame for the Lord.

But Charlie didn't make it. Not long ago they held a massive funeral service for him. People came from as far away as England—a powerful tribute!

So what happened? Why didn't Charlie make it? Why did all of us who prayed for Charlie receive a "wrong" answer? Yes, I know he was healed in heaven; he didn't take that cancer with him. But that doesn't answer my question.

I do have an answer, though—the same one I gave several pages back: *I don't know.* (And neither does anyone else. Don't let anybody tell you otherwise!)

So what am I going to do now? Throw away my Bible? Stop preaching the Good News? Apologize for all the faith-messages I ever preached? No way! God forbid!

Someone asked a doctor whose patient had just died from unknown causes, "What are you going to do now?"

The doctor answered, "I'm going to keep right on practicing medicine!" Amen! Right on! Glory!

If I receive a "wrong" answer, it does not mean God's Word is not true. It only means I don't know as much as He does or see as much as He can. Here is what I'm going to do: I'm going to keep right on proclaiming the Word of God and *standing* on it, because I know "His thoughts are not my thoughts," and "all the promises of God find their Yes in [Jesus Christ]" (II Cor. 1:20)!

Also, I'm thinking of eleven men who sat in despair in an upper room one dark Friday night. They too had received the "wrong" answer. And not one of them said, "Well, *He said* he was going to rise from the dead, and *I believe Him!*" Instead, they gave in to disappointment and despair. Sunday morning proved they were wrong, and if you give in, you're wrong, too!

I'm not giving in to despair. No way! Never! Neither Charlie nor Wanda ultimately will be cheated out of anything! Remember, it is the highest form of faith to hold on during the midnight *when there are no answers!*

So to all you Charlies and Wandas out there—hang on!

Chapter XII

Why Is the Bible So Important to Our Prayer-Life?

*I*f I knew anything about Winston, I knew he was thoroughly honest—so honest that sometimes I fear he spoke his feelings at the expense of others present. He was one of the most open and uninhibited men you could imagine, so I knew there were no shallow excuses behind his comment.

He said, "I'm a Christian. You know that, and Alicia and I pray together every day. But I keep hearing that we must 'get into the Word,' that we must spend more in-depth time in the Scriptures in order for our prayers to be effective."

To assure me of his sincerity, he added, "I love the Bible. I believe it, and I guess I know a little about it from Sunday school. But, Arnold, the truth is, we're busy people. We do well to find the time to pray. So just tell me, if I love God and believe the Bible and we pray together, why is the Bible so important to our prayer-life? Why must we 'get into it' more?"

How would you have answered? I told him this little story.

Albert Einstein once visited in a home where there was a

small boy. After supper the child was having a terrible time with his math homework. His face was flushed with anger and frustration.

Dr. Einstein walked over and said softly, "Perhaps you'd like me to help you."

But the boy snapped, "No, thank you. I've made up my mind! I'm going to do this thing by myself!"

The greatest mathematical mind in the world was a guest in his home that night and wanted to help. Einstein could have changed that boy's entire outlook toward mathematics, but the child missed his opportunity because he had closed his mind to help from other sources.

In the Bible, Winston and Alicia and every Christian in America have a "guest" in their home that can be of more help than any other source in the world. In it are the solutions to any problem life can serve up.

It is the permanent written record of the Word of God Himself, the very author of life. Of all the varied ways the Holy Spirit can answer our questions and keep us on course, speaking to us through the Word towers above them all.

Visualize yourself talking on the telephone. At the other end of the line is the Lord God. You are beset with all kinds of problems, stress, and tension. You have appointments waiting, your in-basket is spilling over with paperwork; or the dishes are piled high in the sink, Junior has to be at Little League practice at 3:30, you have to pick up Missy at Brownies, and your husband wants an early dinner. So you just hang up the phone and get at it.

Each day turns out to be an instant replay of the one before, and the steady pressures of our hurry-up, catch-up, keyed-up culture, like the booster engines on a missile, keep you whooshing through life while God sits at the other end of the wire, dialing. But the line is always busy.

So the written Word, which contains all your answers,

sits on the coffee table and really does not play any major role in your life. God is "dialing your number" but you don't have time to answer the phone.

Then when prayer-time comes around, you find it not only contains mysteries that plague you, but your prayers never seem to be answered, because there is a price to pay—you haven't "paid your phone bill."

Trying to live the Christian life without an ever expanding "heart-knowledge" of the Word is like trying to rollerskate without wheels, sled without snow, or sew without a needle.

It is not my intention to lay a guilt trip on you, but only to be of help in motivating those partners who are trying to make it without knowledge of the Word and of its importance to them. So let's get into some of the reasons I'm coming down on this so strongly.

How Can You Pray Together Effectively If You Don't Know What God Says About Prayer?

When Winston asked, "Why is the Bible so important?" he revealed a major source of the problems he and Alicia were having in their prayer life and, I suspected, in many other areas of their life together.

Put very simply, he did not believe the Scriptures were the written Word of God for humankind. But in this he is not alone. Countless Christians feel the same way, though they would never verbalize it.

Let's throw in some *ifs* here. *If*, as we believe, the Bible is the Word of God, God's instructions to us, then to largely ignore it and try to live out our lives together without it is ridiculous. It would be like trying to operate a computer while ignoring the handbook of instructions that came with it.

If the Bible contains principles in light of which all our decisions can be made according to God's will, and *if* we follow them, we have acted in such a way that He can bless those decisions.

If our decisions are not made on the basis of the principles in the Bible, then we can assume they are in opposition to God's will for us, thus inviting failure and disappointment.

So even though *specific* guidance for every situation we might meet is not provided in this Book, biblical principles are written for us, and the Holy Spirit is always there to guide, correct, and implement. And that is like having a representative from the factory instruct you in specific details the computer handbook may not cover. In effect, the Company Representative comes to live with you! What earthly company has a guarantee like that?

To carry the picture further, if you are not thoroughly versed in the computer handbook's instructions, the representative may be able to talk about your problems, but many times you still will not understand, for you have not learned the fundamental principles of operating your computer.

So couples may *begin* to pray together and be greatly blessed, but their level of maturity, as well as their communciation with Him and with one another, very soon will level off if they do not aggressively pursue what God has to say in His Word.

What Are Some of Those Principles?

Naturally there are many, so we will select only a few of the most important for a life of prayer together. We will suggest the principles and give a few of the Scripture passages that contain them, but we will not quote the passages here. When you look them up and feed upon them, you will have taken your first step toward laying a biblical foundation for your prayer-life.

Forgiveness Is Essential

We always need to pray out of a heart filled with forgiveness. A famous Christian leader of the generation just past, E. Stanley Jones, is said to have remarked, "When I was first converted, I wanted to throw my arms around the whole world and forgive everybody in it!" Jesus made it very clear that the great promises of the Bible are to be cherished in a heart that holds no ill will toward others.

To go to prayer while resentment and ill will fester within is like washing your hands without water. You can go through the motions but the results won't be very pleasing. For what the Lord has to say about this, see Mark 11:25-26; Matthew 6:12-15, 18:21-35; James 5:14-16.

Pray Out of Healed Relationships

The Bible seems to say that prayer, to be really effective, should be entered into *after* you have done all that is possible to remove resentment and ill will toward each other. The Bible makes it very clear that it is vital that couples live in harmony in order to forestall alienation before it takes place, but in no case must it be allowed to linger. Here are some references: I Peter 3:17; Matthew 5:23-24, 18:19.

Give God All Your Attention

We are to do everything we can to concentrate, to give God our full attention. This is a struggle for everybody, so if your mind wanders, or if you are constantly being interrupted, or if you sometimes have great difficulty "shifting gears" for prayer, I assure you again that each of us has the same problem. You are not alone.

109

Here are some of the concentration stealers and other tricks the enemy has used against those who responded to our survey:

TV programs (specials)
Job responsibilities
Too tired and sometimes we just fall into bed
Depression from overwhelming problems
My mind goes blank—I need a list
Sulking in anger
Blasted telephone rings at the wrong time!
Tired kids!

Almost without exception, every person mentioned one or more of these distractions, as well as many others I did not list. We certainly would not want to find comfort in the painful experiences of others, but I must admit it is nice to know we are not "second class" Christians or oddballs simply because we have these problems.

Still, in this spiritual warfare, the Word of God urges us to work toward shutting out the world when we pray together. I am sure this principle is included in the Bible for *our* benefit, not for His.

Study and meditate on these passages: Matthew 6:6; Mark 1:35.

Pray Within the Will of God

If the prayers we offer together are outside God's perfect will for us—that is, His desire and intention—we may be assured that His answers will not be forthcoming. God *cannot* grant answers outside His will, for to do so would violate His nature. And God cannot violate His nature any more than a butterfly can swim under water.

While it is true we do not often know God's perfect will for us in a given situation, still, if we know Him and His Word, the Holy Spirit is free to guide, and then, by faith, we can act. For every situation we face in life, there is a biblical principle that can serve as the springboard for our action. We need to know what that principle is—that is why we seek an in-depth knowledge of the Scriptures.

Let's select an example. We know that God by His nature is not selfish or self-centered. The Cross itself is proof of that.

So suppose some man has made a lot of money. He has more than he can possibly ever need, but he gives only a pittance to the kingdom of God—and even then his motive is to deduct that amount from his taxes. (Believe me, that picture is not overdrawn.)

Now suppose that wealthy man is praying for more money. If the biblical principle here is "Give, and it will be given to you" (Luke 6:38), for the Holy Spirit to honor this man's prayer would be to violate the nature of God, who is not self-centered. Those kinds of people do sometimes become more wealthy, but you can be sure it is not because they prayed for more money. See James 4:2-3 for more on the principle involved here.

So our prayers must be couched within the framework of God's will and nature; but if our prayers *are* within His perfect will for us, then we know by faith that we have received it *already!* If I were to select my top-ten favorite passages in the Bible, the following one certainly would be included. For that reason we will quote it in full:

> And this is the confidence which we have in him, that if we ask anything according to his will he hears us. And if we know that he hears us in whatever we ask, we know that we have obtained the requests made of him.

> *I John 5:14-15*

Pray in the Name of Jesus

Christians need to pray in the name of Jesus. This does not mean merely adding the words "in Jesus' name" at the end of a prayer, though we certainly are free to do so. Rather, it means we should come before God's throne as Jesus' ambassadors, using His authority, and our prayers should be framed accordingly. Here are a few reasons for this biblical principle.

First, to pray in this way is an acknowledgment that, as our Lord said, we can come to the Father only through Jesus Christ (John 14:6*b*).

Second, it is an acknowledgment that we, by faith, have put our trust in the work of Jesus Christ upon the Cross.

Third, to pray in Jesus' name means that, by faith, we believe He will place His approval upon our prayer because we believe we are praying for or about something with which He also is concerned. To pray for or about something we know Jesus could not approve would do injustice to the spirit of His name. Indeed, it would be a mockery and make the prayer more a thing of the occult than of the divine.

Finally, we should pray in the name of Jesus because there is *power* in His name. Read the third chapter of Acts: Peter stood before the lame beggar and, out of the sheer certainty of faith, said to him, "I have no silver and gold, but I give you what I have; in the name of Jesus Christ of Nazareth, walk" (vs. 6). And the crippled beggar leaped to his feet.

We need to be wary when we pray together of letting the phrase "in the name of Jesus" ensnare us in the trap of mere habit or ritual. We need to speak it out of our love for Him, and in full consciousness of the power in that name.

All this does not mean God will not hear us unless we use the name of Jesus. He knows we are Christians; He knows our hearts and understands our thoughts. We use the spoken name of Jesus more for our own sakes than for His. We *need* the reminder of who we are in Christ, and why.

For further insight on this biblical principle, see John 14:13,15-16, and 17:23; Mark 9:39; Philippians 2:10; and many others.

Pray with No Sin in Your Heart

This is a strong principle throughout the Scripture. To pray with a willfully held unconfessed sin is a presumptuous act, a backhanded expression of the belief that one can get away with sin, that God is deceived. Or worse still, that one believes sin is really rather inconsequential—and this attitude blasphemes the very Cross of Jesus Christ.

I am sure the Jewish crucifiers of Jesus went home that night and said all their prayers in preparation for the sabbath the next day. They believed their religious acts would atone for their sin, if indeed they had done anything wrong.

We should not run *from* God when we sin, but rather *to* Him! His forgiveness is so lovingly available—the promise is clear and definite: "If we confess our sins, he is faithful and just, and will forgive our sins and cleanse us from all unrighteousness" (I John 1:9).

Nothing will bore a hole in the bottom of prayer-life together more quickly, letting all the hallelujahs drain out, than the retention in the heart by one or both partners of a known, unconfessed sin.

For more on this, see Psalm 66:18; Proverbs 28:9; Isaiah 59:1-2.

Faith: An Outstanding Principle

By faith, you received Jesus Christ as Lord and Savior—faith in His Person, faith in His redemptive act, and faith in the biblical assurance of John 3:16. Does it not stand to reason, then, that if the Bible, which promises eternal salvation, also promises added benefits if we exercise the faith God has given us, that we should believe *that* also?—that it is *worthy* of our faith?

We have made it clear in an earlier chapter that we are not to "try to have more faith," but are simply to act from our present level of faith. We have said this is the method God has chosen for our growth and that He has established within us all the faith we shall ever need.

So it naturally follows that after asking, prayer partners should begin to praise God for His answers, releasing all the faith possible at their present level, though it may be only of the mustard-seed variety.

That one must have faith seems to be the greatest principle in the Bible. With it, Abraham, obeying God in his old age, pulled up stakes and moved, and out of his seed came the Savior.

With it, prayer partners can have the abundant life. They can tackle the mountains in their lives, remembering that sometimes mountains must be removed one shovelful at a time. With it, they can be overcomers and conquerors—not mere copers.

The message of faith given us by God is more readily released when knowledge of the Bible is established in our hearts: "Faith cometh by hearing, and hearing by the word of God" (Rom. 10:17 KJV). The word *faith* appears in the Bible 245 times, but in the Old Testament we find it *only twice*. Therefore it is in the New Testament, the final, full revelation of God through Jesus Christ, that we find the key to the prayer-life of Christian disciples—faith.

I have no way of knowing what all this meant to Winston and Alicia, but I believe they came to find the answer to the question he had asked with a certain degree of casualness: "Why is the Bible so important to our prayer-life?"

I like to believe that now they know—and so do you!

Chapter XIII

The Joy of Visibly
Answered Prayer

J oy is the splash made by that stubborn mountain in your
life when you finally cast it into the sea; it is the fruit
growing in the orchard of visibly answered prayer; it is the
hilarious ringing of the bells in your heart. That is why we
sometimes call them joy-bells!

Miss Martha and I have heard them many, many times.
We heard them when our baby was healed by the then new
miracle drug penicillin. We heard them when a walnut-
sized tumor disappeared from the pelvic girdle of one of our
children. We heard them when our adult son finally found
the Lord. I could go on and on.

We have listened for the bells sometimes when they did
not ring. But even then we knew they were ringing in the
heart of God, because we believed He was working things
together for our good (see Rom. 8:28 KJV). Even though we
couldn't hear the bells then, we knew we would later on. As
prayer partners, have you ever heard them? If you have not,
keep on listening and believing.

Freda, just beginning the experience of shared prayer,
began, "We have been married twenty-five years. We are

both Christians who attend church regularly and consider Christ our Lord. However, we rarely pray together—only when serious situations arise. This is really my fault, for I have always considered my prayer-life very personal. I am almost secretive about it."

I knew this was very difficult for her, but she continued, "I have recently come to realize that I must reconsider my view, and I feel this will become a powerful new dimension in our lives."

A severe crisis had invaded her family. "Last night we prayed together because our oldest daughter, after ten years of chemical dependency, has developed a life-threatening disease. I prayed only a few words, through many tears, but I felt a lot of comfort within when I heard my husband express his faith," she concluded.

If Freda and her husband will allow the Holy Spirit to develop that new dimension, I believe with all my heart that the hand of God will pull the rope and set the bells ringing. I believe this because I have known Him to do it many, many times.

We marvel at the change the Holy Spirit made in the life of Saul of Tarsus. We are not told, but I like to believe that somewhere devout Christian prayer partners were storming heaven's gates in his behalf. Perhaps they had seen a look on his face as he held the garments of Stephen, murdered by stoning. Maybe they saw something happen in Paul when Stephen cried out that he saw Jesus (Acts 7:56). Who knows?

But there are many modern Sauls. Mike Graham was an alcoholic of the wocst kind, but a little group of prayer partners in his church would not give up on him. One night his pastor went to see him for the umpteenth time, and that was the night the lightning struck Mike. He received the Risen Lord into his heart, and the Lord drove His tent stakes way down deep, for He intended to stay.

That was more than twelve years ago, and now Mike Graham, with his children and proud wife, is at college preparing for seminary. At the age of thirty-eight he consistently tops his class in almost everything, including Greek. He has a brilliant mind, especially adept at memorization, and is an on-fire preacher.

When Mike's will melted under the onslaught of prayer-love, I believe the joy-bells of heaven probably got stuck. And when they sent for the Master Mechanic to stop the incessant ringing, I'm sure He must have said, "No, let them ring. I like the sound!"

But joy does not always set up such a fire storm in the heart. Sometimes it forms like the fresh dew on newly mown hay. A few days ago Miss Martha was having mild back spasms, as she sometimes does, and at the same time I was attacked by a headache, a rarity for me.

We were both going about our tasks when we crossed paths in the kitchen. Suddenly, acting on an impulse of tenderness, I swept her into my arms. She placed her head on my shoulder, and I began to pray for healing for her back. When I finished, she suddenly began praying for healing of my headache.

It was simply an unplanned act of love, and both our problems were healed, though not at that precise moment. But something did happen instantly—joy came stealing in like a rising tide until it filled us both, and thus armed, we went on our way.

There is no joy comparable to that of two people engaged in the lifelong process of loving each other into the fullness of personhood, when together they find an unplanned taste of the fruit of shared prayer to the Father.

So, dear partners in prayer, don't be caught in a ritualistic mold, allowing yourselves to enter into that kind of intimacy only at 6:30 A.M. across the breakfast table or while kneeling at your bedside at 11:00 at night. Do not remain locked up within your deepest selves until that magic hour when, like the little bird in a cuckoo clock, you can come out and be who you are together.

Couples who do so are self-cheated children of God. Throughout the hot, hard hours when the battles are being fought, there they stand, feet sunk in the hard-set concrete of inflexibility. To such people, the joys of visibly answered prayer might be released to their consciousness at only certain prescribed hours.

Pray together any time, anywhere! It can smash down walls of busyness, anger, dark moods, and strange imaginings one can hold about the other. It extinguishes the carelessly flung word-match, which, if left to burn, can eventually cause a great fire.

I have referred to the small tumor that had grown on the crest of the ilium of one of our children. We arrived home from the doctor's office that day, put the children to bed for their naps, and then just sat staring at the floor, trying to comprehend it all.

Suddenly I said to Miss Martha, "Honey, right now is the time for us to find out if there's anything to this praying-together business I've been preaching about!"

We fell to our knees on the kitchen floor and poured out our hearts to God. I do not remember the prayers we prayed, nor would I try to put them into any kind of theological framework. We were just two young parents, squarely up against something we couldn't handle. Together, we were crying out to God.

When we finished, we arose and embraced. Then like the sudden cooling following a hot summer's thunderstorm, joy came upon us. Why do we think joy must always be a king-sized tingle? That day it was more like *peace*—glad peace, assuring peace, peace telling us softly and tenderly, "You have placed it in My hands; now let Me handle it. Don't be anxious about it!"

It is important that within six weeks, periodic X-rays showed the tumor disappearing until finally it was gone. But in our minds, that was not as important as the inrush of joy which told us both that *He had heard!* That was enough.

Sometimes the Night Can Be Very Long!

Almost always the joy of visibly answered prayer comes after a period of long darkness. We shouldn't be surprised at that. The Bible spells it out very clearly: "Weeping may endure for a night, But joy cometh in the morning" (Ps. 30:5 KJV). Sometimes the night can be very long.

One hot August day in 1944, I was a member of the crew aboard a B-17 bomber, high over Germany. One of the four engines had already malfunctioned when suddenly there was a shattering explosion. Another engine had received a direct hit from antiaircraft fire, and we began to fall in a wide, flat spin toward the earth many thousand feet below.

By the grace of God and the skill of our pilot, the crippled plane straightened, and by throwing all our gear overboard, we managed to limp over the border of neutral Sweden where we made a very rough but safe landing.

For almost five months we were held in an internment camp. Though the miles that separated us were many, my prayer-partner's prayers and mine intermingled many times daily, and we both were aware of it. Distance is always a problem to us, but since God made it, it is not much of a problem to Him. Remember that, if your loved one is far away.

Quite naturally, the crux of all our prayers was that we might be reunited. As time ground on the homesickness became worse, and anyone who has ever experienced that malady knows there is only one cure for it, and that is to be home.

By December it became obvious that the Allies were going

to win the war in Europe, and the Swedish government began to allow internees to "escape," a few at a time. One dark night some of us were spirited aboard a waiting aircraft and flown back to England. There we were reprocessed and sent home.

It was the day after Christmas when I walked (with no advance warning!) into the farm home where Miss Martha was spending the holidays with her parents. And I can tell you, that surely became a Holy-day for us. Joy-drops as big as tennis balls rained down! It was a visible answer to our prayers, one "with skin on." Sometimes the night can be very long!

Sometimes Even Short Nights Can Be Long!

It was a hot day in June 1985, when TWA flight 847 took off from Athens bound for the United States. It is now history that Moslem terrorists seized control of the plane and, making radical demands, forced the pilot to fly back and forth between Albania and Beruit, Lebanon.

For more than forty-eight hours the passengers were beaten, cursed, and kicked; one young serviceman was ruthlessly murdered, his body dropped like a sack of unwanted garbage onto the tarmac at Beruit International Airport.

The pilot of TWA flight 847 was Captain John Testrake. He and his wife Phyllis have been friends of ours for many years. Both are completely sold on the Lord Jesus Christ; they are Spirit-filled Christians in the very finest sense.

Untold millions watched that first interview as John leaned out the cockpit window, a terrorist's arm about his neck and a pistol at his head. When a newsman asked if he had a message for his friends, John replied, "Yes, tell all my friends back in Missouri that the Lord has seen us through this thing this far, and He is going to take us the rest of the way!"

Well, of course the Lord did just that. Millions of people joined their hearts in prayer daily, as did Miss Martha and I. I can speak only for ourselves, but from the very first, that same joy—the kind that creeps in slowly, the kind we knew when we first prayed about our child with the tumor—enveloped us. Our prayers from that time on were prayers of praise to God for what He was doing in the hearts and lives of both the hostages and their captors.

The climax came when the last thirty-nine hostages were flown home to greet their loved ones. They had not been gone a month; others have been hostages for several years. But no matter how long the time, the unspeakable agony is the same.

Because that whole TWA 847 episode was personalized for Miss Martha and me, it was Phyllis Testrake for whom we wept many times in the midnight and at the altar of our church. Hers was the vigil of loneliness and uncertainty, the heart that pounded at every bulletin, announcement, or phone call.

Yes, sometimes even when the nights are short, they can be long! So to those of you still waiting in the midnight—waiting in hospitals, waiting for loved ones hostage to sin and those who live from day to day in the clutches of some dread disease—if you have a faithful prayer-partner in marriage, a relationship that has the prayer-carpet of the Word of God on which to kneel, you have been given a priceless gift. There is no gift from God, other than the Holy Spirit Himself, that is so precious.

Or if perhaps you are just beginning and are erratic, uncertain—maybe even still in the shy stage—let me urge you to press on! Don't let lapses of discipline cause you to give up the dream and fall back into the old ways. Don't let distractions, interruptions, delays, or even difficulties in marital communication cheat you of this priceless heritage. Rather, let it be the vehicle through which not only are all your problems met, but through which your sweetest dreams can come true.

How One Couple Grew into Joyful Prayer-Life

In regard to our prayer-lives, we sometimes are like the Israelites of old—helpless, cornered and trapped by the fierce Goliaths of our problems. We keep waiting for God to send us a giant answer of His own. It will come marching out some bright morning, engage our enemy giant in battle, and destroy it in one great, climatic encounter. Then we will all march home, with banners of victory waving in joy at what God has done.

But more often than not, God does not send us His own giants (though He has them aplenty). He usually just sends small answers, like the teenager David, with his slingshot and five rounded stones.

Did you ever wonder why God instructed David to select *five* stones? David must have wondered, too. He knew he would get only one shot at the giant. But David obeyed God and picked five smooth stones from the dry brook. Now, it occurs to me that God was saying, "I know you will need only one stone to handle this enemy, but here are four more, to deal with the next four giants you meet!"

I want you to see how God grew one couple by giving them an ample supply of stones. Below are three of the questions contained in the questionnaire we mailed out, with some of Al's replies to those questions. Watch Al and Ann grow together. Look for the (unexpressed) joy at the visible answers.

TELL BRIEFLY OF YOUR FIRST EXPERIENCES
OF PRAYER TOGETHER.

"This is probably hard for other Christians to believe, but we had been married twenty years before we actually prayed together as husband and wife. My wife was raised in a very rigid, fundamentalist-type home where God was always displeased with everybody and everything. But there came a time when, in her own life, she actually began to know God's grace instead of only His anger and judgment.

"After we prayed together about her joy over this, we did not continue the practice on a regular basis for the next ten years—until finally we were driven to it by the crisis in our family when our children became teenagers."

Al concluded, "So our lasting prayer relationship together grew out of hopelessness, helplessness, and despair. But for ten years now this prayer union has grown in ways that continue to amaze and bless us!"

LIST SOME ADVANTAGES YOUR PRAYER-LIFE
HAS BROUGHT TO YOUR MARRIAGE.

"We have a new solid basis for coping with marital problems and other crises. For example, after we had been praying together for some time, through Ann's prayers, I came to see many subtle ways I had been hurting her without being aware of it. I was forced to say not just 'I'm sorry' but 'I have been wrong!' Believe me, there is a lot of difference.

"It has helped her understand ways she had hurt me, as well. I don't mean we have been using our prayers as a sly way to 'get at each other.' But in expressing our honest hurts to God, the Holy Spirit gives us ears to hear hurts that are unsaid."

Al did not see these as visible, joyful answers, but how much more joyous and visible can you get?

DO YOU READ GOD'S WORD BEFORE YOU PRAY?
HOW HAS IT HELPED YOU?

Al was really enthusiastic about answering this.

"There is no way I could express how much we have grown by sharing God's Word before we pray. It is the way scientists must have felt when they finally split the atom. They must have thought, 'This is it! We have discovered the final secret of everything!' They thought the split atom was the irreducible end of the science of physics.

"But I was reading just recently that we have now discovered twenty-six new levels below the level of the atom. We have developed an entire new science of subatomic physics!

"That is the way it worked for us. After a year or so of Bible study together before prayer, we began to think we had learned just about all there was to know about the New Testament. But then new insights began to come, and we were constantly in awe at the new and deeper revelations we were receiving.

"Briefly, our devotions consist of reading from the Psalms and from the New Testament (a million new treasures every time!). Then we read one or more devotional commentaries, and then have our verbal prayers.

"We keep a prayer list, constantly adding and scratching off as our many, many prayers are answered! We have, after reading, sometimes spent much time discussing healing or Jesus' experiences with people—how much they are like our own. And we have had lots and lots of discussions about the goodness and grace of God. Ann loves that, for it took her so long to accept.

"But here is a new and exciting thing we have recently discovered. We have almost stopped asking God for things for ourselves—we spend most of our time praying about the needs of others. Sure is a switch from what it used to be!"

There we will end Al's answers, though the document was much longer. I would say that every time Al and Ann go to prayer together, they not only see joyful, visible answers to their prayers, but are themselves such answers. Wouldn't you agree?

A Doctor's Family Is Blessed

For years, some very dear friends, a doctor and his wife, lived the typical life of successful young professionals. They were involved in the social life of an exclusive country club and, as the money flowed in, surrounded themselves with more and more of the toys of humankind. Their son and the wife's brother, also doctors, joined our friend to form a clinic, all practicing in the same suite of offices.

Then a wonderful thing happened. Our friend and his wife gradually sickened of their materialistic life-style. And one weekend, without really knowing why, he went to a Christian retreat. There he met the Lord Jesus Christ face to face and gave his soul and all that he had to the Savior.

He soon lost his materialistic-minded "friends" and formed another group of wonderful, supportive, "turned on" people. His wife soon also found the Lord, and now their lives were sparkling.

But there were some burdens. The son and the brother weren't the least bit interested in things of the Spirit, and the son's wife, a brilliant young woman, was hedonistic, an "intellectual."

Then the prayer war began. How our friends longed for the salvation of their loved ones! They made all the mistakes love sometimes makes: They became pushy, they left pamphlets around, they tried to drag them off to meetings. And they met with rebuff every time. Finally, the only hope left was prayer. And Miss Martha and I added the names to our own prayer list.

As the years passed and God seemingly had forgotten them, things went from bad to worse. To mortal eyes, no cases ever seemed more hopeless. But still our friends prayed, sometimes despairingly and sometimes in great faith, but always they prayed.

Then it happened. The Holy Spirit, in His own beautiful

way, prepared the soil—a Billy Graham crusade came to town! During that time when a great anointing was upon the city, God broke through! He came crashing into the lives of the son and daughter-in-law, and they were gloriously converted. They joined a local Bible-believing church and began to grow in Christ, starting a prayer partnership together and a prayer group in their own home.

A year later the brother suffered a serious heart attack, and in his extremity and through the prayers of many partners, he too found his way back to the Father's house.

Our cup overflowed with the pure joy of visibly answered prayer when, the following year at another great Christian retreat, the son and daughter-in-law gave a thrilling testimony about the way Christ had changed their lives, their home, and the lives of their children. To add to the glory, the brother, gifted with a marvelous voice, sang a magnificent anthem of praise to his Deliverer.

Talk about joy! Talk about happiness! Talk about cups running over and sloshing on everyone around—it happened then! I think that was the day my joy-bell developed a crack like that in the Liberty Bell. But the Holy Spirit welded mine back so the sound is sweeter than ever when it rings. And that is pretty often!

A Final Word to Prayer Partners

After forty-four years of prayer-partner experience with Miss Martha, if I had to summarize the greatest thing we have learned, it would be this: *Never forget the fantastic, supercolossal, unspeakable, indescribable power into which you are tapping when you kneel and pray together!*

I fear that sometimes even now, in our fleshly weariness, we tend to come to Him in the eventide as one might approach a rather lackluster meal. It is as if we know the spiritual nutrients we need are there, but—well, we just eat because it's time to eat and we know we need to do so.

But when we take a moment to think about who God is and what He has done for us as stated in John 3:16, it always brings us back to the thrilling realization of what we are about to do, with *Whom* we are about to speak, and in just what kind of love we are about to participate together. This is the Lord God Almighty, the Great I AM, the crusher of the oppressor—the God of the morning stars, the One who made all the quasars and galaxies, who engineered the black holes and the hundred-million universes so huge we cannot even begin to think our way across them!

He is not some unknowable huge gray blob of ectoplasm that swooshes about from galaxy to galaxy, turning all the right knobs and pressing all the proper buttons on a great instrument board. When He receives the news that a little sparrow has fallen to the ground, He does not receive it on some cold, graphlike printout from His ever-working computer. He knows it in His heart because His great heart is *love itself.* He cares.

He cares so very much that when He leaned over the parapets of heaven and saw our unsolvable problem of sin and disobedience, His love was not in the least intimidated. He found a solution that only *He* could put into effect—that God Himself should become a man. I think this passage in Philippians says it more beautifully and succinctly, in one brilliant burst of revelation, than any other passage in the Scriptures:

> *Let this mind be in you which was also in Christ Jesus, who, being in the form of God, did not consider it robbery to be equal with God, but made Himself of no reputation, taking the form of a servant and coming in the likeness of men. And being found in appearance as a man, He humbled Himself and became obedient to the point of death, even the death of the cross.*

Philippians 2:5-8 (NKJV)

This God, the man Jesus, was forsaken by heaven and by earth; so they hanged Him half-way between. Only death would claim Him, so it took Him in its arms and carried Him down the hill to a new tomb and locked the door with a great stone, fitted with the emperor's own seal. But then the plot took a very strange twist.

Death and decay were stopped dead in their tracks by a great burst of cosmic energy, highly charged with love that could not fail. And the life that surged back into Him "was the light of men. The light shines in the darkness, and the darkness has not overcome it" (John 1:4-5).

He folded the graveclothes and blasted the doorway off His tomb forever. He lived again, and heaven, which had forsaken Him, took Him back.

For twenty centuries, earth has tried to push Him into history's tomb. But He won't stay dead! Every time they try to paste him on the pages of some history book, He comes marching back into their lives, banners waving, trumpets sounding, demanding a decision.

So remember Jesus Christ, and one day when your life has been blown apart, you and your partner, in your brokenness, will come together to your prayer-place and find it shining.

And then again you will know from whence the true Light always comes!

IN SEARCH
OF
FAMOUS
SHIPWRECKS

ADVENTURES OF A
Sea Hunter

Previously published as *Adventures of a Sea Hunter*

JAMES P. DELGADO
foreword by Clive Cussler

MJF BOOKS
NEW YORK

Published by MJF Books
Fine Communications
322 Eighth Avenue
New York, NY 10001

In Search of Famous Shipwrecks
LC Control Number 2007941368
ISBN-13: 978-1-56731-893-7
ISBN-10: 1-56731-893-2

Portions of chapters 6 to 14 previously appeared in a different form
in the *Vancouver Sun* newspaper. Part of the introduction previously
appeared in the *Washington Post*. An account of the dive on the USS *Arizona*
appeared in *The USS Arizona* by Joy Jasper, James P. Delgado,
and Jim Adams, published by St. Martin's Press.

QM   10   9   8   7   6   5   4   3   2   1

This is for my mother, who had to tolerate human bones and stone tools in her bathtub as I learned about the past as a teenage archeologist. And for making her cry as a middle-aged archeologist who dives in dangerous places because, as she points out, I'll always be her little boy.

This is also for Ann, who keeps the home fires burning while juggling a career and an often missing-in action archeologist.

And last, for Beau, my faithful feline companion during many an evening's writing marathon. It's not the same without him.

CONTENTS

OCEAN

FINLAND

ENGLAND

RUSSIA

GERMANY

CHINA

JAPAN

AFRICA

INDIAN

OCEAN

AUSTRALIA

ATLANTIC

OCEAN

1. *Isabella*
2. USS *Arizona*, USS *Utah*
3. USS *Saratoga*, *Nagato*
4. USS *Somers*
5. RMS *Titanic*
6. RMS *Carpathia*
7. *Vrouw Maria*
8. Mongol fleet
9. *General Harrison* and *King Philip*
10. USS *Merrimac*, *Almirante Oquendo*, *Vizcaya*
11. *Mittelbau-Dora*
12. SMS *Dresden*
13. *Fox*
14. *Sub Marine Explorer*
15. *Frances*
16. Unidentified Schooner

ANTARCTICA

His stories were what frightened people worst of all. Dreadful stories they were—about hanging, and walking the plank, and storms at sea, and the Dry Tortugas, and wild deeds and places on the Spanish Main.

ROBERT LOUIS STEVENSON, *TREASURE ISLAND*

FOREWORD

by Clive Cussler

Ships and their crews have been sailing off into oblivion since the dawn
of recorded history. Through the millennia, more than a million ships
have sunk or gone missing, along with untold numbers of their crews. A
million ships is an impressive statistic not believed by most landsmen. Yet,
to call the seven seas a vast cemetery is an understatement.

During the ages, storms have wreaked havoc on entire fleets, some
consisting of more than a thousand ships, that were torn apart and hurled
to the bottom. The first tragedy may have taken place when one of our Cro-
Magnon ancestors happily discovered he could float on water atop a log, at
least until he fell off and drowned. From that time forward, huge ships,
small boats and men have vanished in an unending surge beneath the
waves into dark watery depths that have yet to resurrect their dead.

Except for divers holding their breath and diving in shallow water,
shipwrecks seemed as impossible to reach and touch as a rock on the moon.
Finally, less than two hundred years ago, divers in hard hats, breathing air
pumped down from the surface, started working on the sea bottom and
riverbeds. At long last, the sea begrudgingly began to give up her secrets.

Treasure and salvage came into their own. Salvage became a thriving
enterprise, while treasure hunting was about as hit or miss as buying

stocks in a bear market. Suddenly, shipwrecks in shallower waters became accessible. The boom was on, and shipwrecks were discovered and studied in a prodigious number of projects. Soon, modern technology enabled the salvage of wrecks thousands of feet deep beneath the sea's surface.

The dead in the depths of the sea have no tombstones, no grave markers, nothing to identify their remains that quickly cease to exist. There is an eerie feeling about diving on a shipwreck. You can sense the presence of the crew that died with the ship. A wizened old diver once said that swimming through a shipwreck was like walking through a haunted house.

The last to come on the underwater scene were the marine archeologists. These are about as strange and diverse people as you could ever hope to meet. They seldom become wealthy, and their main claim to fame is in their reports on shipwreck explorations, surveys and artifact removal for conservation and study. Some publish books on their expeditions, some teach, while many work in the commercial end, surveying for government or private corporations that develop properties along waterfronts which might contain history. Not until an accredited archeologist declares the site free of historical artifacts can they begin construction.

Nautical archeologists fight like the furies to preserve a wreck and keep it out of the hands of salvers, treasure hunters and sport divers who are out to pillage shipwrecks of historic significance. Mostly they win, but often they lose the battle to protect a wreck from looters. Their biggest problem is money. Few state, local and federal government agencies have the funding to preserve shipwrecks, so the archeologists squeak by on shoestring budgets from one project to the next.

One who has made a difference is Jim Delgado, a man whose dedication and hard-earned efforts have made a contribution to the field of nautical archeology that cannot be equaled. Of all the archeologists I've known in my years of chasing after historical shipwrecks, he is one of the few who has his feet on the ground and knows more about lost ships than the Congressional Library and Lloyd's of London wrapped up together. His exploits beneath the sea have become legendary.

I'm honored and privileged to call him a friend.

THE GREAT MUSEUM *of the* SEA

For the last thirteen years, I have shared my passion for the past with the public through books and newspaper articles, as a television "talking head" and host, and as a museum director. After I learned how to dive and embarked on a career with the U.S. National Park Service, I traveled the United States, and then the world, in search of shipwrecks. Not all of them were famous, but in the last few decades, the wrecks I've been privileged to see and explore have included some notable ones. But what really keeps me fired up with a passion for the past are the connections to everyday people like you and me. Often, it's an unidentified wreck or the mute evidence of a life forever interrupted that moves me, and grounds the scientist in the firm reality of the human condition. Recently, I've enjoyed a new set of adventures "in search of famous shipwrecks," thanks to John Davis, producer of the National Geographic International television series *The Sea Hunters*. Working with John, together with co-host and famous novelist, raconteur and shipwreck hunter Clive Cussler, master diver Mike Fletcher, his diving son Warren and a great crew behind the camera, is a wonderful experience. We've made dives on many of history's legendary ships, from *Titanic* to lost warships and fabled fleets like the one Kublai Khan sent to conquer Japan in 1274. It's great fun to work with Clive, whose passion is wrecks, particularly finding them when no one else can. With his blessing, we've joined the extended National Underwater and Marine Agency (NUMA) family that he founded, working in the field as more of his "sea hunters" scouting the world's waters for shipwrecks.

In those seven seas, we've encountered history and the stories of the people who make history. Part of the record of humanity's achievements, its triumphs and tragedies, rests out of sight on the seabed: the greatest museum of all lies at the bottom of the sea. My desire to see and touch the past and share it with others continues thanks to the friends and colleagues who have joined me on the ongoing quest. What I've learned along the way from these shipwrecks, both the unknown and the famous, is that they all have tales to tell. Sometimes their broken bones tell me who they are and how they died. Sometimes the story of their birth, their careers and the personalities who sailed in them also come to light, resurrected from the darkness of the deep or the back rooms of an archive. Nearly every time I dive, I am reminded of archeologist Howard Carter's famous comment at the door to Tutankhamen's tomb. No one had passed that threshold in thousands of years. Carter opened a small hole and held up a light as he peered into the darkness of millennia, now briefly illuminated again. "What do you see?" he was asked. "Wonderful things," he answered.

No matter how many times I dive, how many shipwrecks I see, the awe, the excitement, the thrill of discovery, are always there. I, too, see wonderful things. And as an archeologist, educator and museum director, I bring back to the surface what I have seen. I bring back photographs, images, impressions, stories and, occasionally, items—artifacts—to share with others. I only raise an artifact after I or my colleagues have studied it on the bottom, mapped it, photographed it and learned how the piece fits into the puzzle that is the wreck as a whole. I raise artifacts that have the power to tell a story and place them in the laboratory for treatment, where the ravages of the sea and time are halted or reversed, so that they can go on display in public museums. There, artifacts—the "real thing" of history, history that people can see with their own eyes—make the past come alive.

I have had the privilege of diving on wrecks around the world and bringing their stories back from the ocean's floor. From 1982 to 1991,

James Delgado in the water examining the Civil War–era submarine Sub Marine
Explorer. *Marc Pike*

as a member of a U.S. National Park Service team called the Submerged
Cultural Resources Unit, I dived with a group of men and women
committed to preserving shipwrecks and telling their stories. They
included iron-hulled sailing ships swept onto Florida reefs by hurri-
canes, ocean steamers strewn along rocky shores on both coasts of the
Americas, wooden-hulled schooners sunk in the Great Lakes and
warships on the bottom of the Pacific. We mapped, photographed,
researched, studied and then shared what we learned with the public
through museum displays, books and magazine articles, television
screens and newspapers. Since leaving government service thirteen years
ago to become the director of a maritime museum, I have continued to
dive and study wrecks. Now, thanks to *The Sea Hunters* show and its
television audience of forty million people around the world, I have an
even greater ability to share these exciting discoveries.

I have dived on many ships in the past two and a half decades.
They include the Civil War gunboat uss *Pickett* in North Carolina, the

Revolutionary War transport HMS *Betsy* (sunk at the Battle of Yorktown in 1788), the steamship *Winfield Scott* (lost off the California coast during the gold rush) and the aircraft carrier *Saratoga* (swamped and partly crushed in a 1946 atomic test at Bikini Atoll). I have dived in the freezing waters of the Arctic to study the wreck of *Maud*, the last command of polar explorer Roald Amundsen. There are many others, and you are about to share those adventures in the pages that follow.

Sadly, in those same years, I have also seen serious damage done to wrecks by thoughtless souvenir seekers and treasure hunters. In Mexico, while studying the wreck of the brig *Somers*—the only ship in the U.S. Navy to suffer a mutiny and whose story inspired Melville to write *Billy Budd*—I discovered that souvenir hunters had ripped into the ship's stern, taking some of the small arms, swords and the ship's chronometer. We never got them back. They either crumbled into dust without treatment, or were treated and sold on the black market. This happens too often. I also have watched countless auctions of artifacts from shipwrecks, raised by treasure hunters and sold off to the highest bidder, usually not museums, as most museums will not participate in activities that turn archeological relics into commodities for sale. Our role is to encourage understanding and appreciation of the past, of other cultures and of who we are. We work to encourage science and knowledge. Wrenching a porthole off a wreck or digging into a ballast pile on the bottom to take a copper spike home is as wrong as systematically mining a wreck of its artifacts and then selling them off with some hype, often abetted by the media.

A few years ago, I went on a trip to Bermuda, a graveyard of lost ships and home to one of the world's great maritime museums. In a souvenir shop, I saw a brick with a maker's stamp from San Francisco. I had only seen that stamp once before, in the ballast of a mid-nineteenth century wreck in the North Pacific that I was still trying to identify. I asked where the brick came from. "A shipwreck off the coast," I was told. Did they know what ship? Where had it come from? How old was it? How had this brick from far-off San Francisco reached the Caribbean? Where had the wrecked ship gone in her travels? The shopkeeper didn't know. A local diver had pulled it off the bottom a long time ago, and others had followed to strip the wreck clean. The souvenir shop, and others like it, had been selling bits and pieces of the wreck to tourists for years. This was an opportunity lost, a story never told. The divers, the shops, the buyers who wanted a "piece of the past," had scattered the pieces of the puzzle all over the globe, and now the puzzle will never be assembled to reveal the whole picture.

It is those pictures, the connections that these wrecks have not just to the great sweep of history but to individual lives, to stories of people like you and me, that compel me to explore and investigate. My life has been defined by a quest to learn about the past and share it. This is the story of that quest, as related by the stories of the lost ships in the great museum of the sea.

CHAPTER ONE

GRAVEYARD *of the* PACIFIC

OFF CAPE DISAPPOINTMENT, WASHINGTON

The long, uninterrupted swells of the north Pacific gather momentum as they surge eastward across thousands of miles of open water to break, finally, on the shoals and rocks of the northern coast of the American continent. On that rough and savage shoreline is the mouth of the Columbia, the great and mighty river that divides Oregon and Washington.

At the mouth of the Columbia, buttressed by the two small settlements of Astoria, Oregon, and Ilwaco, Washington, the river's burden of silt and sand spreads out into the ocean, forming a massive "bar" at the entrance. The bulk of the bar catches the force of the open sea, and as a result the transition zone from ocean to river is a dangerous one that surprises unwary mariners—the area is a graveyard of ships drowned by the force of huge waves that surge over the bar's shallows. More than two thousand vessels, from mighty square-riggers and freighters to hardworking fish boats, have been caught in the bar's trap and lost, along with countless lives. And yet, because this bar is an obstacle that must be overcome to engage in trade on the Columbia, with its ports full of produce, wheat, lumber and fish, for more than two centuries seafarers have braved it and their chances to enter the great river of the west.

Efforts to make the passage safer commenced in the mid-nineteenth century with the installation of a lighthouse at Cape Disappointment and continued with the construction of breakwaters and the marking of a channel through the shoals. But the power of nature can never be tamed, and the government's money has perhaps more effectively been spent upholding the century-old traditions of the United States Life-Saving Service and its successor, the U.S. Coast Guard. There is no rougher or more dangerous place to ply the trade of the lifesaver than here, at the mouth of the Columbia, a grim reality measured by the memorials to those who laid down their own lives so that others might survive, and by the fact that it is here that America's lifesavers come to learn their trade at Cape Disappointment's National Motor Lifeboat School. It is not for the faint of heart or the timid—the sea is a rough teacher, and the Columbia River bar, if you relax your guard, will kill you.

All of these thoughts, and the lessons of history evident in the lists of lost ships and images of crushed, broken and mangled hulls, fill my head as the Coast Guard's motor lifeboat pitches and rolls on the bar. The lifeboat lifts high on a wave, into the bright blue sky, before dropping into the trough of the next wave, so that all I see is the dark gray-green water towering high above, blocking out the sun. Then, as the boat turns, the water crashes down, swirling and thundering as it sweeps over the deck. Then, suddenly, it is gone, as the plucky lifeboat sheds the sea and gives itself a shake, just like a dog, and climbs the next wave. It is both terrifying and exhilarating. The skill of the Coast Guard coxswain and the fact that I'm dressed in a survival suit with a crash helmet on my head and am tied down to the deck by a harness that tethers me tightly so that even if I fall I will not be swept away, add to my confidence. My fellow archeologists share a shaky grin with me, savoring the risk while not acknowledging the fear in our eyes.

The hours we spend in this lifeboat experiencing the waters of the bar are a lesson in the power of the sea and the danger of the Columbia's entrance, courtesy of the Coast Guard and the commander of the "Cape D" station, Lieutenant Commander Mike Montieth. Our team, assembled by the National Park Service (NPS), has come here to the graveyard of the Pacific to dive on a recently discovered wreck that may just be the earliest one yet found on this coast, the Hudson's Bay Company (HBC) supply ship *Isabella*, lost on the Columbia bar in 1830. Montieth, who has already visited the wreck, has arranged this no-holds barred introduction to the Columbia so that we might better understand the dynamic and violent environment in which we are about to dive. As we ride the roller-coaster seas off Cape Disappointment, the team gains a new perspective on the predicament of Captain William Ryan and *Isabella*'s crew more than 150 years ago.

ISABELLA: COLUMBIA RIVER, MAY 3, 1830

The Hudson's Bay Company supply ship *Isabella* had survived a long and hard six-month voyage from London's docks to the "North West Coast," marked by rough seas, a stormy passage around Cape Horn that had damaged the ship and a mutinous carpenter whom Captain William Ryan had clapped in irons for several weeks. Scanning his chart, Ryan squinted at the coast. For over a day, they had maneuvered off Columbia's bar, searching for the channel and a safe entrance. Now, in the predawn darkness, Ryan saw a point of land that he was certain had to be Cape Disappointment. Turning to first mate William Eales, he gave the order to head into the channel.

Now, the end of the voyage was in sight. Ryan's orders were to slowly work *Isabella* up the Columbia River for 110 miles to Fort Vancouver, the Pacific coast headquarters of the Hudson's Bay Company. There, he would discharge his cargo of trade goods and take on bundles of valuable fur, gathered by trappers and traders, for the return trip to England.

But as *Isabella* sailed across the bar, Ryan immediately realized that he had made a mistake. The sea surged and rolled over the shallows, picking up the ship and hurtling it towards a patch of broken water. They were not in the channel, but on the bar itself. Then *Isabella* hit hard at the stern. "She's not answering the helm," shouted the mate.

Looking over the stern, Ryan saw broken pieces of the rudder swirling in the sea. Without her steering, the ship swung wildly. Waves crashed over the side and filled the deck with masses of water. As each wave rolled over the ship, *Isabella* pounded hard on the sand. Ryan had to act quickly, or the ship would be lost. Using the sails to catch the wind and steer off the bar was his only chance. But first, the crew had to lighten the ship. Pinned by her heavy cargo, *Isabella* was slowly sinking into the sand as the waves washed around the hull.

The men set to work, heaving overboard piles of lumber stacked on the deck. With axes, they smashed open the heavy water casks to empty them. Then, laboring in the surging surf, they dumped 30 tons of cargo and stores into the sea, but still *Isabella* would not budge. As the sun climbed into the sky, Ryan saw that they were stuck fast and pounding hard, and that water was flooding into the hold. He later explained to his superiors that as "there appeared little prospect of saving her and being surrounded by heavy breakers fearing she would drive on shore into them when it would be impossible to save ourselves," he gave the order to abandon ship. Grabbing what they could, the crew piled into the ship's two boats and dropped into the sea. "Pull! Pull for your lives!" the mate roared as the boats climbed one breaker, then another, and *Isabella* disappeared behind them in the towering waves.

The men strained at the oars until the boats at last pulled free of the breakers and flying surf. Wiping the stinging salt water from his eyes, Ryan scanned the horizon. Darkness had fallen, and along the shore, he saw fires blazing up. Some of the men saw them, too, and muttered among themselves. Ryan's voice, loud and clear, reassured them: "We are strangers in this uncivilized country, and we shall not land, lest we be murdered by the natives." Just the year before, the Hudson's Bay Company supply ship *William and Ann* had wrecked on the Columbia bar, and none of the crew had survived. The headless body of her captain, identified by his blue uniform jacket, had borne mute witness to what the HBC was sure was the savagery of the neighboring Clatsop people. A search of the native village had turned up items from the wreck, and the HBC men had bombarded the Clatsop with cannon fire to punish them for pilfering the wreck.

Watching the fires on the beach, Ryan shivered at the thought of landing and falling into the hands of the Clatsop, having "heard such evil reports of the savage character" of the natives. So *Isabella*'s crew headed up the river to Fort Vancouver. It took them a full day to reach the fort.

At Fort Vancouver, Ryan and his men reported to Dr. John McLoughlin, the chief factor, or head of the fort, and the officer in charge of the Hudson's Bay Company's activities on the Pacific coast. Tall, with a full head of flowing white hair, McLoughlin represented what was then the most powerful commercial interest on the continent. Chartered in 1670 by King Charles II as the "Company of Adventurers of England trading into Hudson's Bay," the Hudson's Bay Company had royal authority to exploit the resources of a vast area that stretched from the shores of Hudson Bay to encompass much of what eventually would become Canada and some of the United States.

The HBC's first ship on the coast was the 161-ton, Bermuda-built brig *William and Ann*, which started operating in 1824. But the coastal trading effort, as well as the annual supply of Fort Vancouver, had been dealt a serious blow when *William and Ann* wrecked at the mouth of the Columbia River on March 10, 1829, with the loss of the entire crew and most of the cargo. To replace her, the HBC bought *Isabella*, a four-year-old 194-ton brig, for the tidy sum of £2,900 in October 1829. *Isabella* was loaded with a diverse and expensive cargo that reflected the needs of Fort Vancouver's growing agricultural and industrial community: tools, medicines, preserved foods, lead and pig iron, paint and stationery supplies. She was also loaded with the commodities of the fur trade: guns, ammunition, blankets, beads, copper cooking pots, candles, mirrors, tinware, buttons, combs, tobacco and tea.

Following right after the wreck of *William and Ann*, the loss of *Isabella* was a serious blow. But McLoughlin's consternation turned to rage the day after Ryan and his shipwrecked crew arrived at Fort Vancouver. Messengers from Fort George, a small Hudson's Bay Company outpost at the Columbia's mouth, reported they had seen *Isabella* enter the wrong channel and become stranded on the bar. They had raced to the brig's assistance and lit a fire to signal Ryan, but the captain had mistaken it for marauding and murderous natives and had fled up the river with his crew. In the morning, the Fort George men had boarded *Isabella* and found that the ship and her cargo were aground but reasonably safe, then sent word to McLoughlin.

Furious, McLoughlin sent the hapless Ryan and his crew back down the river to their ship to save what they could. In a letter to his superiors, he reported: "When Capt. Ryan arrived here he could not distinctly ascertain where he had left his vessel . . . it was only when I received Mr. Mansons [report] I actually learnt where she was and if Capt. Ryan had remained on board with his crew it is certain the vessel would have been saved as on the turn of the tide they had only to slip her cable and she would have drifted into smooth water."

When Ryan and his crew arrived back at the wreck, they found *Isabella* on her side on a small island just inside the river's mouth. She was full of water and, as the incoming tide washed away the sand that swirled around the hull, was slowly being swallowed up. The first task was to save the valuable cargo still inside the brig.

The next few days were spent stripping the wreck. The masts and rigging were chopped free and stacked on the island, and the crew began to unload the cargo from the dark, wet confines of the hold. Work stopped each day at high tide, when the heavy surf that broke over the capsized hulk made it dangerous to even approach the wreck. The hold flooded each day, making each day a repetition of pumping. After two weeks of back-breaking work, *Isabella* was at last emptied and the task of trying to save the dismasted hull began.

But the sand and the sea would not relinquish the wreck. A survey on May 24 found the brig settled into a deep hole, the hold full of water, beams cracked, decks and bulwarks washed away, and the hull beginning to crack in half. It was hopeless, and the surveyors wrote to McLoughlin that any attempts to save *Isabella* "would be an unnecessary sacrifice of labour... as we consider her a total wreck." With that, the ship was abandoned to the water and the sands of the Columbia bar.

ON THE WRECK OF *ISABELLA*

Although the sands of the bar had swallowed *Isabella*, occasionally they washed away to expose some broken timbers. Charts from 1880 to 1921 mark a wreck at the site where, in September 1986, Daryl Hughes, a commercial fisherman, snagged his nets. Other fishermen had snagged nets there, but Hughes was the first to send down a diver, who reported that Hughes's net was wrapped around the hull of a wooden ship. Hughes, who knew the river's history, thought that he might have found *Isabella* and reported the discovery to the Columbia River Maritime Museum, just across the river from the wreck site.

The museum's curator, Larry Gilmore, enlisted the support of a number of people, notably Mike Montieth, the Coast Guard commander of the "Cape D" station. An avid wreck diver himself, Montieth led a group of volunteers on a series of explorations of the wreck. In the murky darkness, Montieth began to sketch out the sloping sides of a wooden ship with a series of what looked like gun ports, a discovery that puzzled the investigators. Perhaps the hulk emerging from the sand wasn't *Isabella* after all, but USS *Peacock* or USS *Shark*, two warships lost on the deadly Columbia River bar in 1841 and 1846. A sand-encrusted cutlass from *Shark* and a rock with a message carved into it by the survivors of that wreck are among the prize exhibits at the Columbia River Maritime Museum, relics of one of the hundreds of ships lost at this graveyard of the Pacific.

To help resolve the questions, our National Park Service team was called in. The team leader, Daniel J. "Dan" Lenihan, who is an intensely focused, hardworking archeologist with a quiet demeanor, created the U.S. government's first field team of underwater archeologists. The work of Dan and his team has also revolutionized underwater archeology in the United States, both in the way that work is done in the water and how archeologists think about shipwreck sites.

The team that assembles at Astoria in August 1987 includes Dan Lenihan, myself and another adjunct member of his team, Larry Nordby, who looks like a Viking and whose skill in the science of archeology is enhanced by the ability to measure and draw the remains of ships on the bottom in the worst possible conditions. We three are joined by volunteers—Mike Montieth, local shipwreck historian and wreck diver James Seeley White, and other local divers who have already been exploring the wreck of *Isabella*.

As we gear up on the boats that are tied off the line that Mike has rigged to the wreck, he and Dan brief us. The wreck lies in only 48 feet of water on a hard sand bottom. That's the easy part. The tough part is that the current rips through at such a fast pace that a diver can't hold on when the tide ebbs and flows, so we can only go in the water at slack tide, when the current dies down to a dull roar. It's also dark down there. Mud in the water near the surface blocks the light, so we have to feel our way over the broken wooden hulk, guided by a flashlight that illuminates just a few yards ahead. Then there are the fishing nets and crab pots caught on the ship's protruding timbers, along with fishing line drifting in the current, to snag dive gear and unwary divers.

This is not going to be easy. In fact, I'm scared, but not enough to stay out of the water. We all jump in and make our way to the buoy that marks the wreck. The current tugs and pulls at us. Dan looks carefully at each one of us, checking to see if we're ready. With a series of nods, we vent the air from our buoyancy compensating vests and start down the line, into the dark water.

The green water becomes gray and then black. Then, suddenly, I land on a thick wooden beam, encrusted with barnacles and wrapped with the buoy line. I'm on the wreck. Mike and the other divers have done an excellent job of sketching the basic outline of the wreck—the curving side

A site map of Isabella *as the wreck looked in 1987. National Park Service*

of the hull, with ports open in what may be two rows. I turn and put my face close to the hull to examine it better, then switch on my light and follow Larry and Dan as we make a quick inspection of the hull. It is clearly half of a ship, with broken beams and timbers indicating where the decks were. From the weather deck to the bottom of the hull, this half is nearly complete, though we don't yet know which side of the ship it is. Later dives will confirm that it is the starboard, or right-hand side, of the wreck.

Dan has asked me to take a careful look at the ports to see if they are for guns. Six of them, in a row, line the hull below the level of the deck. They are small square ports—they seem too small to be for guns, I think—and I run my gloved hand along the top of one to check for hardware or the hole for a lanyard to pull open a gun port. The wood is solid, and there is no evidence of hinges or other hardware. They look to be cargo ports—square holes cut to load bulk cargo like coal or grain, then plugged with wood and caulked for the voyage. To make sure, I inspect each one. My reward for this meticulous work is a sudden encounter with the rotting head of a salmon, stuck in a wad of net inside one of the ports, its empty eye sockets staring at me as I stick my head into the port. It gives me a start, and I hit my head on the top of the narrow aperture and curse.

Dropping further down, I look for the second row of ports. I find only one opening, and after examining it closely, I decide that this is not a port. It is a roughly square hole that has been cut into the side of the ship. The rounded corners indicate that an auger was used to drill through the thick planks. The preservation of the wood, buried in sand and kept intact by the brackish water of the river where wood-eating organisms cannot survive, is remarkable; taking off my glove, I can feel the edges where a saw has bitten into the wood to cut out the hole. Some of the edges of the planks are splintered, as if an axe was used to help open up the hole. I smile, for this, I am sure, proves the wreck is *Isabella*.

How do I know? The Hudson's Bay Company kept *Isabella*'s logbook, which Captain Ryan had saved from the wreck and in which he made entries each day as they labored to save the brig and her cargo, ending only when it was apparent she was doomed. While reading a copy of the ship's log in preparation for the expedition, I learned that the ship's carpenter had cut a hole in the side. As my fingers trace his crude but effective handiwork in the gloom at the bottom of the Columbia, I think back to that journal entry: "Cut a hole in the side to let the water out, so that we could better get at the cargo."

Dan is signaling that it's time to surface. As we climb out, there are grins all around. This wreck, dark and dangerous as it is, is fascinating. The next few days quickly fall into a routine of early morning breakfasts at a small fishermen's restaurant and two dives a day, which is all we can manage because of the currents and tides.

On one of these dives, I nearly become part of the wreck. Working in the darkness to map the wreck, Larry and I are signaled by Dan to get back to the line. The current has picked up slightly ahead of schedule, and we've got to surface. As we slowly work our way up the line, the current hits hard, and we have to hold on with both hands to fight the current to reach the boats. I'm the last one up. Exhausted, I stand on the ladder at the stern of Jim White's boat. Forgetting my training, I

A side-scan sonar image showing Isabella. *National Oceanic and Atmospheric Administration/Columbia River Maritime Museum.*

pull off my mask and spit out my regulator. Instead of climbing up or handing up my weight belt or tank, I reach down and pull off my fins, one at a time. I fumble the last fin. As I reach out to catch it, the weight of my gear pulls me off the ladder and back into the water.

I fall fast and hit the bottom. Without my mask, I can't see very well, but it looks like I've landed next to the wreck. The strong current is rolling me along the bottom, and I can't reach my regulator, which has twisted and is now behind me. With the desperate strength people sometimes find in these situations, I push off the bottom with my legs and kick for the surface, my lungs burning. My outstretched hands hit the bottom of the boat, and I claw and scratch my way along the fiberglass hull to get out from under it. But the weight of my tank and belt drags me back down into the water. I hit the bottom again and start rolling. My mouth opens convulsively, and I take in a breath of cold water and gag. I'm going to die, I realize, and I'm really angry. Like most accidents, this one is a combination of a foolish move and a deceptively dangerous dive site. My eyes are wide open, but my vision is narrowing, and I know that I'm about to black out.

Finally, my dive training kicks in. I reach down and tug at the clasp of my weight belt. It falls free. Then I reach up to my buoyancy compensator to pull the lanyard that activates a CO_2 cartridge. I start to float off the river bed and remember not to hold my breath or I'll burst my lungs as I rocket to the surface. When my head rises out of the water, I reach up and try to draw in a breath, choking with the water I've inhaled. Hands grab me and pull me into a Zodiac—I've rolled and drifted a few hundred yards away from where I fell in. I lie on the bottom of the inflatable, coughing up the muddy water from my lungs. Shaky, dripping and miserable, I climb onto the deck of Jim White's boat, wipe my face, and ask, "Well, did I die like a man?" Dan makes sure I'm okay and debriefs me to ensure I learned from my mistake, and then we're back at work at the next slack tide.

When everything is all done, we have a beautiful plan of the wreck, drawn by Larry, that confirms this is indeed *Isabella*. The size and construction closely match the known characteristics of the ill-fated brig. The location is exactly where the ship's log placed the efforts to save the stranded vessel, off what is still known as San Island inside the Columbia's mouth. And the remains on the bottom show a determined salvage effort, from the open cargo ports to the hacked-off rigging fittings. But the real indicator, in the end, is that single, crudely hacked hole in the side.

On return dives to *Isabella* in 1994, Mike Montieth and Jerry Ostermiller, the director of the Columbia River Maritime Museum, discovered that more of the wreck had been exposed by shifting sand. So ten years after the first dives, I returned to Astoria with a team of divers from the Underwater Archaeological Society of British Columbia. With more of the hull exposed, we could see that the brig had literally unzipped along its keel, splitting in two as the bow and stern broke apart in the flying surf that battered *Isabella*. I also found the ship's rudder post, torn free

James Delgado examines the exposed bow of the British four-masted bark Peter Iredale, *wrecked near the entrance to the Columbia River in October 1906. Unlike* Isabella, *whose wreck is shrouded in underwater darkness in the nearby river,* Iredale *is a visible victim of the "Graveyard of the Pacific." © Darryl Leniuk Photography*

and broken, the thick fastenings for the rudder shattered by the force of the ship's stern hitting the bar. We had hoped to find some of the brig's fur-trade cargo, as the Hudson's Bay Company archives showed that not everything had been recovered from the wreck in 1830. But the hull was empty of artifacts, and the only tale this shattered wreck could tell was the sad one of just how she had died.

CHAPTER TWO

PEARL HARBOR

DECEMBER 7, 1941: A DAY OF INFAMY

"Yesterday, December 7, 1941—a date which will live in infamy—the United States was suddenly and deliberately attacked by naval and air forces of the Empire of Japan... The attack yesterday on the Hawaiian Islands has caused severe damage to American naval and military forces. Very many American lives have been lost... Always we will remember the character of the onslaught against us. No matter how long it may take us to overcome this premeditated invasion, the American people in their righteous might will win through to absolute victory." The indignant and stirring words of President Franklin Delano Roosevelt as he addressed Congress on December 8, 1941, ring through my mind as my plane crosses the United States. I'm on the way to Pearl Harbor to join a long-standing National Park Service survey of USS *Arizona* and other ships that lie beneath the waters of that battlefield.

Being an archeologist thoroughly at home in the mid-nineteenth century, I am surprised by the realization that I've worked on more World War II wrecks than any other type of ship. That includes a decade of work for the National Park Service, studying and documenting World War II fortifications and battle sites. Recently, I have been posted to Washington, D.C., as the first maritime historian of the National Park Service, to head up a new program to inventory and assess the nation's maritime heritage, and the work included dozens of visits to preserved warships and museums.

I've already studied one shipwreck, the Civil War ironclad USS *Monitor*, for historic landmark status. Now I'm on my way to Pearl Harbor to carry out a similar study of the battle-ravaged *Arizona* and the nearby USS *Utah*, both sunk on December 7, 1941. Dan Lenihan and the Submerged Cultural Resources Unit of the National Park Service have invited me to join them to dive at the site of the first action in America's war in the Pacific. Congress had passed a law making *Arizona*, still the responsibility of the Navy, a memorial to be jointly administered by the Navy and the National Park Service.

Most of the initial survey work on *Arizona* and *Utah* has been done, but I will dive with the team on both wrecks as part of the historic landmark study. I'll also be participating in a side-scan sonar survey of the waters outside Pearl Harbor to search for a Japanese midget submarine that was sunk just before the attack commenced, a warning that was not heeded in time. The midget sub sank in deep water and has never been found.

BATTLESHIP ROW: USS *ARIZONA*

Standing on the narrow concrete dock while a group of tourists slowly files into the *Arizona* Memorial, I look across the waters of Pearl Harbor's Battleship Row. The battleships are gone, their places marked by white concrete quays that the U.S. Navy has kept painted for more than four decades. The names on the quays are those of the battleships that were moored to each on the morning of December 7, 1941: USS *Nevada*, USS *West Virginia*, USS *Tennessee*, USS *Oklahoma* and, directly in front of me, USS *Arizona*. Unlike the other ships, which have only a painted name to mark their passing, *Arizona* rests in the water below me.

Around me is a group of other divers drawn from the ranks of the National Park Service and the U.S. Navy, all of us preparing our gear and suiting up to jump into the dark green waters of the harbor. The water is too warm for a wetsuit, but bare skin is no protection against

A perspective view of USS Arizona *from the stern. Drawing by*
Jerry L. Livingston, courtesy USS Arizona *Memorial Association*

barnacles and rusted steel, so I pull on a pair of Park Service dark green coveralls before strapping on my weight belt, tanks and gear.

After reading dozens of books and poring over files and interviews with men who fought here on that tragic day, I'm ready to explore a ship that precious few have been allowed to visit. *Arizona* is a war grave, and as many as nine hundred of her crew are interred within the crumbling steel of the battleship. This is sacred ground for Americans, and a potent symbol of a long and terrible war that, for the United States, began here. Only a handful of divers have been allowed to go beneath the surface and explore the ship.

The large American flag flying over the wreck of *Arizona* waves lightly in the warm breeze against a bright blue sky. I pause for a second, then turn back to my gear checks and final preparations. With my dive partner on one side, we stride together off the dock, splashing into the murky water and sinking 45 feet to the soft muddy bottom. We can't see more than a couple of yards ahead as we adjust our buoyancy. Floating gently over the mud, we swim slowly towards the wreck.

My subconscious registers the looming presence of the hulk before I realize that I see it. Perhaps it is the shadow of the wreck's mass in the sun-struck water, masked by the silt, but there, suddenly darker and cooler. My heart starts to pound and my breath gets shallow for a second with superstitious fear. This is my first dive on a shipwreck with so many lost souls aboard. I flick on my light and the blue-green hull comes alive with marine life in bright reds, yellows and oranges, some of it the rust that crusts the once pristine steel. As I rise up from the muddy bottom, I encounter my first porthole. It is an empty dark hole that I cannot bring myself to look into. I feel the presence of the ship's dead, and though I know it is only some primitive level of my subconscious at work, I can't look in because of the irrational fear that someone inside will look back.

Not once throughout this dive, nor ever in the dives that follow, do I forget that this ship is a tomb. But the curiosity of the archeologist overcomes the fear, and I look into the next porthole. As my light reaches inside, I see what looks like collapsed furniture and a telephone attached to a rusted bulkhead. This is the cabin of Rear Admiral Isaac Kidd, who died on that long-ago December morning. His body was never found. Salvage crews found Kidd's ring partly melded to the steel at the top of *Arizona*'s conning tower, apparently blown there by the force of the blast that sank the ship.

From here, we rise up to the deck and follow it to the rim of the No. 4 turret. The turret, stripped by U.S. Navy salvagers during the war, is now a large round hole in the heart of the battleship. Half filled with silt, it has been designated as the receptacle for the urns of *Arizona*'s survivors, who, years after the battle, choose to be cremated and interred with their former shipmates for eternity. It is a powerful statement about the bonds forged by young men in service together, bonds that even the passage of decades and death itself cannot fully sever. I gaze at the first urn placed inside here in March 1984 and pause for a respectful moment of prayer before rising again to the deck. I turn to my right and head for the stern, and there, in water that is only a couple of yards deep, I float on the surface and look down at the empty socket for the jackstaff where *Arizona*'s flag once flew.

After the blast that split open *Arizona* and set her ablaze, the crew abandoned ship. Flooded and sunk to the bottom, *Arizona* rested in the soft mud, which gradually, as the next few days passed, yielded to the weight of the massive ship. Ultimately, the decks disappeared beneath the water. Today, they lie just a few feet below the surface and nearly half the hull is buried in the mud. But on the evening of December 7, even as fires blazed forward, the stern was not touched and the ship's huge American ensign hung off the jackstaff. One of *Arizona*'s officers, Lieutenant Kleber S. Masterson, was ashore during the attack. He returned to assist with first aid and muster the surviving crew members. "There weren't many," he later said. "Out of eight-four men in my fire control division, I think there were only five survivors."

After being temporarily reassigned to the battleship *Maryland*, Masterson decided to return to *Arizona* to take down the flag. "It was the big Sunday ensign flying from the stern, and it was dragging in the water and getting all messed up with oil." With another *Arizona* survivor, Ensign Leon Grabowsky, Masterson motored over to the still-burning ship in a launch. Jumping aboard, they found only an eerie silence. "We heard no noises, because there were, of course, no survivors under that little bit of deck we could walk on." As the sun set, Grabowsky lowered the flag while Masterson gathered up the oily cloth in his arms. They returned to *Maryland* and handed over the flag to the officer of the deck, who sent it off to be burned. Drifting over the spot where the two officers performed that final ceremonial duty, I think not only of Masterson and Grabowsky but of all the men who died that day.

Backing up, I drop down to look at the fantail. A buoy chained to the wreck here marks the stern to passing boats. The buoy's mooring chain drags across the steel hull, back and forth, scraping off corrosion and marine growth. The thick steel letters that spell out the name ARIZONA are bright and shiny, polished by the incessant movement of the chain. They reflect some of the sunlight that drifts down through the water, and for brief moments, the name of the ship blazes as if on fire again. It is an awe-inspiring sight, and I hang there listening to the beat of my heart and the air moving through my regulator.

Swimming back to the edge of the deck, we follow it along the starboard side, coming up to an open hatch near the No. 3 turret. I hover over it, looking down into the darkness, my light picking up the tangle of debris that blocks it. Then, to my surprise, I see something rising up to meet me. It is a blob of oil, no bigger than a child's marble. It passes the edge of the hatch and floats to the surface, where it turns into an iridescent slick. Six seconds later, another globule of oil follows it, and I, like so many others who have watched this phenomenon, am struck by the fact that *Arizona* still bleeds.

The light-filled warm waters on the shallowly submerged deck give way to darkness as we pass beneath the memorial. I look up through the water and notice visitors staring down, some of them seeing me, others gazing out and a few tossing their offerings of flower leis into the sea. We pause here for a drop over the side, past the empty mount for a 5-inch gun, and drop down to the top of the torpedo blister. The blister, a late addition to the ship's armored sides, was supposed to protect *Arizona* from submarine attack by absorbing the impact of a torpedo. The defenses of Pearl Harbor were focused on a submarine attack, not an aerial assault.

The hatches that line the top of the torpedo blister are open, but what we are looking for should be resting atop the blister. In April 1982, the widow of an *Arizona* survivor who wished to rest with his shipmates dropped his urn from the memorial onto the wreck. With the decision to place urns in the open well of No. 4 turret, the National Park Service has just received her permission to relocate his urn from the blister. I think I see the urn, but it lies inside a corroded section of hull that cuts deep into my thumb when I try to pull it free. We leave the urn there. It is wedged in too deeply, so this is where it will remain.

The dropping of that urn and the decision to allow the interment of other survivors inside the hull of *Arizona* attest to the ongoing emotional pull of the wreck. I am reminded of that as we drift past the overhanging memorial again and look down at the deck, lit brightly by the sun. Combs, sunglasses and camera lens caps lie where they were dropped accidentally. Coins carpet the deck, so many coins, in fact, that the National Park Service sends in snorkeling rangers to collect these offerings to the sea and donates them to charity. But as we swim along, we spot photographs, some weighted down, others waterlogged and moving loose with the swell. They show women whose hair has gone gray or white, some with younger men and women and babies. I wonder for a second, why these are here, and then it hits me. These are wives and sweethearts, now grown old, sharing children and grandchildren with *Arizona*'s dead.

We continue on over the remains of the galley. The stubs of the legs of the steam tables, mess tables and the bases of ovens protrude through the mud. Here and there, bright white hexagonal tiles are uncovered as our fins sweep the deck clear of silt. Broken dishes, coffee cups and silverware lie scattered, reminders of a breakfast forever interrupted. The tile on the decks gives way to teak, unblemished and still polished in places. Despite the passage of decades and the onslaught of corrosion, there are places that time has not touched. In addition to the teak decks, we find a porthole with its glass in place, and inside it, the steel blast cover set tight and dogged down in condition "Z" for battle. Between the steel and the glass, the space is only partially flooded with oily water.

Another moment stopped in time lies on *Arizona*. Snaked-out lines of fire hose show where some of the crew fought not against the attacking enemy but to save their ship. As thick, choking smoke smothered the decks, men dragged out hoses to deal with the fires caused by the several bombs that hit the ship. Those men were wiped clean off the decks by the final blast that sank *Arizona*. Seven bombs hit the battleship before the last blow, at least three of them massive 1,750-pound, armor-piercing bombs made from 16-inch naval projectiles taken from the magazines of the Japanese battleship *Nagato*. Flying high above the harbor, Petty Officer Noburo Kanai, in the rear seat of a Nakajima B5N2 bomber from the carrier *Soryu*, trained his sights on the stricken *Arizona*. He released his bomb from 9,800 feet and watched as it spiraled down and struck the battleship's decks. He yelled *"Ataramashita!"* (It hit!)

The bomb struck *Arizona* near the No. 2 turret and punched through three decks before exploding deep inside the bowels of the ship, setting off about a thousand pounds of high-explosive black powder stored in a small magazine. The force of the blast smashed through an armored deck and ignited the ship's forward powder magazines. Each 14-inch gun magazine held 10 tons of powder, and each 5-inch gun magazine held 13 tons. Nine of these magazines, holding altogether 99 tons of powder, erupted in a low, rumbling roar that released heat so intense it softened steel. The blast and the wave of heat bucked the ship out of the water, nearly taking off the bow as it twisted. The decks collapsed as the armored sides of the battleship blew out. The No. 1 turret, engulfed by the inferno, fell forward into the maw of the explosion's crater. A massive fireball climbed into the sky. Fragments of bodies and debris from the ship fell onto nearby Ford Island, onto the decks of other ships and into the water. A few survivors, most of them badly burned, were hurled through the air and into the water.

Many men never made it out from their battle stations inside the ship. Trapped below, they were either incinerated by fire or drowned as water poured into the ruptured hull. I think of them as we swim past the side of the No. 2 turret, its guns stripped away by U.S. Navy salvagers, and arrive at the top of the No. 1 turret, whose three 14-inch guns angle down. The U.S. fleet at Pearl Harbor was sent to the bottom by a new force in naval war: aircraft. In a matter of minutes, aerial torpedoes and bombs devastated the American ships at Pearl Harbor. In a heartbeat, *Arizona*, a mighty battlewagon bristling with huge guns capable of hurtling massive steel shells across the horizon, died, and few of her complement of 1,177 men escaped. Inside this turret, the gun crew, like their ship, sleeps for eternity.

As we drop down into darkness, we see no trace of the fatal wound, the hole punched through the decks by the last bomb, but the destruction of the magazines and the fierce flames that burned for forty-eight hours created a deep depression into which the No. 1 turret has fallen Moving forward, we reach a twisted mass of metal that looks like a tangle of giant flower petals and ribbon. This is the peeled-back armored deck, once horizontal but now vertical, and its sheared supports. We see more evidence of the force of the blast at each side, with hull plates pushed out as much as 20 feet. I rise along this wall and reach the gaping maw of the hawse pipes, which stand open and empty of anchor chain. Forty feet of the bow survives intact.

At the bow, we turn and head back, swimming up to the decks. As we swim, I think again of those who survived this tragic day. One of them, Don Stratton, was the farthest forward of *Arizona*'s crew to live through the blast. Stationed inside a gun director with a shipmate, Stratton felt the concussion of the magazine explosion. He and his shipmate watched in horror as the steel that surrounded them grew red, then white hot. Both sailors, dressed in T-shirts, shorts and boots, started to bake. Stratton's shipmate wouldn't stand and wait to die, so he rushed to the hatch and grabbed the steel "dogs" that latched it shut. He left his charred fingers on the steel but managed to push open the hatch as the flames reached in and took him. Stratton pulled his T-shirt over his head and ran through the flames and jumped over the side of the ship. The heat stripped the skin off his exposed legs, arms and torso, but he lived.

In 1991, I met Don Stratton and his wife at the fiftieth anniversary reunion at Pearl Harbor and sat through an interview as he again recounted his story. At the end, he unbuttoned his shirt to show us his seamed, scarred flesh. His wife, tears in her eyes, told us not only did *Arizona* still bleed, so too did her husband, who had just undergone yet another operation on his burned skin. As she talked, I thought back to my dive and how I had drifted past the spot where Stratton made his dash for life. Don Stratton's ordeal makes that spot of deck special, just as all the lives lived and lost on *Arizona* make the whole ship special.

USS *UTAH*

On the opposite shore of Ford Island, off Battleship Row, lie the remains of USS *Utah,* sunk on December 7 and, like *Arizona,* never raised after the battle. Unlike *Arizona, Utah* is rarely visited, and the memorial to the ship and her dead is in a non-public area on the island's shore.

The remains of USS Utah, *sunk at Pearl Harbor on December 7, 1941. Photo by Gary Cummins,* USS Arizona Memorial/National Park Service

Lenihan, Larry Murphy, Jerry Livingston and Larry Nordby had made a number of dives on *Utah*, and in the summer of 1988, took me on my first and only dive there. Commissioned as battleship BB-31, *Utah*, by the time of the Pearl Harbor attack, was serving as a target ship: aerial bombers practiced by dropping dummy bombs on her decks. For protection, the decks were covered by thick timbers. They were no protection on December 7.

Japanese planners had ordered their pilots to ignore *Utah*, but despite this, two torpedo bombers skimmed along the surface of the water and launched their weapons. Ensign Tom Anderson was running on the deck to sound the alarm when the first torpedo struck the port side, "staggering the ship." A geyser of water shot up the side and came down on him. Picking himself up, Anderson reached the alarm gong

and pulled it. *Utah* continued to list to port as the second torpedo detonated. Captain James Steele was ashore, and Lieutenant Commander
Solomon S. Isquith was in command. As *Utah* started to go down,
Isquith gave the order to abandon ship over the starboard side, so that
the capsizing hulk would not roll over on top of them. Eleven minutes
after the first torpedo hit, *Utah* sank.

Utah's crew had more chances to escape than the men on
Arizona, but it was often a harrowing, near thing. Seaman 2nd Class
James Oberto started to climb through a hatch as "an alarming amount
of seawater came cascading in the hatch opening just above our heads.
We started to climb in single file to the second deck. Compounding our
situation were the tons of water pouring in on use from the open portholes on the port side. We were standing in water nearly to our knees."
Oberto made it to the deck, as did Radioman 3rd Class Clarence W.
Durham. But as Durham climbed out, he looked back and saw that the
steel "battle bar" grates had broken free and blocked off the escape
route of some of the engine room crew. "I will never forget the faces of
those men trapped in the Engine Room. I knew there was no way I could
lift those steel grates and I also knew at that point that my chances were
very slim of getting out of there myself." Durham made it out as *Utah*
rolled. He slid down the "rough barnacle-encrusted steel hull," ripping
himself open.

One of the trapped men, Fireman 2nd Class John Vaessen, got
through a battle grate just before it slammed shut, trapping his shipmate Joe Barta. As the ship capsized, Vaessen said, "Batteries began
exploding. I was hit with deck plates, fire extinguishers, etc." Climbing
up into the bilge, once at the bottom of the hull and now exposed to the
air, he "could hear the superstructure break and the water would rush
closer." Taking a wrench, he beat against the hull to call for help. "I got
an answer then silence, then rat-a-tat-tat. I thought that was a pneu-
matic tool. It was strafing." Japanese planes, firing at men in the water
and across the hull of the overturned battleship, were claiming more
lives. Vaessen's rescuers did not give up and used a blowtorch to cut
open the hull and pulled him out of the steel tomb. But fifty-eight of his

shipmates did not make it, including Chief Water Tender Peter Tomich, who stayed at his post to shut down the boilers and prevent an explosion. Tomich's sacrifice so that others might live was recognized by the posthumous award of the Medal of Honor. He still lies inside *Utah* with most of the ship's dead.

I think about those men inside the hulk as we motor towards the ship. After the battle, salvage crews tried to right the hull and refloat *Utah,* but she could not be freed. Abandoned, the ship rests on her port side, festooned with salvage cables; some of the starboard air castle and some of the forward superstructure rise out of the water. We approach the exposed rusting decks and roll out of our boat into the water. Larry Murphy leads me past open hatches to the armored top of the No. 2 turret. Although the battleship's original guns had been removed when she was converted into a target ship in 1931, the turrets remained. In 1940, the Navy installed new 5-inch/25 caliber antiaircraft guns atop the turrets, part of a new battery that *Utah* was to test. Dan and Larry point them out to me as a reminder from our predive briefing that, ironically, *Utah,* with her new guns, was perhaps one of the best equipped ships at Pearl Harbor that morning to fight back, had she not been mistakenly hit and sunk so early in the attack.

The remainder of this summer at Pearl Harbor is spent searching, without success, for crashed Japanese aircraft and the deeply submerged remains of the Japanese midget submarine. Built to be a stealth weapon, the sub remains hidden, even after a highly publicized search by our colleague Bob Ballard in November 2000. But after he leaves, the sub is found intact (just as Murphy's 1988 side-scan sonar image showed it) by a hardworking team from the University of Hawaii's Undersea Research Lab. The sub's two-man crew presumably rests inside, reminding us that like *Arizona* and *Utah,* these lost ships are more than historic monuments. They are war graves

Working at Pearl Harbor, which is steeped with the emotionally charged memories of that day of infamy, had a deep impact on me, an archeologist who hitherto had dealt with a more distant past. The tragedy of the attack and the sunken ships and the memorials reminded me that humanity is at core of what I do—archeology is far more than a scientific reappraisal or a recovery of relics. Lost ships, historic sites and sacred places like memorials are mirrors in which we examine ourselves. Human weakness, human arrogance, heroism, sacrifice and perseverance dominate the story of the Pearl Harbor attack. Diving on *Arizona* and *Utah*, which had sunk in a handful of minutes as their crews were propelled from peace to war, and from the here and now to eternity, was a potent reminder of the human cost when nations collide.

— CHAPTER THREE —

SUNK *by the* ATOMIC BOMB

AT BIKINI ATOLL

We've been flying for hours over an empty ocean, far out in the middle of the Pacific. Now, the plane's slow turn signals that we are approaching our destination. Leaning over to look out the small windows in the crowded cabin, we all scan the horizon. The dark sea is giving way to the greenish-tinged hues of shallow water. In the midst of these sparkling waters, the white sand of islands appears. A chain of islands, like pearls on a string, mark the top of a volcano's rim, now submerged. The shallows of the atoll merge into darker water inside the ring, the drowned maw of the volcano, that now forms a deep lagoon.

This atoll, with its beautiful islands, beaches and a lagoon teeming with marine life, is a place with a famous name. It is Bikini, the setting for many American atomic tests between 1946 and 1958, including those of the first nuclear weapons. In July 1946, less than a year after Hiroshima, Bikini Atoll, in the middle of the Pacific Ocean, 4,500 miles west of San Francisco, was the setting for Operation Crossroads, a massive military effort to assess the effects of the atomic bomb on warships. The atoll's 167-person native population was evacuated. The fallout from those first blasts miraculously fell into the sea and did little to contaminate Bikini.

My eyes are not drawn to the beauty of this tropical paradise, however. Abruptly, the rim of the atoll is interrupted by a dark blue hole. Nearly a mile across, it is the site of a vanished islet. It is also the site where in March 1954, the most powerful nuclear bomb ever was detonated on the surface of the earth by the United States. In an instant, an atomic bomb capable of incinerating an entire city vaporized the islet and cracked the reef. The pulverized coral and sand ejected by the 15-megaton blast traveled high up into the atmosphere, raining down as atomic fallout over thousands of square miles of ocean, nearby islands and ships at sea. Conducted in the name of science, the blast, code-named Castle Bravo, was a Cold War test of America's new hydrogen bomb. It killed and sickened Pacific islanders, the crew of a Japanese fishing ironically named *Lucky Dragon* and left behind a horrific legacy.

Bikini is now a deadly place, its abandoned shores littered with rusting machinery and cables, its islands covered by thick concrete bunkers and regimented rows of decaying houses and replanted palm trees intended for the returning Bikinians, who are known as the "nuclear nomads" of the Pacific. Craters from nuclear blasts pock the bottom of Bikini's lagoon. Inside the shallow dish of one of those craters rests the sunken fleet of Operation Crossroads. Like the debris on the islands and along the shores of the atoll, the sunken ships of Bikini are an archeological legacy of the beginning of the nuclear age. Our National Park Service team, about to land on the atoll, will be the first to survey this ghost fleet now that the radioactivity has diminished to a safe level. Looking down at the crater made by Castle Bravo, we all silently cross ourselves and wonder just what we will find and what other legacies may lurk in the water and the ships.

OPERATION CROSSROADS

Operation Crossroads was the result of months of inter-service rivalry and a postwar scramble to assess the military potentials and perils of the atomic bomb. The *New York Herald Tribune*, in a post-Hiroshima editorial, commented: "The victory or defeat of armies, the fate of nations, the rise and fall of empires are all alike, in any long perspective only the ripples on the surface of history; but the unpredictable unlocking of the inconceivable energy of the atom would stir history itself to its deepest depths." Editorials suggesting that the advent of the atom bomb had forever changed warfare alarmed military officers, who did not like reading that "it should make an end of marching, rolling, and even flying armies, and turn most of our battleships into potential scrap." The atomic tests at Bikini would test the truth of that argument.

The tests were appealing for more than technical reasons. They would demonstrate to the world, particularly the Soviet Union, the power and wealth of the United States. In April 1946, Admiral William H. Blandy, commander of the joint Army-Navy task force conducting the tests, told the nation in a live radio broadcast that the upcoming tests would "help us to be what the world expects our great, non-aggressive and peace-loving country to be—the leader of those nations which seek nothing but a just and lasting peace." More bluntly, commentator Raymond Gram Swing stated that Operation Crossroads, "the first of the atomic era war games . . . is a notice served on the world that we have the power and intend to be heeded."

The decision to use the atomic bomb test to destroy ships of the once-feared Imperial Japanese Navy would also emphasize America as the principal victor in the war. One newspaper account, accompanied by an Associated Press photograph of twenty-four battered-looking destroyers and submarines, crowed: "Trapped Remnants of Jap Fleet Face Destruction in United States Navy Atom-Bomb Tests." The use of Japanese warships as atomic targets was a "symbolic killing" with the same weapon that had forced Japan's capitulation. The battleship *Nagato* particularly fulfilled that role. The onetime flagship of the Imperial Japanese Navy and the scene of operational planning for the attack on Pearl Harbor, *Nagato* had been "captured" as a bombed-out derelict on Tokyo Bay in September 1945. The capture, an event staged by military press officers, symbolized "the complete and final surrender of the Imperial Japanese Navy." Sinking the same battleship with an atomic bomb would ritually "destroy" the Imperial Japanese Navy in a more dramatic manner than prosaic scrapping or scuttling at sea. The battle-ship's intended fate was so important that, at Bikini, American support vessels were moored alongside *Nagato* since "there was some danger that the captured Japanese ships ... might actually sink ... if they were left unattended."

At the same time, military planners wanted to show that the United States Navy would survive in the coming nuclear age. According to Admiral Blandy, testing the bomb on warships would improve the Navy: "We want ships that are tough, even when threatened by atomic bombs; we want to keep the ships afloat, propellers turning, guns firing; we want to protect the crews so that, if fighting is necessary, they can fight well today and return home unharmed tomorrow."

To further test the effects of the bomb, the military loaded twenty-two of the target ships with fuel and ammunition as well as 220 tons of equipment: tanks, tractors and airplanes; guns, mortars and ammu-nition; radios, fire extinguishers and telephones; gas masks, watches and uniforms; canned food and frozen meat. They also placed sixty-nine target airplanes on the ships and moored two seaplanes in the water near them.

The first test took place on July 1, 1946. The B-29 *Dave's Dream* dropped a 20-kiloton plutonium bomb on the target fleet, slightly to star-board of the bow of the attack transport *Gilliam*. Caught in the explosion's incandescent fireball and battered down into the water by the shock wave, *Gilliam*, "badly ruptured, crumpled, and twisted almost beyond recogni-tion," sank in seventy-nine seconds. The blast swept the nearby transport *Carlisle* 150 feet to one side and nearly wiped away the superstructure and masts. *Carlisle* began to burn and sank in thirty minutes. The destroyer *Anderson*, hit hard by the blast, burst into flames when her ammunition exploded. Burning fiercely, *Anderson* capsized to port and sank by the stern within seven minutes. The destroyer *Lamson*, its hull torn open, sank twelve minutes after the blast. The Japanese cruiser *Sakawa*, badly battered, caught on fire and sank the following day.

The second test took place three weeks later. The Navy remoored the target ships around a bomb lowered 90 feet below the surface.

When the underwater atomic bomb erupted at 8:34 on the morning of July 25, a huge mass of steam and water mounded up into a "spray dome" that climbed at a rate of 2,500 feet per second and formed a 975-foot thick column. Its core was a nearly hollow void of superheated steam that rose faster than the more solid 300-foot thick water sides, climbing 11,000 feet per second and acting as a chimney for the hot gases of the fireball. The gases, mixed with excavated lagoon bottom and radioactive materials, formed a mushroom cloud atop the column. The upward blast crushed, capsized and sank the battleship *Arkansas* in less than a second.

The blast also created "atomic tidal waves." The first wave, a 94-foot wall of radioactive water, lifted and crashed into the aircraft carrier *Saratoga* with such force that it twisted the hull. The falling water also partially smashed the flight deck, and *Saratoga* sank within seven and a half hours. *Nagato,* its hull broken open, sank two days later. Beneath the water, the immense pressure of the bomb's burst crushed three submarines that settled onto the seabed, leaking air bubbles and oil.

On the surface, a boiling cloud of radioactive water and steam penetrated the surviving ships. Radioactive material adhered to wooden decks, paint, rust and grease. For weeks after the tests, the Navy tried to wash off the fallout with water and lye, sending crews aboard the contaminated ships to scrub off paint, rust and scale with long-handled brushes, holystones and any other "available means." In August, worried about radiation, Admiral Blandy cancelled plans for a third test and gave orders to sink badly damaged ships. As Operation Crossroads steamed away from Bikini, it towed the battered, irradiated fleet of targets to nearby Kwajalein, and then to Pearl Harbor, Bremerton in Washington, and Hunter's Point and Mare Island in California. There, sailors stripped the hulks of ammunition and left them to rust.

Starting in 1948, the Navy began taking the Crossroads target ships to sea and sinking them. The explanation was that the sinkings were part of training exercises and tests of new weapons. That year, Dr. David Bradley, M.D., a radiological safety monitor at Bikini, published his journal of the tests in a book titled *No Place to Hide*. It stayed on the *New York*

Times best-seller list for ten weeks. *No Place to Hide* was a forceful book that told the "real" message of Bikini. According to Bradley, Operation Crossroads, "hastily planned and hastily carried out . . . may have only sketched in gross outlines . . . the real problem; nevertheless, these outlines show pretty clearly the shadow of the colossus which looms behind tomorrow." Bradley's metaphor was the target ships rusting at Kwajalein, many of them seemingly undamaged but "nevertheless dying of a malignant disease for which there is no help."

The "cure," being enacted as Bradley's book was printed, was to sink the contaminated ships. In February 1949, *Washington Post* columnist Drew Pearson called the tests a "major naval disaster." He reported that "of the 73 ships involved in the Bikini tests, more than 61 were sunk or destroyed. This is an enormous loss from only two bombs." Pearson, like Bradley, pointed to what he viewed as a military effort to keep the true lesson of Operation Crossroads—the virtual destruction of the target fleet by radioactivity—from being fully apprehended by the public. Although the story had ultimately leaked out, it was downplayed by the government, and the credibility and patriotism of those who spoke out was questioned.

DIVING THE GHOST FLEET

I traveled to Bikini as part of Dan Lenihan's National Park Service team in 1989 and 1990. Lenihan, Larry Nordby, Larry Murphy, Jerry Livingston and I were the first to visit most of the wrecks since Operation Crossroads, and we were undertaking the survey at the request of the U.S. Department of Energy and the Bikini Council. The Bikinians, in their exile on the remote island of Kili, far away from their contaminated homeland, were eager to work with the Department of Energy to see if the sunken "swords" could be transformed into tourism plowshares. The National Park Service had the government's only team of diving archeologists at the time, and our park-oriented approach was not at odds with tourism. Since I was the NPS maritime historian, I easily wrangled my way onto Dan's crew. As well, my proximity to the

National Archives and my love of research meant that I could do advance work to learn about the history of the ships and the tests, and thus help the team to figure out just what we would be seeing in the blue depths of Bikini lagoon.

In 1989 the U.S. Navy did a magnificent job of surveying the lagoon's 180-foot depths to relocate the sunken ships of 1946. There was no chart documenting the location of the wrecks, so the Navy started with nothing but the generally known location of the aircraft carrier USS *Saratoga*, whose mast rose to within 50 feet of the surface and whose grave is marked by oil leaking from its fuel tanks. Our first dive at Bikini was on *Saratoga*.

Anchored over the wreck of USS *Saratoga*, we bob in the slight swell as each diver checks his gear under the blazing hot sun. Rolling backward into the water is a welcome relief. Clustered together like a group of skydivers, we fall in unison onto *Saratoga*. The carrier is huge, its 900-foot length the largest thing I have yet seen underwater. The superstructure towers above the flight deck, and in the clear water, it feels as if we are flying down the side of a tall building. Open hatches and deadlights invite inspection, but for now, we focus on the gaping maw on the hangar deck. Landing on the flight deck, we pause, and then one by one, drop down farther into the hangar. The flight elevator, bent and collapsed, lies at the bottom of the huge shaft. I turn left and head into the dark cavern of the hangar, following Dan and Murphy's lights.

Lying on the deck is a rack of 500-pound bombs. Wedged beneath their noses is a smaller depth bomb. I suck in a little more air and, inflating my lungs, float just a little higher to avoid going near them. The deck below me is covered with silt, and I try not to stir it up. In the distance, I notice that Dan and Murphy's lights have stopped moving. As I swim up, I see why. They have halted at a plane. Sitting upright on its wheels, wings folded up for storage, is a Helldiver, a dive bomber introduced late in the war. The cockpit is open and the gauges on the pilot's panel are clearly visible. The plane is ready to roll out onto the

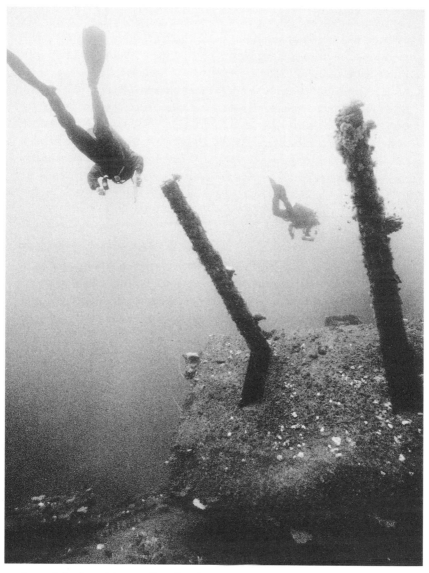

James Delgado and Dan Lenihan drop down to the wreck of USS Saratoga *at Bikini Atoll.* © *Bill Curtsinger*

elevator, rise to the flight deck and be readied for combat. If that is not exciting enough, there are two more intact planes in a row behind the Helldiver. *Saratoga* carried planes on the deck and in the hangar when the atomic blast sank her on July 25, 1946. Since the flight deck above us is largely empty, the survival of these planes in the hangar is something we had not envisioned. Rather, we had figured that being picked up and flung across the water by a nuclear tidal wave had smashed everything inside *Saratoga*. Not so, and as if to underscore this fact, Dan floats up to a row of unbroken light fixtures.

We move on to a hole punched through the flight deck. Rising up through the hole, we pass scattered equipment lying on the deck and look for the lines dangling from our dive boat. We hang there, above the wreck, decompressing to quiet down the gas in our blood and prevent the bends. We are many miles away from a decompression chamber, so we're being careful to avoid a dive accident that could cripple or kill us. Bikini is a challenging dive location, to be sure. There are the unexploded bombs, and the fear of residual radiation. And there are the risks of entering rusting hulks that might collapse on us. In addition, the ships are artificial reefs that attract hundreds of potentially aggressive white tip sharks. Then there's the greatest danger, the depth. The wrecks lie on the bottom of a 180-foot-deep lagoon, with the shallowest depth at *Saratoga's* multistory hull as it rises up from the seabed. These are beyond the limits for most divers, particularly when using regular air and not a mixed gas. In 1989 90, our team breathes regular air, all that is available at our remote location, and we decompress with pure oxygen to scrub our blood clear of the nitrogen bubbles that build up on long dives.

Thankfully, no one gets the bends, though we have a few close calls. One dive team member runs out of air and nearly panics until another diver assists with a spare regulator from his tank. A few days later, I carelessly go too far, fascinated by a deck full of test equipment, and turn back dangerously low on air. I make it back to the decompression line with an empty tank and the reminder that as fascinating as wrecks are, you can't appreciate them when you're dead.

Fortunately, the bombs turn out to be no danger at all. A Navy team disarms a bomb that looks menacing, and later I learn from the archives that the bombs carried by *Saratoga* were filled with plaster, not explosives. If marine growth and corrosion had not covered the bombs, we might have seen the stenciled message that I find on the photos of the tests—rows of big bombs marked "INERT." But the sharks can be aggressive, as we discover when we get too close. They are not "Jaws" size, but they can still tear out a big chunk of flesh, so we usually avoid them. One day, a shark gets too close, but I lash out and punch him in the gills, a sensitive spot. It hurts and he backs off—as do I. Another time, a shark swims by and rips into a fish, tearing it in two. He glares at me, half a fish dangling from his mouth, as if he's daring me to try and take it. "No, go ahead," I mumble in my regulator. "It's your fish."

The only other close call on *Saratoga* comes years later, on a dive with Fabio Amaral, as we probe a passageway inside the wreck during a Discovery Channel filming expedition. Dropping down *Saratoga*'s small bomb elevator, we make our way to a hatch that we are able to squeeze through, into a long corridor running off into the darkness. Fabio has been here before and laid down a line to guide us back should the silt stir up. We follow the line to deep inside *Saratoga*. More than halfway down, we stop in alarm at the sound of a loud bang behind us. When I look back, my lights pick up a wall of silt racing towards us. Fabio and I grab each other by the shoulder and go mask to mask as the silt washes over us, blacking out the corridor. The powerful glow of our lights is useless in the turbid, muddy water. Holding my light up to my face, I can just make out Fabio's eyes, wide open and doubtless a mirror of my own fear. Dive training takes over, though, and we grope for the line. Slowly tracing it with our fingers, we move back until we reach a mass of fallen rusty steel. The deck above us has collapsed, burying the line and probably trapping us inside the sunken ship.

Then we both get an inspiration. The deck above us has fallen down, but that means another corridor has opened up. We slowly rise up out of the cloudy silt and find ourselves in a murky but clearer passageway. Following it, we come up to a sealed hatch that must lead

Larry Murphy approaching the wreck of the Japanese warship Nagato *at Bikini Atoll.*
Dan Lenihan, National Park Service

into the bomb elevator. Straining against rusty hinges, we push it open to find ourselves floating above a mess of bombs at the bottom of the elevator. After a "thumbs up" sign, we swim straight up and out, breathing a sigh of relief.

The thrills of a close escape, however, do not compare with the emotional impact of looking at these historic ships and the dramatic damage wrought by the atomic bomb. *Saratoga* has a huge dent in the flight deck caused by the falling column of water and silt thrown out of the lagoon by the bomb. It's just one dent, but it's a big one: 230 feet long, 70 feet wide and 20 feet deep. It looks like Godzilla stomped on the flight deck. The battleship *Arkansas,* a quarter mile away, is in even worse shape. The armored hull is upside down, warped and smashed nearly flat. A hundred feet of superstructure, masts and turrets lie buried in the coral sand, with only several feet of clearance between the main deck and the seabed. The force of the blast flipped and smashed *Arkansas,* then hammered her down with such violence that she is nearly one with the bottom of the lagoon. The attack transport *Gilliam* is something else altogether. Caught in an atomic fireball and swept by extreme temperatures equal to those on the surface of the sun, the ship has partially melted. It looks like a child's plastic toy left out on a hot sidewalk, thick steel drooping and deformed. A bulldozer from the ship's deck, tossed off by the blast, lies nearby with its thick blade twisted into an "S" by the heat.

On our first dive on the massive Japanese battleship *Nagato*, Lenihan, Nordby, Murphy, Livingston and I realize that we're the first to visit her since the 1940s. We swim around the stern, past the huge bronze propellers that are surrounded by a swarm of sharks. Dan Lenihan and I drop down to the seabed and slip under the overhang of the stern to make our way in the gloom towards the barrels of the aft gun turret. As we hover in front of the gun muzzles, we both think of our dives at Pearl Harbor. Japanese ordnance experts modified some of the 16-inch shells from *Nagato*'s magazines into the aerial bombs dropped at Pearl. One of the bombs punched through *Arizona*'s decks and set off the magazine explosions that destroyed her. I can't help think that this is a full circle for us, particularly Dan, who has worked very hard to document *Arizona* and bring more of her story to the public.

That full circle feeling comes back on a later dive that we start aft from *Nagato*'s bow. As I slip out from under the deck, my eyes catch something ahead in the gloom. Dan and Murphy also see it, and we all swim forward at a fast clip. The entire superstructure of the ship, instead of being crushed like that of *Arkansas,* is laid out on the white sand. It's the bridge; it's the bridge of *Nagato*, where Admiral Yamamoto heard the radio message that the attack on Pearl Harbor was successful: "*Tora, tora, tora!*" It's incredible. Sometimes, science be damned, you just get excited by what you find.

My last dive at Bikini Atoll takes place a decade after the National Park Service survey. With John Brooks, a former NPS colleague, and Len Blix, the assistant dive master at Bikini, I drop down to look at the destroyer *Anderson*. (Since our 1989–90 survey, Bikini has been opened to the world as a unique dive park for those with the skill and the cash to journey to what has been called the "Mount Everest of wreck diving.") *Anderson* is a famous ship that fought in many battles, screening aircraft carriers in some of the greatest sea fights of the Pacific War, including the Coral Sea and Midway. She shelled Japanese shore installations at Tarawa and survived the war only to die beneath the dragon's breath of the atomic bomb.

Anderson lies on her side in the dark blue gloom. We approach the stern, passing over a rack of depth charges that have tumbled free and lie scattered on the sand. The decks seem undamaged, except for a torpedo-launching rack that has fallen off. The bridge lies open, its hatches blasted off. When I look down into the bridge, the dark interior swarms with hundreds of small fish that have sought shelter inside this sunken warship. Moving forward, I see a subtle reminder of the power of the atom. One of the destroyer's 5-inch guns has been twisted by the heat of the blast so that it points straight back to the bridge.

As I sail away from Bikini for the last time, I pause to reflect on all that I've seen there over the years. The crushed hulls, toppled masts and abandoned test instruments are material records that preserve the shocking reality of Operation Crossroads in a way that can never fully be matched by written accounts, photographs or even films of the tests. This ghost fleet is a powerful and evocative museum in the deep. It is a very relevant museum, too. Operation Crossroads and the nuclear age that followed have had and continue to have a direct effect on the lives of every living being on the planet. The empty bunkers and the abandoned homes of the Bikinians remind us of David Bradley's 1948 comment that the islanders might not be the last "to be left homeless and impoverished by the inexorable Bomb. They have no choice in the matter, and very little understanding of it. But in this perhaps they are not so different from us all." As I leave Bikini, I hope that it is a record of the past and not the harbinger of a terrible future.

CHAPTER FOUR

A CURSED SHIP

MUTINY ON THE USS *SOMERS*: NOVEMBER 26, 1842

On November 26, 1842, Captain Alexander Slidell Mackenzie of *Somers* adjusted his uniform and stepped forward to the young midshipman. "I learn, Mr. Spencer," he quietly said, "that you aspire to the command of the *Somers*."

Philip Spencer smiled slightly. "Oh, no, sir."

"Did you not tell Mr. Wales, sir, that you had a project to kill the commander, the officers, and a considerable portion of the crew of this vessel, and convert her into a pirate?" Mackenzie pressed.

"I may have told him so, sir, but it was in joke."

Mackenzie glared at the boy. "You admit then that you told him so?"

Spencer's smile vanished. "Yes, sir, but in joke."

"This, sir, is joking on a forbidden subject," Mackenzie said. "This joke may cost you your life." Now furious, he leaned forward. "You must have been aware that you could have only compassed your designs by passing over my dead body, and after that, the bodies of all the officers; you had given yourself, sir, a great deal to do; it will be necessary for me to confine you, sir." Mackenzie turned quickly to First Lieutenant Guert Gansevoort. "Arrest Mr. Spencer, and put him in double irons."

Soon, Spencer was sitting on the open deck next to the ship's wheel, hands and feet manacled. Mackenzie and his officers searched the ship, looking for incriminating evidence and for co-conspirators. They found both, or so they believed. The first was a note, written in Greek, with the names of those said to be "certain" or "doubtful," and those to be kept, "willing or unwilling." The night before, Spencer had approached Purser's Steward Josiah Wales to confide his plan, joke or not, and had alluded to a plan on paper hidden in his neckerchief. Wales, fearful and sleepless, had reported his conversation with Spencer and told about the paper. A search of Spencer failed to find it, but a hunt of his berth turned up the incriminating document. As for co-conspirators, several of the crew had acted sullenly or had expressed contempt for the captain—led by Spencer, who had from the start of the voyage called the captain a "damned old granny" behind his back.

Then, the next evening, there was an accident with the rigging and a rush aft by the crew to fix. The crew's dash to the quarterdeck, stopped by Lieutenant Gansevoort, who cocked his pistol and aimed it at the advancing men, was taken by Mackenzie as evidence that Spencer's fellow plotters were trying to free him. The following morning, Mackenzie arrested two more men: Boatswain's Mate Samuel Cromwell and seaman Elisha Small. On November 29, four more men joined them in chains. Mackenzie, on a small, 100-foot vessel with a 120-member crew—an extremely crowded ship—faced a real problem. He had no safe place to keep his prisoners, and he was not sure that there were not more mutineers in the ranks. He asked his officers for their opinion. They interrogated members of the crew and offered their advice on November 30: execute Spencer, Cromwell and Small as punishment, and quickly, to re-establish control of the ship.

The following day, in the afternoon, Mackenzie mustered the crew on deck. Most of them were young boys, teenagers, on a training cruise as part of an experimental program to create seagoing schools instead of the rough-and-tumble, often sordid, world of the between decks of a man-of-war. Now these boys were getting a strong lesson on the Articles of War, the rules that regulated naval life, and on the consequences of defying the absolute authority of a captain and his officers. Spencer, Cromwell and Small, with hoods over their heads and nooses around their necks, stood on the deck. Mackenzie asked Spencer if he wanted, as an officer, to give the order to fire the cannon that would signal the crew to haul on the lines and hang them. Spencer had accepted, but now, at the end, found that he could not.

The crewman at the cannon approached Mackenzie, saluted and said: "Mr. Spencer says he can not give the word; he wishes the commander to give the word himself."

Mackenzie did not hesitate. "Fire!"

The gun roared, and the crew grabbed the lines and ran forward, hoisting three kicking bodies up the yardarm. There they struggled, slowly strangling, until life left them.

Mackenzie climbed up onto the trunk, the cover of the passageway leading below to the officer's quarters. It was the highest spot on the deck. From there, he spoke to the assembled boys and men, reminding them of the dead men's crimes and how all men were masters of their own fates, and not to follow the example of those three. He ended by pointing to the flag fluttering at the stern. "Stand by, to give three hearty cheers for the flag of our country." Three cheers, and the crew went below to dinner. The bodies, lowered to the deck, were cleaned and prepared for burial. Cromwell and Small were lashed into their hammocks with weights. Spencer, dressed in his uniform, was laid in a wooden coffin made from two mess-chests. A sudden squall sprang up, covering the decks with rain. When it ended, the crew, called up from dinner, stood in ranks. Darkness had fallen, and battle lanterns illuminated the scene as Mackenzie led them in prayer. Then, one by one, the bodies splashed into the sea.

When *Somers* reached New York on December 14, news of the "mutiny" spread quickly. At first, the press acclaimed Mackenzie's actions. The *New York Herald* of December 18 enthused: "We can hardly find language to express our admiration of the conduct of Commander Mackenzie." But questions soon arose over the hasty nature of the executions, as well as their necessity. And then there was the matter of just who Philip Spencer was. The nineteen-year-old midshipman was the son of Secretary of War John Canfield Spencer. A difficult boy, Philip's short but notorious naval career had been punctuated by drunken behavior and brawls. *Somers,* ironically, had been his last chance. Mackenzie and his officers had not been overjoyed, to put it mildly, by his arrival. Nonetheless, Spencer remained despite their protests and sailed with *Somers* on a voyage that took him to eternity.

Mackenzie's actions aroused outrage among his detractors and concern from his friends when, in response to questions as to why he could not have kept the prisoners in irons until *Somers* reached port in the Virgin Islands just four days later, he explained that the quick executions at sea had been necessary because Spencer, as the son of a prominent man, probably would have escaped justice ashore. A damning letter in the *Washington Madisonian* of December 20, probably penned by Spencer's angry and anguished father, whipped up sentiment for the dead midshipman, summing up his transgression as "the mere romance of a heedless boy, amusing himself, it is true, in a dangerous manner, but still devoid of such murderous designs as are imputed." The actions of Mackenzie, on the other hand, were characterized as "the result of unmanly fear, or of a despotic temper, and wholly unnecessary at the time"

Debate over the "mutiny" and Mackenzie's actions raged in the press, on the streets and throughout the nation. Anxious to clear his name, he asked for and received a court of inquiry. The month-long hearing absolved him of wrongdoing, but not sufficiently to satisfy him, his defenders, his detractors or the Secretary of the Navy, who immediately agreed to Mackenzie's request for a full court-martial. The court-martial, on charges of murder, illegal punishment, conduct unbecoming an officer, and general cruelty and oppression, lasted two months. Some influential citizens rallied to Mackenzie's support, while others, notably the famous author James Fenimore Cooper, railed against him as a tyrant and murderer. The court-martial finally acquitted Mackenzie of all charges, but not unanimously. At the heart of his own near-hanging was the fact that he did not have the legal authority to execute his men at sea; they had been denied the very court-martial that now protected the captain from a similar fate.

Alexander Slidell Mackenzie's career was, however, effectively over. He retained his rank but not his ship, nor was he given any other command save a brief one years later.

One significant result was the decision to abolish training ships. Instead, in 1845, Secretary of the Navy George Bancroft authorized the creation of a school ashore, now the United States Naval Academy, at Annapolis, Maryland. And a literary reference to the affair appeared in a book written by Herman Melville, cousin of Guert Gansevoort, *Somers*'s first officer. Melville mentioned the "mutiny" in *White Jacket* in 1850: "Three men, in a time of peace, were then hung at the yard-arm, merely because, in the Captain's judgment, it became necessary to hang them. To this day the question of their complete guilt is socially discussed."

But the most famous use of the *Somers*'s story by Melville came in his last tale found in his desk after his death and not published until 1924 as *Billy Budd:*

> O, 'tis me, not the sentence they'll suspend.
> Ay, ay, all is up; and I must up too
> Early in the morning, aloft from alow.

On that dark December afternoon in 1842, Mackenzie's decision to hang three members of his crew was a controversial one. Sailors are a superstitious lot, and a seaman's poem, published in the *New York Herald* in May 1843, sums up their view of this ship after the hangings:

> The stains of blood are on thy deck,
> Thy freight is curses dark!
> And other hands than flesh and blood
> Thou numberest 'mongst thy crew;
> And a ghostly "mess" thou'lt always hear
> Across the ocean blue . . .

And ill luck, and misfortune dire
Will follow in thy wake,
Till the ghostly three, where lie their bones,
Thy last dark haven make.

Then they started, the tales of a haunted, cursed ship. Much later, a member of the brig's final crew, Midshipman Robert Rodgers, recalled his shipmates' reactions when he told them he had been posted to *Somers:* "Get rid of that craft as soon as you can, for sooner or later she's bound to go to the devil. Since the mutiny damn bad luck goes with her."

As for *Somers*, the brig sank a few years after the notorious "mutiny," with Rodgers aboard.

OFF VERACRUZ, MEXICO: DECEMBER 8, 1846

Ever since the war between the United States and Mexico had broken out in the spring of 1846, *Somers* had stayed off Veracruz, enforcing the U.S. Navy's blockade of the port. Now, winter had come, and with it, more tedium punctuated by occasional excitement.

"He's heading in, sir!" cried the lookout on *Somers*. As *Somers* tacked to pick up the wind and surge towards the incoming ship, the men loaded the guns. Lieutenant Commander Raphael Semmes was sure the other ship was going to try to bypass *Somers* and run into harbor, and it was his job to stop it. Lieutenant Parker, standing on the bulwark, telescope trained on the horizon as they tracked the suspected blockade runner, turned to Semmes. "It looks a little squally to windward, sir."

A black cloud was racing across the sea, heading directly for them. The squall would bring powerful gusts of wind as well as rain, and Semmes knew that his ship was in trouble. *Somers* was "flying light" with little ballast, and the tall masts were full of canvas, spread to the wind, to give her the speed she needed to intercept the other ship. *Somers* was built for speed, but running with a full rig was a risky business. "Shorten sail, Mr. Parker," Semmes ordered.

An engraving depicting the wreck of the U.S. warship Somers, *from* Gleason's Pictorial Drawing Room Companion, *December 1847.*

"All hands!" Parker bawled. "To the yards. Strike the mainsail and brail the spanker!" Men scrambled up the shrouds and spread out onto the yards, hands clutching at the billowing canvas of the mainsail as the helmsman eased off a bit to slack the sail. With jerks and lurches, as men grabbed handfuls of the thick canvas, the main sail climbed up the mast. After the men lashed the sail in place, they turned their attention to the spanker, its canvas spread out on the boom sling off the back of the mast. As they lowered the sail to half its full length, they tied off the loose canvas with the brails, rows of line sewn into the sail.

Then the squall hit. A blast of wind slammed into *Somers*, and the brig rolled. As a sailor screamed "She's going over!" the man at the wheel called out: "She will not answer the helm, sir." The decks canted sharply, throwing men and loose gear. In seconds, the brig lay on her side, water pouring into open hatches. Clinging to the rigging, Semmes knew he had one chance to save his ship. "Cut away the masts!" he ordered. Balancing above the waves on the bulwark, the men grabbed knives and axes and started hacking at the thick, tarred lines that supported the masts. But it was too late. The masts and yards lay flat on the sea, and the brig was filling fast, settling deeper into the water. *Somers* was sinking. When the hull started to go under, Semmes yelled out, "Every man save himself who can!" As the men threw themselves into the sea, *Somers* sank. Just ten minutes after the squall hit, the most notorious ship in the U.S. Navy was gone, taking thirty-two men with her.

Somers's last captain, Raphael Semmes, was a son of the South. He survived the sinking and later, during the Civil War, to acclaim (or distress, depending on which side of the war you fought on), as Admiral Semmes of the Confederate States Navy, he helped to sweep the high seas free of Union merchant shipping, capturing and burning any ship flying the American flag in his raider css *Alabama*.

REDISCOVERING *SOMERS*

In 1986, the governor of Mexico's Veracruz Province, Acosta Lagunes, asked art dealer, explorer and filmmaker George Belcher to search out historic shipwrecks for the Provincial Museum in Jalapa. Thoughts of Spanish galleons full of rich treasures for the museum's galleries inspired the governor's request, but instead of them, Belcher discovered the forgotten grave of *Somers* in 107 feet of water on June 2, just as a squall rolled over his survey boat and covered the scene with darkness and rain. Belcher knew the story of the infamous brig, and the significance of his find inspired him to seek protection for the wreck from both the Mexican and U.S. governments. But first, he had to firmly establish its identity, and so in May 1987, he returned to Veracruz with a small team that included shipwreck archeologist Mitch Marken and me.

Our dives proved conclusively that this was indeed *Somers*, setting off three years of negotiation between the United States and Mexico over who owned the wreck and what would happen to it. The Mexicans agreed to protect the site, in response to news that local divers had been plundering the wreck, taking weapons, bottles and the ship's chronometer, which I had last seen lying in the sand at the stern, exactly where it would have dropped from the deteriorating binnacle at the wheel. It has never been seen again, a reminder that significant finds, if not acted on immediately, end up being taken by looters and souvenir hunters. While I condemn the souvenir hunters, I also blame bureaucratic circumstances when governments stand by, either for lack of funding or lack of interest, and leave sites like *Somers* unprotected and unexcavated.

Eventually, the two nations agreed to share the costs, such as they were, of documenting *Somers*. This was no mean feat for Mexico, as it had far less money than the United States. The Armada de Mexico provided a patrol boat, *Margarita Maza de Juarez,* its crew, their SEAL team (the Commandos Subacuaticos) and a team of underwater archeologists from the National Institute of Anthropology and History, headed by Dr. Pilar Luna Erregucreña. I led the U.S. team, loaned by the National Park Service's Submerged Cultural Resources Unit, with archeologists and wreck mappers Jerry Livingston and Larry Nordby, and photographer John Brooks. George Belcher and his brother Joel, the discoverers of the wreck, came as our guests but paying their own way. In July 1990, we gathered in Veracruz. It had been three years since I had last dived *Somers,* and, like George, I was both excited and uneasy about what we would find.

— —

The thoughts of Billy Budd as he waits in the ship's brig for his execution come to mind as I perch on the edge of the patrol boat, preparing to drop "fathoms down, fathoms down" to where "oozy weeds" do twist, not around a dead boy, but amidst the bones of *Somers,* the ship that inspired Herman Melville's haunting tale:

> But me they'll lash in hammock, drop me deep.
> Fathoms down, fathoms down, how I'll dream fast asleep.
> I feel it stealing now. Sentry, are you there?

> Just ease these darbies at the wrist,
> And roll me over fair,
> I am sleepy, and the oozy weeds about me twist.

I turn to George Belcher and nod. Together, we roll off backward, splashing into the warm blue water. Other splashes follow us, and soon a cluster of divers is hanging on the anchor line. A final check of the gear, then we let the air out of our buoyancy vests and drop into the murky depths. Sixty feet down, I'm in a cloudy haze of grayish-green water, my dive partner a blurry form. Ninety feet, and the blur clears as I switch on my dive light. The bottom is approaching, so I give the buoyancy vest a quick hit of air. My descent slows and stops, and I'm hovering over a large iron anchor, nearly 110 feet below the surface. In front of me, the curving form of a ship's bow rises up out of the silt, sweeping sharply back like the edge of a knife blade.

Sleeping in her grave, the clipper brig *Somers,* perhaps the most notorious ship in the history of the United States Navy, lies before me at the bottom of the Gulf of Mexico. Canted on her side, the wooden hull largely consumed by marine organisms, *Somers* is now truly a ghost ship, her form outlined by the copper sheathing that once protected her hull from the voracious appetite of marine creatures. Impervious to the attack of the teredo worms that eat wooden ships' hulls, the copper has leached its metallic salts into a thin layer of wood so that this fragile remnant of *Somers* still holds her form perfectly more than 140 years after she went down. A slow and steady decay, this, and as a result, everything lies on the seabed exactly as it once did on the decks and in the holds: iron cannon, anchor chain, the ship's stove and other gear, even the iron fittings and blocks from the masts. Everything inside *Somers,* after she sank, lay trapped in the hull as it deteriorated and collapsed over the decades, and presumably much of it should still be here, buried in layers of rotten wood, sand, silt and thick masses of corroded iron. Indications of what was once inside the ship, and of lives interrupted and lost, include a small white plate, an oval serving platter from the officers' wardroom and a small black glass bottle.

I drift past the iron davits for the port quarter boat. Lying flat on the sand, they are a reminder of the only boat to get away from the sinking *Somers*. It ferried several men to the safety of the nearby island of Isla Verde. Many others never made it, trapped below by the rushing water or drowned in the open sea as their heavy boots and uniforms pulled them under. I also recall, as I float for a moment over this spot, that this is where young Philip Spencer lay manacled to the deck on that long-ago night of November 26, 1842, in the first of a chain of events that cost three lives and ruined others. Spencer, Cromwell and Small were all chained at the stern, Small next to the aftermost 32-pounder carronade on the port side. That gun lies here now, and I swim up to take a look at it.

As I continue my tour of the wreck, I see that three of the four carronades on the starboard side lie buried muzzle down in the sand, showing that *Somers* sank sideways, never righting as she dropped into the depths, and landed on the starboard side. I stop and carefully run a small iron probe up inside the barrel of one of the guns. The probe stops 24 inches into the 4-foot bore of the carronade. I turn to another gun and try it. It, too, is blocked. I smile and turn to Pilar Luna, who is shining a light on the gun to help me guide the probe. These guns are loaded, as we expected. After all, *Somers* was ready for action, in the middle of a chase, when the squall hit.

A long metal tube, topped by what looks like an open trough, is the brig's pump, once used to remove water from the hold, but useless on that fateful morning. Lying on the bottom, it is now being mapped by Larry Nordby and Jerry Livingston. Their tape measure indicates it is just over 11 feet long—a perfect match for the depth of the hold. A metal flange, almost halfway up the iron tube, would not be noticed by most people, but Larry instantly recognizes that it means the area below decks was divided into a berth deck, where the men lived, and a lower hold. This flange marks the location of that divide, a feature not recorded in the few surviving plans of the brig. It is also an indicator of just how small and crowded this vessel was, particularly on that winter voyage in 1842, with 120 men and boys packed on these decks and in

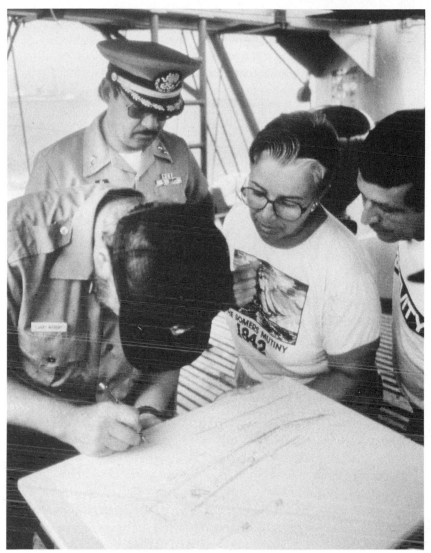

Captain Santos Gomez Leyva of the Armada de Mexico and Dr. Pilar Luna Erreguereña
watch as Larry Nordby works on the map of the wreck of Somers *aboard the patrol vessel*
Margarita Maza de Juarez, *1990. James P. Delgado*

these berths. Confronted by the small size of *Somers*, we gain a new perspective on how just a handful of men, suspected of plotting a mutiny, could inspire the near-panic that led to three hasty hangings.

We find more reminders of the crew as we swim forward. Lying on its side is the huge cast-iron galley stove of the brig, its flue still attached. The hinged opening of the stove has fallen away, and when I flash my light into the stove, I can see that the drip pan and range grates are still in place. My light startles a small fish, which darts out of the stove, and I chuckle at the thought of its making a home where once it would have been cooked. A scatter of bottles and a ceramic jug are all that remain of the ship's provisions, including a bottle with a lead foil cap from "Wells Miller & Provost, 217 Front St., New York." That New York merchant was the nation's leading manufacturer of preserved foods and condiments in its day, and finding the bottle is the sort of human connection across time that makes history special. This bottle probably held a popular condiment, a special touch to make a sailor's meal just a little tastier. I like making discoveries like this.

As we turn to leave, I look down, and my heart stops. There are bones scattered in the wreckage, yellow and mottled. Thirty-two men died on *Somers*, and the wreck is a war grave. Have we found the remains of some of the crew? We've been told to respectfully collect any human remains and return them home for analysis and reburial, so I take a closer look. There are three vertebra and a short, small bone that could be from a radius or ulna. But I can tell that they're not human. These are from a large hog or a small cow, part of the rations of salted meat packed in barrels and carried as provisions. *Somers*'s log shows she had nine barrels of what sailors liked to complain was "salt horse" when she sank. This is what's left of some of it.

As I begin my slow ascent to the surface, stopping to decompress, I think about *Somers* and the stories locked in her decaying timbers. Powerful events played out on those decks and changed the course of a navy. Our team never loses sight of that tragedy over the next few days as we continue our inspection, complete our chart and finally bid the wreck goodbye.

After our departure from Veracruz, the Armada de Mexico closes the site to all divers and vows to keep a close watch on the site. A return visit by the National Park Service a few years ago found *Somers* looking much as we had left her, but with more evidence of unauthorized visitors who have taken souvenirs. With the exception of these few illegal divers, *Somers* rests alone in the eternal darkness. If that broken hull could speak, I'd like to think that, just like Billy Budd, she would ask to be left in the solitude of the sea.

CHAPTER FIVE

TITANIC

ABOVE THE ABYSS

It's 6:00 a.m., and the first hints of light on the horizon reveal scattered clouds in a gray sky and the flecks of whitecaps on the ocean's dark surface. I'm aboard the Russian research vessel *Akademik Mstislav Keldysh*. We're slowly steaming in a wide circle, barely making headway in the rolling sea. For the last week, we've kept the same course, 368 miles southeast of St. John's, Newfoundland, constantly retracing our wake on this patch of ocean, far from sight of land.

Featureless it may be, but this area of ocean is famous because of what happened here on the late evening and early morning hours of April 14 and 15, 1912. Two and a quarter miles below us, at the bottom of the sea, lies the wreck of *Titanic*. And in a few hours, I will slowly descend to the ocean floor, sealed in a small deep-sea submersible, to visit the wreck in the freezing, pitch-black, crushing depths.

Ever since *Titanic*'s shattered hulk was discovered in 1985, only about a hundred people have made the risky dive into the abyss to visit it. That's far fewer than the number of humans who have flown into space.

The name itself says it all: *Titanic*. The second of three enormous steamships designed and built to be the world's largest, *Titanic* was the epitome of an age of confidence and achievement. The ship was 882 feet,

9 inches long, with a beam or width of 92 feet, 6 inches. From her keel to the top of her funnels, *Titanic* towered 175 feet, and the distance from the waterline to the boat deck was the same as a six-story building. The hull displaced or weighed 66,000 tons. Each steel plate that went into the hull was 30 feet long, 6 feet wide and an inch thick.

The wreck itself, deep down in the eternal darkness of the bottom of the North Atlantic, has continued, as author Susan Wels points out, "to fire and torment the public's imagination." "The location of her sinking," said Wels, "an imprecisely known patch of the Atlantic, vacant and menacing . . . became part of the world's geography. Unknown and unreachable, her abyssal grave and her fatal voyage obsessed dreamers and adventurers for more than seven decades."

When the news of finding *Titanic*, by the joint French-U.S. team of Jean-Louis Michel and Robert Ballard, was announced in the early morning hours of September 1, 1985, the world's press provided, at first in brief snippets, and then in more detail, images and information from the bottom of the Atlantic. From a few simple views of the bow and a single boiler to dozens of images of empty decks, empty lifeboat davits and scattered debris, the eerie scenes gave immediacy to what was, for a new generation, a distant and abstract tragedy. Robert Ballard himself felt it, just hours after his euphoria over finding the wreck faded. "It was one thing to have won—to have found the ship. It was another thing to be there. That was the spooky part. I could see the *Titanic* as she slipped nose first into the glassy water. Around me were the ghostly shapes of the lifeboats and the piercing shouts and screams of people freezing to death in the water."

The wreck of *Titanic*, in all its twisted, rusting splendor, like many other historic sites—Pompeii, Tutankhamen's tomb or other shipwrecks—gives people a "temporal touchstone." In this case, it is a time machine that provides a physical link to the "night to remember." I've joined other viewers of many television specials, the IMAX film *Titanica* and James Cameron's movie *Titanic* to watch as submersibles and cameras pass various spots mentioned in the history books and survivors' accounts. The crow's nest where lookout Frederick Fleet picked up the telephone and gave warning of an iceberg. The boat deck with its empty lifeboat davits. The remains of the bridge, where Captain Edward John Smith was last seen. But being an archeologist who has spent two decades exploring the seabed and lost shipwrecks, I wanted to see this wreck for myself. Zegrahm DeepSea Voyages, a subsidiary of Zegrahm Expeditions in Seattle, Washington, has offered adventurers the opportunity to participate in Russian scientific dives to the wreck of *Titanic* since 1998. The price—$35,500 in 1999—was out of my range, but Zegrahm offered me the chance of a lifetime. As a lecturing archeologist and "team leader," I could join the year 2000 scientific expedition and get a dive, if I would share my experiences and observations with my fellow passengers.

At the heart of the research vessel *Akademik Mstislav Keldysh*'s operations are two extraordinary submersibles, *Mir 1* and *Mir 2*. "Mother ship" to the two subs, and a floating workshop and scientific platform, *Keldysh* is the center of Russia's deep-sea program. The participation of *Mir 1* and *Mir 2* in the IMAX film and Cameron's *Titanic* made both submersibles famous, as well as *Keldysh* and her crew. Their star status notwithstanding, the men and women of *Keldysh* are excellent scientists and technicians whose work has advanced the frontiers of science. The ocean covers two-thirds of the planet, yet during the last century of oceanographic research, humans have gained detailed knowledge of only 5 per cent of its depths.

In the nineteenth century, scientists dropped dredges and nets to grab samples from the deep, while divers wearing heavy helmets, thick rubberized canvas suits and lead-weighted boots walked the shallower depths. In 1930, the first submersible to go deep, William Beebe's round steel bathysphere, made a 3,280-foot dive off Bermuda, suspended on a steel cable from a surface ship. It was followed in the late 1940s and 1950s by bathyscaphes—self-propelled undersea vehicles with tanks for buoyancy and ballast. In the 1960s, the Cold War with Russia inspired the development and construction of deep submersibles, as the ocean depths became a strategic frontier. The famous *Alvin,* as well as France's *Nautile,* both deep-ocean submersibles developed during the Cold War, were involved in the earliest dives on *Titanic*. Back home, at my own Vancouver Maritime Museum, is another Cold War–era submersible, built in 1968: *Ben Franklin* is capable of diving to 3,280 feet and staying down for thirty days, the largest deep-diving submersible ever built.

Mir 1 and *Mir 2* were built in Finland in 1985–87 at a cost of $25 million each, for Russia's Shirshov Institute of Oceanology. The builder, Rauma-Repola, was awarded the contract after the United States pressured the Canadian government to block the sale of Vancouver-built Pisces submersibles to the Soviets. Each 18.6-ton *Mir* is an engineering marvel capable of diving to (and returning from) depths of up to 4 miles. The heart of each sub is a 6-foot diameter nickel-steel pressure sphere 1 ½ inches thick. Inside that small sphere, three persons—a pilot and two observers, as well as life-support equipment, sonars and the sub's controls—have to fit. It is a tight, cramped workspace.

After we load our gear, *Keldysh* clears the harbor of St. John's and begins the twenty-hour cruise to the *Titanic* wreck site. We arrive in the early morning hours of September 1. The crew of *Keldysh* prepares for the dive by dropping three acoustic transponders around the wreck to help the two *Mirs* to navigate and to give mission control aboard *Keldysh* an indication of where we are 2 ¼ miles below them.

Five days of diving—a total of ten dives, each with two passengers and a Russian pilot—follow. As we slowly circle this famous patch of ocean, I stare out over the dark blue water and then up at the clear night sky, the stars burning brightly, unobscured by city lights. I can't help thinking about what happened at this very site eighty-eight years ago. Ballard was right when he said this is a spooky spot on the ocean. The power of the human imagination, and the fact that I am exactly where the tragic events happened, bring to mind that ill-fated ship poised on the brink of her final plunge, the silently bobbing bodies, deck chairs, broken wood and steamer trunks. The next morning, some people confess that during the evening they came up on deck, or like me, looked out of an open porthole, and felt the impact of being *here*—it was an emotional moment. Those of us who will be diving in the subs are wondering how we will feel, how we will react, when we reach the ocean's floor and see *Titanic*.

In conversations with the other divers and participants, the motive for their presence on the expedition is a constant and early question. Each of us wants to know why the others chose to do this dive. One motive is historical interest—a British non-diving passenger is a keen student of *Titanic*'s history, and many others have more than a passing acquaintance with the ship's famous story. Another is that it is an opportunity to participate in the exploration of a shipwreck and to see a part of our world that few ever visit. There is a powerful intellectual curiosity afoot, stoked not just by this famous shipwreck but also by working with a top team of scientists and technicians to experience first hand these amazing submersibles and to view the ocean depths. By volume, the sea covers 99.5 per cent of our biosphere, with 78.5 per cent of that taken up by deep ocean.

There is probably more diversity of life in the deep sea than on land, and the opportunity to see some of that life, as well as the very real possibility of discovering a new species through observation as the subs drop through the water, interests a few of the diving passengers. For others, there is the rarity of what we are about to do. And for most, if not all, there is the passionate desire to learn more, to connect with the past, by visiting the wreck in person and not just seeing it on film. This is a visit to an undersea museum and graveyard, made all the more powerful by the nature of the tragic event that left the wreck and its scattered contents as a moment in time.

Driving the need to visit the wreck now is a concern over reports that *Titanic* is deteriorating rapidly. A *USA Today* story, published just before we departed, quoted scientists who think that *Titanic* will collapse within two years. There is also a concern that the ongoing salvage of *Titanic*'s artifacts by RMS Titanic Inc., an American salvage firm, is diminishing the "time capsule" effect of the wreck. Since 1987, RMS Titanic Inc. has made over a hundred dives and pulled nearly six thousand artifacts from the sea.

RMS Titanic Inc. is seeking to cover the costs of its dives through public displays of these artifacts, as well as film deals and souvenir sales that include small pieces of coal from *Titanic*'s bunkers. Recently, the company, which has no museum or permanent home for the collection, raised the possibility of selling the artifacts. While that sale idea has been blocked, for the time being at least, by the U.S. courts, there is a risk, whether through nature or by human activity, that the opportunity to explore the ultimate *Titanic* museum—the shipwreck site itself and the associated artifacts—is at risk.

DIVING ON *TITANIC*: A DAY TO REMEMBER

We assemble in the lab at 9:30 a.m. *Mir 1* is loading, and we watch as the huge crane picks up the submersible, swings it over the side and then, timing the waves, lowers it into the water. As the support boat *Koresh* ("friend" in Russian) comes alongside, a Zodiac roars up and a wet-suited diver leaps out from it onto the partially awash *Mir*. After unhooking the huge umbilical that connects *Mir* to the crane, he fastens a towline and straddles the sub, riding it as *Koresh* pulls it clear of *Keldysh*. Then he unhooks the towline, and, as the Zodiac quickly swoops in, he makes a flying leap into it as *Mir 1* starts her dive.

Now it's our turn. My dive partner is Scott Fitzsimmons, president of Zegrahm. After a quick chat with Anatoly Sagalevitch, the senior scientist, and our pilot, Evgeny "Genya" Chernaiev, we climb up the ladder one by one, at 9:45 a.m. At the top, two technicians take our shoes (no shoes are allowed inside in order to keep the sub's delicate electronics dust-free) and hand us our gear as we lower ourselves through the narrow hatch. A thick rubber O-ring is positioned on the hatch's tapered rim to make a watertight seal. Looking at it, I can't help but think about the explosion of the space shuttle *Challenger*. Faulty O-rings doomed *Challenger* and her crew in a disaster caused by an over-reliance on technology—and many observers have compared *Challenger* to *Titanic*. I take a hard look at the O-ring but am reassured by the careful inspection that the Russian crew give it.

Scott follows me in, and we take up positions on either side of Genya as he preps the sub for launch. We lie, half-flexed, on narrow padded bunks that have me tucking my feet into a crowded corner between cables and stowed gear. The crew lowers the hatch and Genya secures it, then he folds up the internal ladder and locks it over the hatch. He switches on life support, and as the air gets richer with oxygen, the muffled bumping above us signals the arrival of the crane. Peering out the tiny view ports, we watch the deckhands unshackle the cables that hold *Mir 2* to the deck, then we rise up and over the gunwale. It is a smooth ride, and not until we hit the water do we feel any movement. We roll with the waves as *Koresh* tows us clear of *Keldysh*. Genya reaches overhead and floods our ballast tanks with 3,300 pounds of sea water, then suddenly, just 9 feet beneath the waves, the sub stops rolling. We're dropping now, at a rate of about 105 feet a minute, slowly picking up speed as we free-fall all the way down to the ocean floor. The slow spin of the sub's compass shows we're spiraling, just the way that water does when it goes down a drain.

It's hot inside the sub—about 75°F—and as we fall, Genya rechecks the systems. Only one small light is on, and Genya is playing light jazz on the CD player. In two minutes, we pass 213 feet, the maximum depth I've reached as a scuba diver. Scott exchanges a grin with me—we're looking forward to hitting bottom in a couple of hours. The feet click away on the electronic display behind me, and we both watch at 492 feet as the last light disappears from the water. Light blue gave way to dark magenta, but now it is pitch black outside. The light from inside the sub dimly outlines the manipulator arm and video camera mounted near my view port, and as I watch it, I notice the occasional flash of a bioluminescent sea creature as we continue to fall.

At 10:50 a.m., we reach 6,560 feet. Genya switches on the powerful external lights for a check and examines the motors of Sergeytch, our small remotely operated vehicle (ROV), in its external "garage." The ROV is a small robot camera linked to *Mir 2* by a cable. It has not worked all week, and technicians spent long hours fixing a thruster problem so that we can get some close-in interior photos of *Titanic*. All systems are "go" as Genya fires up Sergeytch and tries the thrusters. At 11:17, *Mir 2*

The deep-sea submersible Mir 1 *being lowered to dive on* Titanic. *James P. Delgado*

reaches 9,840 feet, and Genya turns on the sonar and pings the seabed below us. At 11:42, Genya starts *Mir 2*'s thrusters, and we slow to lightly touch down at 11:45.

We're at a depth of 12,465 feet. That's 2 ¼ miles down, the average depth of the world's oceans, and the deepest I've ever been. The pressure outside the sphere is 6,000 psi. If we spring a leak, we won't live long enough to worry about it. Outside *Mir 2*, in a net bag lashed to a sonar, we carry some forty Styrofoam cups as souvenirs for the crew and passengers on *Keldysh*. The intense pressure collapses and shrinks the cups, complete with the written inscriptions and decorations people have added to them, to less than half their original size. But this environment, though perpetually dark and crushing, does support life. The seemingly barren, yellow-white clay and silt bottom is the habitat for some species, including a large, ashy gray rattail fish that slowly swims before us as Genya lifts the sub off the bottom and we start moving forward. The sonar, reaching ahead of us, clearly shows the sharp angle of *Titanic*'s bow 1,640 feet away in the dark.

We start to climb a mound of tumbled clay. Suddenly, without warning, a wall of rusting steel looms out of the darkness. It fills the view ports as our bright lights pick out the edges of the hull plates and the rivers of rust bleeding from them and onto the seabed. The mound we have climbed was created when *Titanic*'s bow slammed into the seabed and ploughed it up as she slid along, until the thick clay arrested the motion of its long fall from the surface. Genya slowly pilots *Mir 2* up past the huge anchor, still in its hawse pipe, then here we are, at the tip of the bow made famous by Leonardo DiCaprio's "king of the world" exuberance and his lingering kiss with Kate Winslet in the movie *Titanic*. The size of the massive spare anchor nestled atop the bow stuns me. It is bigger than our sub, and despite seeing numerous photos and videos of it, nothing has quite prepared me for the scale of the anchor—or the ship.

We pass over the bow, the anchor chain, the capstans with their brass covers, the No. 1 cargo hold and the anchor windlass. We stop for an hour at the cargo hold, latching on to the edge of the hatch with one of *Mir*'s arms. Genya switches on the tiny ROV Sergeytch and sends it down into the hold. Despite working perfectly earlier, the ROV now has a problem. One of its thrusters is not working, and try as he can, Genya cannot easily maneuver Sergeytch. But we do get a view of the inside of the wreck. It is a rust-filled cavern, with dangling rusticles everywhere. We cannot penetrate far in without fear of losing Sergeytch, though, so finally Genya slowly backs it out and returns it to its small "garage." We fire up our motors, unhook from the hatch and continue our dive.

Forward of the windlass rests the broken base of the ship's mast, and we follow the steep angle of the fallen mast up into the gloom. An open oval hatch in the mast marks the location of the crow's nest. We shine a light in, and see the rungs of the ladder that the lookouts once climbed to reach this perch. I think of the opening act of the drama that started here at 11:40 on that long-ago evening—"Iceberg, right ahead!" Then we pass over the folded arms of the cargo cranes and stop, hovering, over the bridge deck.

The ship's bridge is gone, either smashed by a falling funnel or swept away by the sea as *Titanic* sank. Captain Smith was last seen here, and I think of the scene in the film where he locks himself in and gazes in horror as the cold green sea presses against the windows, with just the creaking of the dying ship to keep him company before the glass shatters and the sea engulfs the bridge. Now, all that remains is the brass telemotor, or steering gear, the wooden sill of the bridge's bulkheads, and a tangle of electrical wires from the lights and controls. Five brass memorial plaques and a bundle of plastic red roses and ferns, placed here by other expeditions, are a powerful reminder that for a number of people, this ship is a gravesite.

There are other, equally affecting reminders of the tragedy. Lifeboat davits stand at the edges of the boat deck, their empty falls a silent indictment of too few boats and boats lowered in haste only half full. Proceeding along the port-side boat deck, we come to a davit lying over the deck. Up until now, I have been intently observing, shooting photos and focusing on the physical reality of the wreck. But I realize this is not just any davit. This is the davit for lifeboat No. 8. What happened at this exact spot on the deck is one of the great and haunting stories of that night. Isidor and Ida Straus, with their maid, came to this boat. Mrs. Straus and the maid climbed in, but Mr. Straus could not, of course, given the rule of "women and children first."

The boat was not full, and there were no other women or children to load, but rules were rules. There was also a powerful social convention that would have branded Straus a coward had he climbed into that boat. But Mrs. Straus believed that their place was together. They had been married for more than fifty years, and so, filled with love, Mrs. Straus climbed out of that lifeboat and walked away with her husband, presumably back to their cabin to wait for the end together. In the James Cameron film, they are lying dressed in their coats, on their bed, holding each other and weeping as the cold sea pours in. As we drift over that davit, what happened to the Strauses ceases to be a story. It is real, as real as the deck and that fallen davit from the boat that they did not take to safety.

I have tears in my eyes as we pass over the davit. Some people think archeology is all about science, while others argue that it is about humanity. I tend to agree with the humanists, for though science does play in a role in what we do, we should never lose sight of the fact that the focus of our work is people. The power of Mrs. Straus's sacrifice is a reminder of that, and as I cry, I notice I am not alone. The wreck of *Titanic*, down here in the darkness and silence, preserves a sense of immediacy and a link to tragedy, both large scale and individual, that you do not often experience.

We then rise, passing over the gaping doorways and windows of the officers' quarters. Glass in the panes brightly reflects our lights. Ahead is the skylight that looks down into the Marconi Wireless Room, where the sos was broadcast from the sinking ship. Here, some of the heroes of the disaster, like senior wireless operator Harold Bride, worked to the very end, trying to get help.

We turn around and move aft to where the first-class staircase, in all of its ornately carved splendor, once led below. At the edge of one deck, two chandeliers are visible, hanging from their wiring, a reminder of former elegance in this ruin. We follow the sloping deck to the break in the hull where the ship ripped apart as the stern rose high into the air. For years after the tragedy, some people argued that *Titanic* sank intact, while others insisted that the ship was torn apart. The arguments ended with the discovery of the wreck in 1985.

We descend to the seabed again, turning forward to look into the severed bow section's boiler room. Here *Titanic* fractured: the torn and crumpled steel, the half crushed and twisted water and steam pipes, and the five massive boilers that rise before us as high as a three-story-tall wall, are impressive not only in their mass but in the gargantuan scale of the damage. The steel is deformed and stretched in some areas like saltwater taffy on a hot summer's day. Other hull plates have jagged edges like a shattered porcelain plate. Everywhere is a tangled mess of electrical wires. As we edge along this open wound, we look up to see the towering mass of the decks above us. The danger of a sudden collapse and our burial in the debris spurs Genya to pull away at last and head out across the abyssal plain to examine the stern.

The debris field that lies between the two sections of the hull is an array of hardware, hunks of steel, lumps of coal and occasional items that speak to the splendor of the ship and the lives changed by or lost in the disaster. I see linoleum tiles, a ceramic sink bowl, plates, a section of brass bench and shoes. I also see a copper pan from the ship's galley, looking amazingly bright after nearly nine decades in the sea. The shifting sands keep it polished, Genya suggests. I have been told that the debris field looks as if a small city exploded in space and rained down, and it is an apt description.

The bow section of *Titanic* is separated from the stern by some 1,790 feet. That distance seems to go on forever down here, but gradually, the pieces of debris get larger. We pass a crank from an engine that seems to be as big as an average family minivan, and then one of the ship's boilers. Finally, we reach the stern. The stern is a mangled, deformed mass of steel, but in its wreckage we can discern the form of the hull as it swept back to the rudder, the deckhouses, a half-fallen cargo crane, the stub of a mast and the graceful curve of the poop deck. We edge forward to view the massive reciprocating steam engines. The cast iron is fractured because the cylinders, each the size of a large truck, imploded with the pressure of the sea as the stern sank. Nestled between the cracks and broken pipe is a beautiful ceramic teapot; its handle is intact but the spout is broken. Lighter debris, like the teapot, rained down for hours after the ship sank, falling onto the heavier wreckage that had plummeted to the bottom first.

Titanic is such a part of the mass-media world in which we live that my mind keeps flashing back to the various written stories and films. Here, inside the engine room, as I look at the teapot, I think back to a scene in the 1958 classic movie *A Night to Remember*. The chief engineer is talking to the men who are running the electrical system. The chief is asked, "How are things up top, sir? Any chance for us?" He stops and says, "Whatever happens, we've got to keep the lights going. I'll give the word when it's time to go, and then it's every man for himself." He pauses and goes on. "But it won't be so bad, they say the *Carpathia* is on her way to us, should be here any time now." As he leaves, the engineer in charge turns to his men and says, with a slight smile, "Well, let's hope they're right, eh boys? If anyone feels like praying, you'd better go

The bow of RMS *Titanic at the bottom of the North Atlantic. James P. Delgado*

ahead. The rest can join me in a cup of tea." It's just a movie, but I remember that scene of understated British heroism as I look at the teapot in the wrecked engine room.

Slowly, we pull back from the engines, past warped walkways, torn pipes and hanging wires. We turn, and Genya pilots us back to the stern. A narrow opening between the sea floor and the overhanging steel mass of the stern beckons us, and as Genya slowly pilots *Mir 2* into the gap, we enter a rusting cave. I ask Genya what our clearance is. He glances at the sonar, makes a quick calculation, and answers that we have 20 inches of clearance from the bottom, and the same between us and the steel wreckage above. We edge in without a bump, stopping just ahead of one of *Titanic*'s 21-ton bronze propellers, half buried in the silt. Genya not only manages to get us in but extracts *Mir 2* without a scrape, then takes us to the propeller on the other side of the stern. Despite Genya's skill, the maneuverability of *Mir 2* and the reassurance of looking at hull plates still covered with black paint and with very little rust, Scott and I breath a sigh of relief when we're out.

Genya nudges the controls and we drift up past the tip of the stern, where the words "Titanic, Liverpool" once were. The edge of the poop deck, with its collapsed railing, marks the last piece of the ship to sink, and we stare silently, thinking of the struggling crowd of people who clustered here, hands grasping that railing, clinging on as the stern climbed higher and higher, then dropped into the deep. I also think of the ship's baker, Charles Joughlin, who balanced himself on this rail, clad in a thick fur coat and drunk as a lord. He stepped off the rail just as the stern sank and reportedly didn't even get his head wet. Lubricated by the alcohol and insulated by his coat, he was not killed by the cold water. He was pulled into a lifeboat and survived.

Before we start our ascent, we briefly tour the debris field around the stern, noting huge pieces of hull, a broken-off engine cylinder, a cargo crane, the ornate bronze end of a deck bench, wine bottles and plates. Off to one side is a pair of boots. Small, flat-heeled and calf-length, they are the boots of a working-class woman, perhaps a steerage passenger. They lie side by side and are still laced tight. We pass over them in respectful silence, for while the body is long gone, consumed by the sea, this is a place where one of *Titanic*'s dead came to rest. It's much colder now, and I pull on a sweater, wondering as I do if it is really the lower temperature or what we've just seen.

My thoughts are on many things as Genya powers the thrusters and we start to rise, pumping seawater out of the ballast tanks all the way as the outside pressure relents, bit by bit, during the two-hour ride to the surface. We're elated with excitement because of our visit to this undersea museum, historic site and memorial, but we're also reflective and somber. After years of studying *Titanic*, reading the history books and watching hours of video of other dives, this dive has put all the pieces together for me.

We reach the surface at 6:50 p.m. After thirty minutes of bobbing and rolling on the surface, we rise dripping, out of the sea to land on the deck of *Keldysh*. At 7:25—after nine hours and forty minutes inside *Mir 2*, we step out into the last light of day. It feels good to breathe in the sea air and watch the sun set over the North Atlantic.

This place is more than a memorial, more than a museum. It is a place that, like a battlefield, the pyramids of Egypt, or the Forum in Rome, is a reminder of humanity's achievements and the price we often pay in our quest. *Titanic* should not be left to the salvagers, nor should it be surrendered entirely to the dark solitude of the deep. We must keep the stories and the lessons alive and ever present.

Back in St. John's, I pack my bags for a flight home to Vancouver. There, I repack my bags and prepare for a return trip to the east coast of Canada. A new venture I'm involved in, a documentary television series called *The Sea Hunters*, has started what we hope will be a long-running series based on Clive Cussler's best-seller of the same name. We will search the world's oceans for famous shipwrecks. While I've been out exploring *Titanic*, some of the crew members of *The Sea Hunters* have been searching for *Carpathia*, the ship that rescued *Titanic*'s survivors.

— CHAPTER SIX —

CARPATHIA

THE NORTH ATLANTIC: APRIL 15, 1912

Harold Thomas Cottam's watch was long over, but the wireless operator of the Cunard liner *Carpathia* was still at his post, listening to the dot-dit-dot-dit Morse transmissions of other ships and the shore. Cottam's late night wakefulness was unusual, but he wanted to catch the latest news flashes from the station at Cape Race. As he reached down to unlace his boots, he suddenly stopped, stunned by the message coming in over the airwaves.

The news he heard changed his life—and probably saved those of more than 700 others. The White Star liner *Titanic*, bound to New York on her maiden voyage with 2,224 persons aboard, was calling for help.

As Cottam acknowledged the signal, *Titanic*'s wireless operator, John George "Jack" Phillips called back: "CQD—CQD—SOS—SOS—CQD—MGY. Come at once. We have struck a berg. It's a CQD, old man. Position 41.46 N, 50.14 W." CQD was the wireless distress call, and SOS was the new call just introduced to replace it. MGY was *Titanic*'s call sign. There was no mistaking the news, as much as Cottam could scarcely believe his ears. The new and "practically unsinkable" *Titanic* was going down.

"Shall I tell my captain?" Cottam wired back.

"Yes, quick," came the reply.

77

Racing to *Carpathia*'s bridge, Cottam blurted the news to First Officer Dean, who, without knocking, went straight into the cabin of Captain Arthur Rostron. In the 1958 classic movie *A Night to Remember*, the scene, as re-created, has Rostron yelling out, "What the devil!" and sitting up angrily in his bed, but Cottam's quick explanation stops him from taking the wireless operator to task. In his memoirs, Rostron wrote: "I had but recently turned in and was not asleep, and drowsily I said to myself: 'Who the dickens is this cheeky beggar coming into my cabin without knocking?' Then the First Officer was blurting out the facts and you may be sure I was very soon doing all that was in the ship's power to render the aid called for."

Rostron, a seasoned master known to his peers as "the Electric Spark," was both decisive and energetic. He did not hesitate now. Again, as *A Night to Remember* reconstructs the scene, he ordered: "Mr. Dean, turn the ship around—steer northwest. I'll work out the course for you in a minute." The film's script matches the decisiveness of the captain's published memoirs. Rostron recalled that he asked Cottam if he was sure it was *Titanic* calling. "Yes, sir." "You are absolutely certain?" "Quite certain, sir." "All right, tell him we are coming along as fast as we can."

Carpathia was not the only ship to receive *Titanic*'s distress call, but she was the closest of them all. Still, she was 58 miles away. The 13,564-ton, 558-foot *Carpathia* was a ten-year-old veteran of Cunard's fleet, three days out of New York with 750 passengers bound to Gibraltar and the Mediterranean. As Rostron worked out his position in relation to *Titanic*'s, he realized that at *Carpathia*'s top speed of 14 knots, it would take four hours to reach *Titanic*. That just wasn't good enough. He knew that many people would not survive in the icy waters unless help arrived soon.

Rostron called for more speed. Every off-duty stoker was roused and sent into the boiler rooms to shovel coal into the furnaces. To squeeze every bit of steam out of the boilers and into the engines, Chief Engineer Johnston cut off the heat and hot water throughout the ship, and pushed his men and machines to the limit. *Carpathia* surged forward at 15, 16 and finally 17 knots, faster than she had ever gone.

RMS Carpathia, *the ship that rushed to save the survivors of* Titanic. *Vancouver Maritime Museum*

As *Carpathia* raced northwest towards *Titanic*, Rostron was well aware that he was steaming into danger. Numerous warnings of ice from other ships and *Titanic*'s own collision with an iceberg made him wary. But he couldn't slow down. Rostron posted extra lookouts, including Second Officer James Bisset, who stood in the open, the frigid wind blasting his face as he stared into the darkness. When Bisset looked back at the bridge, he saw his deeply religious captain, hat lifted, lips moving quietly in silent prayer.

Carpathia's crew was at hard at work, clearing the ship's dining saloons to receive *Titanic*'s passengers, gathering blankets, uncovering the lifeboats and running them out. Stewards manned each passageway to calm *Carpathia*'s passengers and keep them in their rooms, out of the way. The galley staff brewed coffee and made hot soup, while the ship's doctors readied emergency supplies and stimulants in makeshift wards. The deck crew rigged lines, ladders and slings to bring survivors aboard.

Aboard *Titanic*, the end was fast approaching. At 1:45 a.m., Phillips called Cottam to plead, "Come as quickly as possible, old man; engine room filling up to the boilers." The last boats had pulled away—many only half full—as a crowd of some fifteen hundred people raced towards the stern, which was rising out of the sea as *Titanic*'s bow went under.

Cottam kept trying to raise Phillips, but *Titanic*'s faint signals showed that power was failing aboard the sinking liner. At 2:17 a.m., Cottam heard the beginning of a call from *Titanic*, then nothing but silence.

On *Titanic*, Phillips and assistant wireless operator Harold Bride stayed at their posts nearly to the very end, frantically working the radio to urge the ships racing to *Titanic* to hurry. As *Titanic*'s stern rose higher in the air, the engineers—all of whom had remained at their posts, knowing that they would die, but who nonetheless kept the dynamos running to keep the lights burning and to give "Sparks" every remaining bit of electricity to call for help—lost their battle as the machinery tore free of its mounts. The lights blinked out, surged on briefly, then went out forever. Once the power was gone, Phillips and Bride joined the crowd of people on the sloping decks. *Titanic*, straining in the water, half submerged, tore apart. The stern bobbed free for a minute, then joined the bow in a 2 ¼ mile fall to the ocean floor.

It was 2:20 a.m., and *Carpathia* was still nowhere in sight. Hundreds of people huddled in twenty lifeboats, while in the water more than fifteen hundred people thrashed, struggled and screamed for help until the icy water took their lives. "The cries, which were loud and numerous at first, died away gradually one by one . . . I think the last of them must have been heard nearly forty minutes after the *Titanic* sank," reported survivor Lawrence Beesley, floating in the distance in the relative safety of a lifeboat.

Two of those struggling in the water were Phillips and Bride. They made their way to one of the ship's collapsible boats that had been washed off the deck when *Titanic* sank. Floating half submerged on the overturned boat through the night, they suffered from the cold with a handful of passengers and crew. As the long night wore on into early morning, Phillips died. Second Officer Charles H. Lightoller, washed into the sea as the ship sank, had also struggled onto the overturned lifeboat and took command of the precarious perch. "We were painfully conscious of that icy water, slowly but surely creeping up our legs. Some quietly lost consciousness, subsided into the water, and slipped overboard . . . No one was in a condition to help, and the fact that a slight but distinct swell had started to roll up, rendered help from the still living an impossibility."

Lightoller hoped that help would come soon. "We knew that ships were racing to our rescue, though the chances of our keeping up our efforts of balancing until one came along seemed very, very remote."

Rostron kept a careful lookout as *Carpathia* rushed into the darkness. "Into that zone of danger we raced . . . every nerve strained watching for the ice. Once I saw one huge fellow towering into the sky quite near— saw it because a star was reflected on its surface—a tiny beam of warning which guided us safely past." At 2:40 a.m., he spotted a green flare on the horizon, just as the first icebergs came into view, but he did not slacken speed. Firing rockets and flares to signal his arrival, Rostron dodged the ice and he pressed on. He knew that the *Titanic* was probably gone, but he also knew that every minute counted for the survivors on—or in—the frigid sea. "It was an anxious time," he later recalled. "There were seven hundred souls on the *Carpathia*; these lives, as well as all the survivors of the *Titanic* herself, depended on a sudden turn of the wheel."

At 3:50 a.m., *Carpathia* slowed, and at 4:00 stopped. She was at *Titanic*'s position, but the ship was gone. Then, ahead, just a few miles off, a green flare blazed up from the water, and the dim outline of first one, then several lifeboats, came into view. In the boats, the survivors, many of them sitting in stunned silence, watched as *Carpathia* slowly approached, picking her way through the ice. As the profile of the ship, portholes filled with light, came into sight of the survivors in the boats, *Titanic* passenger Lawrence Beesley recalled: "The way those lights came into view was one of the most wonderful things we shall ever see. It meant deliverance at once . . . everyone's eyes filled with tears . . . and 'Thank God' was murmured in heartfelt tones round the boat."

As *Titanic*'s lifeboats rowed towards *Carpathia*, the sun rose to reveal that rescuer and rescued were in the midst of a field of ice—it lay everywhere, from bergs 200 feet high to chunks "as big as a man's fist" bobbing in the swell. Beesley said that when his boat rowed past a berg and alongside their rescuer, "We could read the Cunarder's name—

CARPATHIA—a name we are not likely ever to forget." Another passenger, Colonel Archibald Gracie, reported that when he climbed up a ladder and into an open companionway hatch, he "felt like falling down on my knees and kissing the deck in gratitude for the preservation of my life."

As No. 2 lifeboat came alongside, the first to reach *Carpathia*, *Titanic*'s fourth officer, Joseph G. Boxhall, went to the bridge to report to Captain Rostron. Rostron knew the answer, but he asked Boxhall a "heartrending inquiry." Had *Titanic* sunk? "Yes," answered Boxhall, "she went down around 2:30." His composure broke when Rostron asked how many people had been left aboard. "Hundreds and hundreds! Perhaps a thousand! Perhaps more! My God, sir, they've gone down with her. They couldn't live in this icy water." Rostron thanked the distraught officer and sent him below to get some coffee and warm up.

By 8:00 a.m., *Carpathia* had taken aboard more than seven hundred of *Titanic*'s crew and passengers, many of them stunned by shock.

As *Carpathia* stood by, *Titanic*'s survivors waited at the rails, looking out at the water. Husbands, fathers, sons—as well as women and children—would never return. Rostron held a service of thanksgiving for the saved and a memorial service for the lost, then left the scene of the disaster at 9:00 a.m., just as the Leyland Line's *Californian* arrived to offer assistance. Ironically, *Californian* had been closer than *Carpathia* to *Titanic,* and her deck officers had seen the sinking liner's distress signals—but the wireless operator had gone to bed so they had not received *Titanic*'s frantic calls for help.

Carpathia headed for New York, her passengers divided by the gulf of the tragedy. Many of *Titanic*'s survivors kept to themselves. J. Bruce Ismay, chairman of the White Star Line, sequestered himself in *Carpathia*'s doctor's cabin, refusing contact. His actions on *Carpathia*— and his survival when so many others had died—only reinforced the criticisms leveled against him in the aftermath of *Titanic*'s loss. Sadder yet, and perhaps more typical, was the reaction of two women who sat wrapped in blankets on *Carpathia*'s deck chairs, staring at the sea as a steward approached to ask if they wanted coffee. "Go away," they answered. "We've just seen our husbands drown."

After running through a storm at sea, *Carpathia* arrived at New York, reaching Pier 54 at 8:00 p.m. A crowd of thirty thousand had gathered. The news of *Titanic*'s sinking was the focus of world attention. Wireless operators ashore had intercepted the distress calls, and Rostron had broadcast a brief message to the Associated Press, informing the world *Titanic* was gone, along with two-thirds of the people who had sailed in her.

At the Cunard Pier, a clutch of anxious families and eager reporters stood by. After *Carpathia*'s own passengers disembarked, *Titanic*'s survivors filed off, many of them wearing clothes donated by *Carpathia*'s passengers and crew, some of the children dressed in makeshift smocks sewn from steamer blankets.

The daring dash through the dark and ice-filled seas to rescue the survivors of *Titanic* earned world fame for *Carpathia* and her captain. Both received a number of awards—plaques, engraved silver cups and plate, and medals, many of them displayed in a special case aboard *Carpathia*. The ship returned to her regular run between New York and the Mediterranean, sailing again on April 20 to resume her interrupted voyage.

CELTIC SEA: JULY 17, 1918

The coming of war in 1914 disrupted *Carpathia*'s usual routes, and in 1915 she began running from Liverpool to New York and Boston. After leaving Liverpool with just fifty-seven passengers as part of a convoy on July 15, 1918, *Carpathia*'s luck finally ran out in the Celtic Sea as she left the British Isles. Just after midnight, in the early moments of July 17, the German submarine U-55 intercepted *Carpathia* with two torpedoes. The first ripped into the port side and the second went into the engine room. The blasts killed five of the ship's firemen and injured two engineers. Dead in the water, *Carpathia* began to sink by the bow as the sea poured in. Captain William Prothero gave the order to "abandon ship" and fired distress rockets to warn the other ships in the convoy that a submarine was nearby.

Carpathia's passengers and the 218 surviving crew members climbed into the lifeboats as the ship sank. The U-boat surfaced and fired another torpedo into the ship to hurry the end, and *Carpathia* finally went under. The submarine was approaching the lifeboats when the armed sloop HMS *Snowdrop* hove into view and fired her deck guns to drive away *U-55*, then came about to pick up *Carpathia*'s survivors.

At 12:40 a.m., *Carpathia* sank at a position that *Snowdrop* recorded as 49.25 N 10.25 W, off the southern coast of Ireland about 120 miles west of the famous Fastnet. The loss of the famous ship was one of many during the war and was overshadowed by the sinking of other liners, such as the well-known tragedy of *Lusitania* and the loss of *Titanic*'s sister ship *Britannic* in the Mediterranean. But the memory of the gallant liner never faded. Her former captain, Arthur Rostron, eulogized *Carpathia* in 1931: "It was a sorry end to a fine ship . . . She had done her bit both in peace and war, and she lies in her natural element, resting her long rest on a bed of sand."

THE SEARCH FOR *CARPATHIA*

Exactly where *Carpathia* rested spurred the efforts of many shipwreck hunters, particularly Clive Cussler, the famous author whose bestseller *Raise the Titanic* had launched not only the fictional career of Dirk Pitt of the National Underwater and Marine Agency (NUMA), but also fueled Clive's real-life NUMA and its quest, funded largely by his book royalties, to search for famous shipwrecks. *Carpathia* was high on Clive's list of ships to find, and in 1999, when John Davis of Eco-Nova Productions proposed a television series based on Clive's book *The Sea Hunters,* they chose *Carpathia* as the first wreck to look for. When *The Sea Hunters* crew was assembled, I had the good fortune to be selected as Clive's co-host for the show and as the team's archeologist, joining veteran diver Mike Fletcher.

The search for *Carpathia* was more daunting than it sounds, because the general location of *Carpathia*'s loss was a U-boat killing ground during two world wars, and hundreds of sunken vessels lay on the seabed. It would take systematic searching and as comprehensive a survey as possible to try to find *Carpathia*.

Under NUMA's sponsorship, British explorer Graham Jessop mounted a search for *Carpathia*. In September 1999, he thought that he had discovered the wreck in 600 feet of water, 185 miles west of Land's End, England, but bad weather drove off his ship before he could verify the discovery by sending down underwater cameras. When Jessop later returned to the site, he found that it was not *Carpathia*. A dinner plate lying on the sand, marked with the crest of the Hamburg-America Line, was one of several clues that finally identified the wreck as Hamburg-America's *Isis*, lost in a storm in November 1936. Only one of the crew, a cabin boy, survived the sinking.

— —

Mike Fletcher headed out to sea in May 2000 for another try at finding *Carpathia*. He watched the side-scan sonar pen trace black-and-white images of the ocean floor. At the same time, he also checked a magnetometer as it scanned the seabed for a large metallic object—like a sunken ship. After a month of surveying, slowly running straight lanes in what ocean searchers call "mowing the lawn," he felt that at last the survey was narrowing down where *Carpathia* should be.

Finally, on May 22, 2000, as Mike watched the side-scan sonar and magnetometer, he was rewarded by the ghostly outline of a sunken ship in profile, rising clear of the bottom, and by the shadowy image of it from reflected sound waves. But the weather was getting bad, and again there was no opportunity to drop in a camera to take a look at the wreck up close. The wreck was the right size for *Carpathia* and was in the right spot, just a few miles from where *Snowdrop* had placed it. However, *The Sea Hunters* kept the news under wraps until we could mount a second expedition to confirm the facts. "You don't know till you go" is tried and true wisdom in the difficult task of shipwreck identification.

In September, John Davis of Eco-Nova headed for England to visit the wreck we all hoped was that of *Carpathia*. Nine days later, John and his team set out in the teeth of a storm. Working under difficult conditions, they were able to deploy a remotely operated vehicle with a camera to dive down to the wreck and capture four hours of video. With the precious footage in hand, John flew to Halifax, to meet with the rest of the team.

— —

John, Mike, Clive and I all gather in the theater of the Maritime Museum of the Atlantic, after hours, as the guests of its director, Michael Moore. The large-screen television in front of us the center of attention as John Davis takes the videotape out of his bag (he has already made a copy in case something goes wrong) and pops it into the machine. I'm ready, leaning forward, with photos of *Carpathia* and the ship's plans spread out before me. After more than two decades of shipwreck hunting, diving and research, I'm still as excited as a child at Christmas by a new discovery. So is everyone else.

We watch as the ROV moves across a mottled sand and gravel bottom. Then, suddenly, coming out of the dark gloom, we see a propeller. It is covered with encrustations of marine life, but the outline is clear: three blades, one buried in the sand, attached to a shaft that is braced by a strut that comes out of the hull. So far so good—it's the right shape, has the right number of blades and is off-center, showing that it is one of two propellers that should be on either side of the rudder.

The ROV swings around, looking up at the hull that curves out from the keel. Then it turns, and we see the rudder, still attached to the sternpost. As John freezes the video frame, we study the ship's plans and match the rudder—its shape, fastenings and size—to them. Just beyond the rudder, we spot the second propeller. As I watch the screen, I think of how fast those propellers were spinning in the early morning hours of April 15, 1912—faster than they ever had either before or after—on that heroic dash to aid *Titanic*. *Carpathia*'s engineers and captain pushed her so hard that the hull rattled and shook—"she was excited as we were," said one engine-room hand.

The ROV climbs the stern, which has a very distinctive shape. There is no mistaking it, and the curving lines before us match what until now we had seen only on black-and-white photos taken in a bygone age. Moments like this remind all of us how privileged we are to relive history, as stories and faded photographs come to life. The ROV is on the deck now, and a pair of davits for a lifeboat comes into view. They are in the right place to help confirm that this is *Carpathia,* but even as I note that technical fact, my mind is back at *Titanic,* looking at her empty davits.

Our first disappointment comes when the ROV encounters a mass of wreckage where the superstructure once was. We were hoping the superstructure was not damaged, but it is gone. The ROV passes over an intact bronze porthole lying on the deck, its glass unbroken. After marine organisms consumed the wood that held this porthole in place, then it fell free to lie where we see it. We go back and forth as the robot traverses the deck, revealing fallen bulkheads and electrical wire, broken glass and ship's hardware. *Carpathia*'s deckhouses and bridge have collapsed, and I think of those plaques and awards, now buried beneath tons of rusting steel.

The ROV moves off the deck and follows the hull, whose steel plates are torn and mangled, but it is hard to say if the damage came from the torpedoes that struck the ship or from the red-hot boilers exploding as the cold sea flooded them. Gradually, it becomes clear that we're looking at damage from a torpedo that struck *Carpathia* on the starboard side. The ROV does not completely survey the port side, but another hole, perhaps from the first torpedo hit, shows up near the area of the vanished bridge. It's a sad moment as we inspect these wounds of a long-ago war.

When the ROV's lights pick out a row of portholes along the hull, I am struck again by a voice from the past, recalling Lawrence Beesley's description of watching from one of *Titanic*'s lifeboats as the lights blazing from *Carpathia*'s portholes signaled that help had at last arrived. The ROV climbs back to the deck and passes the steam winches of *Carpathia*'s forward cargo cranes—there is no doubt now, as we look at their position next to the No. 1 cargo hold, that this is *Carpathia.* But forward of the hold, the bow is in bad shape, and it is clear that the liner's final plunge was bow first—like *Titanic*'s. But instead of falling thousands of feet into the depths, *Carpathia* sank in water shallower than her own length: the 558-foot ship went down in 514 feet of water.

Her bow hit the bottom—hard—before her stern left the surface. It is ironic to see that *Carpathia*, while not torn in two like *Titanic*, is in worse shape than the liner she had once rushed to help.

The videotape is nearing the end now, and as we gaze into the murk, John Davis points out the most interesting discovery of all. There, lying on the bottom near the hull, half buried in the sand, is the ship's bell. It is a riveting sight. We strain our eyes to see if we can make out if the name is there, but marine growth has covered the bell's surface. More details are filled in: *Carpathia*'s fallen stack lies off her starboard side, with the ship's brass whistles lying flat in the sand nearby, and debris blown out of the hull by the blasts is scattered over the seabed. Later, a group of British technical divers descend to the wreck and find some of the ship's dishes, which they say have the Cunard crest on them.

To confirm that this is *Carpathia*, I look for ten exact matches between the wreck and the ship's plans. Not only is this ship the right size but her decks are laid out exactly like those on *Carpathia*'s plans. The position of the deck gear, the single stack, the twin screws at the stern, are also identical—and then there's the torpedo damage and the fact that the ship sank bow first. The excitement of the discovery and confirmation that this other important part of *Titanic*'s story has come to light is on all our minds as the tape ends.

In the morning, we will announce the news of the discovery, and once again *Carpathia*'s name will flash through the airwaves and appear on the front page. My hope, as I look at the fleeting images from the bottom of the sea, is that people in the modern, fast-paced world we now live in will remember the tragedy that led to *Carpathia*'s fame and the special mettle of her officers and crew who, despite the dangers, acted in the best traditions of the sea. In the days that follow, we are not disappointed. *Carpathia* again dominates the world's stage, if only briefly, as we prepare for more sea hunting.

CHAPTER SEVEN

CATHERINE THE GREAT'S LOST ART

OFF FINLAND: OCTOBER 4, 1771

Reynoud Lorentz and his ship *Vrouw Maria* were in serious trouble. The ship was stuck fast on a rock, and from where Lorentz stood near the stern, he could hear water pouring into the hold. Everywhere he looked, he saw more rocks surrounding the ship like giant teeth waiting to devour her. *Vrouw Maria* was already badly damaged, and the violent surf threatened to overwhelm the efforts of the crew, who strained at the pumps to try to keep the flooding down. Panicked, the men shouted up at Lorentz, demanding that he give the order to abandon ship. Better to save their own lives than the cargo, they argued. Lorentz did not want to leave his cargo behind, particularly not this cargo. The narrow stack of crates in the hold, loaded quietly on the dock in Amsterdam, was far too precious. But, in the end, he conceded that it was time to go.

The voyage that was now foundering along with *Vrouw Maria* had begun on August 12, 1771, as workers began to load her with cargo for St. Petersburg. On September 5, as a strong southwest wind filled the sails, *Vrouw Maria* raised anchor and headed out to sea, "in the name of God," as Lorentz wrote in the logbook. Heavy winds and stormy weather battered the tiny ship as she made her way up the North Sea, passing Jutland in a driving rainstorm. Finally, on the morning of September 23,

Vrouw Maria anchored off the Danish port of Elsinore, where all ships running through Danish waters had to stop and pay customs duty.

The records of the custom house list *Vrouw Maria*'s cargo as sugar, "Brazil wood," cotton, cambric, calico, linen, zinc, cheese, paper, indigo, mercury, butter and other items—a nondescript array that would hopefully fetch a good price in the Russian winter capital. No mention was made of the ship's "special cargo," a shipment for the Russian Imperial Court. Its presence on *Vrouw Maria* may have been a secret, or, as Finnish historian Christian Ahlström has noted, because royal shipments were usually exempt from customs duties, it simply may have not been listed by the Danish authorities.

Heading up the Baltic towards the Gulf of Finland, *Vrouw Maria* sailed into a storm on the September 30. For the next three days, the ship beat through heavy seas and rain. Lorentz did not realize that *Vrouw Maria*, drifting in the storm, was off course. Then, on the evening of October 3, the ship hit a submerged rock. The collision brought *Vrouw Maria* to a sudden stop, and Lorentz wrote in the ship's log that "at first we thought that we would sink when a high wave lifted us." As she drifted along, the ship hit another rock: "We struck hard and lost our rudder and part of the stern." Leaking badly, *Vrouw Maria* drifted off again, and the crew anchored her. Every man took a turn at the pumps to try and get rid of the water that was rapidly filling the ship. They pumped all night, but by the early morning, the storm was still blowing and the crew was exhausted. "Since we could not continue pumping and save the ship and its cargo," said Lorentz, he gave order to abandon ship.

Crowded into a small dinghy, the crew rowed over to a small island, not much bigger than a rock, and spent a cold night. When help arrived the next morning, Lorentz and his men learned that they were stranded off the southern coast of Finland in the Turko Archipelago, a maze of twenty thousand islets, islands and rocks. The ship, surprisingly, was still afloat, though there was little chance of saving her as the decks were close to the water. But some of the cargo might be saved, so Lorentz ordered the crew back to *Vrouw Maria*. For the next three days, they worked the pumps to keep the rising water in the hold from swamping the ship. The sugar cargo was certainly ruined; when Lorentz tasted the water pouring out of the pumps as the men labored, it was sweet. His dismay deepened when each stroke of the pumps brought up gouts of coffee beans. The crates, bundles, bags and boxes in the flooded hold were banging and bumping around, and breaking up.

Lorentz's luck held long enough for the crew to open the hatches and start pulling out the top layer of cargo. Taking their knives in hand, the sailors also cut down *Vrouw Maria*'s sails and some of her rigging, salvaging everything they could before the ship slipped into the deep. Finally, on October 9, as they rowed to the ship after spending the night ashore, they found the sea was empty. In the night, alone in the darkness, *Vrouw Maria* had finally sunk. There was no trace of the ship, not a scrap of floating debris, to mark her passing.

ST. PETERSBURG: OCTOBER 16, 1771

Count Nikita Panin, Russia's foreign minister, sat at his desk, signing a confidential letter to the Swedish government. His letter asked the Swedes, who controlled the Turko Archipelago, to assist the Russians in an "unusual" matter. *Vrouw Maria*'s secret shipment had included not only silver, snuffboxes and art for members of the Imperial Court but also, Panin explained, "several crates with valuable paintings belonging to Her Imperial Majesty the Empress."

Empress Catherine the Great was in the midst of assembling one of Europe's greatest collections of art and treasure for her small Hermitage (or retreat) in the Winter Palace at St. Petersburg. She had married Peter, grandson of Peter the Great and heir to Russia's throne, when she was sixteen. But Catherine soon grew disaffected with her husband, who was said to be weak-minded, indecisive and not conjugally interested in his passionate Prussian princess. After Peter was crowned tsar in 1761, his unpopularity grew. Catherine plotted with a group of nobles and army officers led by her lover, Count Grigory Orlov, to depose the tsar. When their coup toppled Peter from his throne in 1762, Catherine seized power. Her reign was a time of sweeping change in Russia. The empress, like her predecessor Peter the Great, was interested in modernizing and westernizing the nation, which was still a feudal state. Among her accomplishments was the introduction of smallpox vaccine to Russia in 1768. Under Catherine, the Russian court became a center for European culture. The empress invited prominent intellectuals to St. Petersburg, encouraged public building projects, and was a patron of the arts and literature both in Russia and abroad. An admirer of the French philosopher Voltaire, Catherine regularly corresponded with him. When Voltaire died in 1778, Catherine purchased his entire seven-thousand volume library and had it shipped to St. Petersburg.

In her lifetime, Catherine the Great amassed collections so diverse and magnificent that she had to build an addition to her Winter Palace to house the paintings, sculptures, porcelain, antiquities, exquisite furnishings and silver. The secret cargo of *Vrouw Maria* had come from one of the most famous art collections of its day, making the loss all the more painful.

When wealthy Dutch shipping merchant Gerrit Braamcamps died in Amsterdam on June 17, 1771, he left behind a home filled with that his contemporaries called a "treasure cabinet" of more than three hundred paintings, porcelain, silver and other valuables. But the heirs of Braamcamps wanted cash, not the collection, so they sold it at auction. Catherine ordered Russia's ambassador to the Netherlands, Prince Galitsyn, to "look after her interests" at the sale. On her behalf, he acquired a number of European Old Masters of the sixteenth and seventeenth centuries, including paintings by Rembrandt and Rubens.

Now, those paintings rested at the bottom of the Baltic Sea. "As these pictures are very sensitive to injury and need care," Panin wrote, he was sending an officer, Major Thier, to co-ordinate a search with the Swedes. "I do not doubt that you will do your utmost as this matter concerns her Majesty the Empress personally," Panin told the Swedish royal chancellor.

Thier's trip to Finland was in vain. Winter was fast approaching, and little could be done. The Swedes sent a number of expeditions out to the archipelago to search for the wreck. Boats towed grappling irons to try and snag the hulk, but the vast area and deep seas made it an impossible task. An obstruction at 30 fathoms was repeatedly snagged by searchers, but it proved to be a rock. The Swedes and Russians abandoned their efforts to find *Vrouw Maria,* and the ship, despite the rumors of riches aboard, was in time forgotten.

VROUW MARIA AND A PRECIOUS CARGO

We're anchored above a small wooden shipwreck that Finnish researchers believe is *Vrouw Maria.* The story of the tiny Dutch ship with her secret cargo of precious paintings resurfaced in 1982, when Christian Ahlström, Finland's leading shipwreck researcher and historian, discovered the tale while working through Swedish diplomatic records. Ahlström spent years meticulously reconstructing the tale of *Vrouw Maria,* and his discoveries encouraged diver and researcher Rauno Koivusaari to start searching for the wreck in 1998. In June 1999, while towing a side-scan sonar behind his ship *Teredo,* Koivusaari finally located the intact wreck of a small wooden ship near Jurmo Island.

Under Finnish law, all such finds are the property of the state. Koivusaari reported the discovery to the Maritime Museum of Finland, which acts on behalf of the National Board of Antiquities. The museum conducted a two-week survey of the exterior of the wreck in the summer of 2000. Lying in a deep hole surrounded by rocks, the wreck was missing its rudder and the deck hatches were open. Reaching inside the main cargo hatch, archeologists carefully recovered three clay tobacco pipes, a metal ingot and small round lead seal. A clay bottle lying on the deck was also mapped and recovered.

Back in the laboratory of the maritime museum, analysis of the artifacts showed the researchers that they were on the right track. The pipes were Dutch, and one of them had a maker's mark that indicated the pipe was made by Jan Souffreau of Gouda, Holland, whose factory was in business from 1732 to 1782. The ingot was zinc, and *Vrouw Maria* was known to have been carrying nearly forty "ship pounds" of that metal. The lead seal, probably from twine that wrapped a bale of cloth, was marked "Leyden," from the Dutch town of the same name. The clay bottle, no older than the 1760s, held mineral water from the German town of Trier.

But more work was needed. The museum assembled a team under the direction of senior curator and archeologist Saalamaria Tikkanen, who invited *The Sea Hunters* to participate in the first detailed look both inside and outside the wreck.

＿＿

We're aboard the research vessel *Teredo,* heading for the site of the wreck of *Vrouw Maria* with an expert team of Finns who are volunteering their time, and archeologists Matias Laitenen and Minna Koivikko. I'm here with *The Sea Hunters* to join the expedition and to film the work of the Finnish team as part of our television series. We're all excited by the uniqueness of the wreck of *Vrouw Maria* and her story, and by the fact that, despite its importance, the story is not well known outside Scandinavia. That's about to change. Our producer and team leader, John Davis, helps Mike Fletcher suit up for his dive. Mike's son Warren and my daughter Beth both haul gear and work to prepare for Mike's 140-foot plunge into darkness. We rig Mike's helmet, lights and underwater video camera.

As we watch a small color monitor on *Teredo*'s bridge, it's almost as though we're there when Mike jumps off the ship and starts his fall into the depths. The water is clear, and soon the form of the wreck comes into view. The rounded hull sits nearly level on the bottom, with a slight list to starboard. The lower part of the masts rise halfway to the surface, and one anchor rests against the port side of the hull. The ship is surprisingly intact, thanks to the special conditions of the Baltic. *Vrouw Maria* is an example, like the famous Swedish warship *Vasa,* of how the Baltic's waters preserve old shipwrecks. *Vasa* capsized and sank in Stockholm harbor in 1628. Swedish researchers discovered the intact hulk and raised it in 1961. Stained black with age, but looking just as she did when she sailed nearly four centuries ago, *Vasa* is one of the world's great archeological treasures and one of Sweden's major tourist attractions in its own museum on the Stockholm waterfront.

The Baltic preserved *Vasa* and *Vrouw Maria* so well because it is a deep, cold sea with a low salinity level. In some areas, the Baltic is practically fresh water because of the many lakes and rivers that drain into it, and cold fresh water preserves wood better than salt water. But most important, the low salinity levels keep out the *teredo navalis,* a sea worm that eats wood and will consume a wooden wreck within a matter of decades. That's why we're all smiling at the wry Finnish humor evident in naming their research vessel *Teredo.* But unlike its namesake worm, this vessel's mission is to document and preserve wrecks. The fact that when the Swedes raised *Vasa,* they found coils of rope, leather shoes and a crock of still-edible butter inside the ship, provides some hope about the state of *Vrouw Maria*'s precious cargo after more than a couple of centuries in the water.

As Mike makes his way around the wreck, we are able to follow, step by step, the actions of Reynoud Lorentz and his nine-man crew as they struggled to save the cargo. It becomes increasingly clear, as we carefully survey the wreck, that this is *Vrouw Maria.* The stern is damaged—rudder missing and planks broken. It's not enough damage to quickly fill the ship, but it is enough to slowly flood her. The ship appears to have sunk at anchor, and we know that Lorentz and his crew had anchored *Vrouw Maria* before the last time they left her. They believed that the thick anchor cables had parted and that the ship had drifted off and sunk, but we can see that the ship filled and sank by the bow, practically on top of an anchor.

Air trapped inside the sinking ship's stern damaged it when she sank. The quarterdeck was ripped free, leaving the captain's cabin an empty shell. A hatch at the back of the stern burst open, and loose planks litter the seabed. Yet the sinking did little to disturb the decks, though some of the planks are missing, others loose, again perhaps part of the frantic work by the crew to pull cargo out of the flooded hold. Loose bits of rigging—blocks, tackle, a coil of rope and the ship's sounding lead, used to determine the depth of water—lie against the starboard rail, perhaps where the crew stowed them as they worked to salvage the ship. Looking at the lead line, I think of the entries in the logbook for

A drawing of Vrouw Maria *sitting upright on the
ocean floor off Finland. Piirtänyt Kalle Salonen, Nauvo Trunsjö*

October 3, 1771, when Lorentz wrote that after hitting the rock, they "sounded and could not find the bottom," a scary proposition. But working the ship "with great difficulty," they "sounded again to approximately 13 fathoms, dropped the anchor, which gave way for a long while, we let out the whole rope and it finally began to hold, we fastened the sails and all hands went to the pump." The lead line on the deck is a reminder that time is standing still on the bottom of the Baltic.

A tangle of spars and the topmast lie against the hull. The windlass at the bow is still rigged for handling the anchor, though the rope cable has rotted away. A wooden handspike is still in its socket in the windlass, which was used to winch up the anchors, as if a crew member working it had just walked away. The pumps, with their handles alongside them, are visible near the stern, next to the dislodged tiller (ships of this period did not always have a ship's wheel) that was used to steer *Vrouw Maria*.

This wrecked ship looks as if she could be pumped free of water and, with a few repairs, rerigged and fitted with sail, resume a voyage interrupted 230 years ago. Discovering that *Vrouw Maria* is so intact raises the big question as Mike approaches the open cargo hatch. What will we find? The camera on Mike's helmet reveals a tightly packed hold with very little space between the top of the cargo and the deck. It looks like Lorentz and his crew did not get very far in unpacking *Vrouw Maria*. We can see hundreds of clay tobacco pipes and an open crate that displays piles of eyeglass lenses. We can also see other crates, tall and narrow, standing on end.

Thanks to Christian Ahlström's research, we know what Lorentz and his crew managed to pull out of the hold; some of it matches what had been declared to the Danish customs officials at Elsinore—and much of it does not. Among the diverse cargo that *Vrouw Maria*'s crew salvaged were rolls of cloth (both coarse and fine), lead chests of coffee, a chest of tea, a chest of bound books, a box of cheese, a box of snuff, a box of "mirrors with gold frames, one round box of cartouche-packed tobacco, one round box with a small musical mechanism, twelve small ivory eggs, one linen package containing six pairs of cotton stockings," plus a large painting with a gilt frame and five smaller pictures. These items were listed in the archives because the Swedes ended up auctioning them under the provisions of admiralty law. The Russians were eager to retrieve what they could, particularly the Empress Catherine's treasures, but the Swedish governor of Turko, Baron Christopher Rappe, reported that "unfortunately, Her Majesty's paintings are not included."

As I look at the tin crates standing on their ends, trapped by other cargo, I know I'm not alone in hoping that they hold Catherine's paintings. No one knows just how many paintings the Russian agents bought in Amsterdam and placed in *Vrouw Maria* for shipment to St. Petersburg. In 1961, Dutch researcher Clara Bille studied the fate of the Braamcamps collection in her doctoral dissertation, and working from that, Maritime

A drawing of the bow of Vrouw Maria. *Piirtänyt Kalle Salonen, Nauvo Trunsjö*

Museum of Finland curator Ismo Malinen has suggested that as many as thirty-five of the Braamcamps paintings ended up on the ill-fated ship.

Vague descriptions exist for many of the paintings, outside of brief notations in the Braamcamps auction catalog printed in July 1771. There were two paintings by Coedyk, a tableau and a scene of a man and woman sitting at a table. There was a Rubens portrait of "one of the four evangelists," and a "portrait of a man" by Rembrandt. There was a painting of a "lady at a table" by Gerard Douw, a pupil of Rembrandt's, and a scene of a man driving a herd of bulls by another Dutch master, Paulus Potter. Van Balen and Bruegel's *The Virgin and Infant Jesus,* and three other Bruegels of unidentified landscapes and people, were packed in with paintings by Joseph Laquy, Jan van den Helden, Adriaen van Ostade, Jan van Gooyen, Adriaen van de Velde, Philips Wouwerman, Guido Reni, Lo Spagnoletto and several other artists. One of the paintings was an appropriate subject to be in a shipwrecked and sunken art collection: Abraham Stork's *Ships at Sea*.

The narrow tin crates in the hold of *Vrouw Maria* may very well contain these paintings, but we will not know for sure until the archeologists methodically excavate the ship and every crate is raised to the surface, then carefully and scientifically opened in the lab.

Mike approaches the bow, and the bluff, almost apple-cheeked shape of the old ship comes into view. The open hawse pipes gape like empty eye sockets. Trailing off the bow is a fallen section of mast that has an end shaped like the side of a giant cello. The age of the ship is apparent, and for me, it is thrilling to see, close up and in detail, a type of ship that has not sailed the oceans for centuries and which most of us have only seen as an engraved drawing in an old book. Mike moves along the port side of the wreck, and there, cemented to the hull planks by rust, is one of *Vrouw Maria*'s iron anchors. From its position, it looks as if the anchor was lashed up against the hull, its hooks pointing skyward and not hanging down, as we might expect. The anchor may have been tied by rope that has disintegrated, because something had to hold it against the planks long enough for the rust to bind with the wood. But why it is where it is, and how it was set, are mysteries.

As Mike continues back to the stern, we see that the lintel above the entrance to Lorentz's cabin is beautifully carved with a scroll decoration. It is a lovely touch on a utilitarian, hardworking ship, and a reminder that people loved and cared for her. That hint of a long-ago emotion has survived the wreck and *Vrouw Maria*'s long slumber in the deep.

The time has come for Mike to start ascending, but he pauses for a moment to gaze back at *Vrouw Maria*, lying silent in the cold greenish-blue gloom of a Baltic grave. Then he begins the long slow climb back up to the surface, pausing to decompress as we share notes and observations.

We'll repeat this process tomorrow and in the days that follow, and the Finnish team also will send down their divers, with cameras and measuring devices, to meticulously plot and document every loose plank, every artifact on the deck, every fallen spar, to create a detailed record of *Vrouw Maria* as she now is. This level of painstaking documentation is absolutely essential before anything is disturbed or removed, a scientific protocol that separates us from souvenir hunters. If the lead line was taken away or some of the crates yanked out, we'd lose important clues as to what had happened. We'd lose some of those evocative connections across time, like the single handspike in the windlass, indicating where a sailor stepped away from working the anchor lines to start pumping. It is one thing to read about events in an old logbook; it is another thing altogether to have the privilege to see the scene exactly as that writer left it.

The discovery of *Vrouw Maria* poses a unique opportunity and a challenge. This intact wooden ship of 1771 is a time capsule. Packed full of merchandise as well as Catherine the Great's collection of paintings, the ship, when excavated, will yield valuable details about European trade of the time and Russia's rapid pace of westernization. As for the thirty-five or so lost paintings that still rest in *Vrouw Maria*, they may very well not be in as good condition as the ship. Even if the panels and canvas have survived, the paint may not. Conservators, the scientists who meticulously battle the ravages of time and the elements to restore and repair antiquities, are sure that any watercolors are gone. Other paints may have emulsified or washed away after two centuries in the sea. But paintings have survived Baltic immersion, including one from a seventeenth-century shipwreck, and Catherine's paintings may have been sealed in waterproof containers. It will be years, however, before *Vrouw Maria* and her cargo are raised and every crate is carefully unpacked in the laboratory.

Our last day on the site comes as the Maritime Museum of Finland crew also prepares to leave for the winter. Soon the ice will come and lock up the Turko Archipelago. That's one form of protection for a rare treasure. Another is the surveillance cameras that the Finnish Coast Guard has installed around the wreck, feeding continuous video images back to land to ensure that no souvenir hunters or looters seek to plunder the site.

Meanwhile, the Finnish government is examining plans to raise and restore *Vrouw Maria* and display her cargo, perhaps in a new state-of-the-art museum in Helsinki. If that course is pursued, it will take years of planning and cost millions to raise the ship and then to preserve it, because the moment the ship is lifted out of her grave, she will begin to deteriorate, and in a matter of minutes, if not seconds, some delicate bits will disintegrate.

The costs are huge, but the revenues could also be significant. *Vasa* is a major attraction in Sweden's tourism market, and the unique sight of the tiny *Vrouw Maria* from 1771, still laden with the goods she was carrying, would also appeal to tourists. Some supporters, including Finland's Minister of Culture, believe that the time has come to bring *Vrouw Maria* ashore, but how to accomplish that job is unclear. Some argue for a slow excavation at the wreck site, but the depth limits diving time and places humans in a stressful and dangerous environment. Others think that the ship could be braced and moved to shallower water, or placed in a large tank and studied at a shore (and publicly accessible) facility, but whether or not the hull would withstand the stress of bracing and moving is unknown. More studies and more discussions are needed.

As we pack our gear and leave, I am still in a state of awe over what we've just seen. Never before in my career have I seen a wreck as intact as this. It's only our third foray as *The Sea Hunters* team, but everyone agrees that the privilege we've been extended is rare and wonderful. I've always thought that the seabed was the greatest museum in the world, and now I've literally seen a shipwreck that is a museum in its own right, including paintings originally intended for an empress's private gallery. I wonder if our next adventure and the ones that follow can ever top this experience.

CHAPTER EIGHT

KUBLAI KHAN'S LOST FLEET

AT HAKOZAKI SHRINE IN JAPAN

A gentle breeze sighs through the trees and leaves flutter gently in response. Robed priests slowly walk through the shrine's precincts, stopping in front of the main altar to clap loudly and bow. The smoke of incense fills the air, and wooden placards painted with the prayers of the devout line the walkway. I am inside Hakozaki, one of Japan's three most sacred Shinto shrines. Established in 923, Hakozaki has existed for more than a thousand years. The grounds of the shrine are filled with monuments and buildings, and it is in front of one of them that I stand gazing at a stone weight for an ancient ship's anchor. A small plaque, in English and Japanese, explains that it came from a lost ship, part of a fleet sent by China's Mongol emperor, Kublai Khan, to invade Japan in 1274.

A stone tablet nearby has musical notes and writing in *kanji,* or traditional Japanese script. I am told that it is a traditional song about the Mongol invasion. To my surprise and delight, our host stops a tour group of Japanese schoolgirls and requests them to sing the song. I ask my host and translator what the words are, and, with less grace than the girls but with gusto, he sings the song for us in English. The last stanza is the most significant:

Heaven grew angry, and the ocean's
Billows were in tempest tossed;
They who came to work us evil,
Thousands of the Mongol host,
Sank and perished in the seaweed.
Of that horde survived but three;
Swift the sky was clear, and moonbeams
Shone upon the Ghenkai sea.

There it is, the story of how the gods sent a divine wind to sink the Mongol invasion fleet and save Japan. The anchor stone is displayed at Hakozaki as proof of that long-ago event and as a reminder of how Japan's shores were protected by that wind—a wind whose name in Japanese is *kamikaze.*

The story of the kamikaze was used to lethal effect in the Second World War. In the name of that "divine wind," nearly two thousand young Japanese men strapped themselves into airplanes and dove out of the sky to suicidally crash onto the decks of American and Allied warships. The deadly toll they wrought did not turn the tides of war, however. In defeat, the Japanese were told that their emperor was not a god and that the ancient story of the kamikaze was a myth. But the story of the Mongol invasion and the kamikaze remains a powerful part of the national consciousness of modern Japanese.

I've journeyed to Japan with fellow members of *The Sea Hunters* to visit an archeological site where a lost ship of Kublai Khan's fleet has surfaced from the gray-green waters near Takashima, a tiny island off Japan's southwest coast. History, myth or a combination of both? The remains of the ancient ship will tell us much about what really happened off these shores more than seven centuries ago.

THE MONGOL INVASIONS OF JAPAN: 1274 AND 1281

Under Chinggis Khan, a great horde of "barbarians" swept out of the Mongolian plains in 1206 to win a series of military conquests that made them not only the masters of much of Asia but also of an army poised on the doorstep of Europe and the Middle East. History would have been very different had the Mongols achieved Chinggis Khan's dream of absolute conquest. As it was, the world will never forget the saga of the Mongols and of battles like their capture of the Turkmen city of Merv in 1221. In revenge for the death of his son-in-law, Chinggis ordered the death of every living thing in the city, and seven hundred thousand people were put to the sword.

Battles against the Muslims, the Russians and other eastern European kingdoms continued under Chinggis's son Ögodäi; however, the death of Ögodäi's successor not only doomed the Muslim campaign but stalled the conquest of China. The next Mongol leader, Kublai Khan, soon controlled more territory than any sovereign in history. But he wanted more territory, more riches and, above all else, recognition of his supreme status as ruler of much of the world.

Even while he was engaged in a bitter struggle to conquer China, Kublai sent envoys to the Japanese court in 1268 to demand subservience. The Japanese military dictatorship, the *bakufu*, ignored the Mongol demands. In response to this defiance, Kublai Khan ordered his vassals in the subjugated Korean state of Koryo to build a fleet of nine hundred ships to invade Japan. The relatively narrow straits of Tsushima, spanning 284 miles between Korea and the coast of Japan's Kyushu Island, had been a trade route for centuries. Now it would become a highway for war.

The invasion fleet departed from Koryo on October 3, 1274, after embarking twenty-three thousand soldiers and seven thousand sailors. Two days later, the fleet attacked the island of Tsushima in the middle of the strait, overwhelming the eighty Japanese troops stationed there. The island garrison of Iki, closer to the Japanese coast, fell next. On October 14, the Mongol fleet attacked the Kyushu port of Hirado, and then moved north to land at various points along Hakata Bay (near modern Fukuoka). Groups of samurai and their retainers rushed to meet the invaders at Hakata Bay—in all, historians estimate that some six thousand Japanese defenders stood ready to fight the far more substantial Mongol army.

Among the defenders was a samurai named Takezaki Suenaga. He left the only contemporary pictorial records of the Mongol invasion on two scrolls that he commissioned later in order to petition the government for a reward for his services. The scrolls, known as the Moko Shurai Ekotoba, are one of Japan's great cultural treasures.

Dating to around 1294, the first scroll unrolls to reveal samurai in armor riding off to battle in 1274. The battle was unequal not only in numbers but in weapons and tactics. Mongol weapons were more advanced than those of the samurai: their bows had greater range, firing poisoned arrows, and they also had explosive shells hurled by catapults. In battle, the Mongols advanced en masse and fought as a unit, while the samurai, true to their code, ventured out to fight individual duels. In a week of fighting, the Japanese were slowly forced to give way. The scroll shows the Mongol forces firing arrows as horses and men fall, and Suenaga himself bleeding and falling from his horse as a bomb explodes in the air above him. The Japanese retreated, falling back to Daizafu, the fortified capital of Kyushu. The Mongols sacked and burned Hakata, but time was running out for them: Japanese reinforcements were pouring in from the surrounding countryside. The Mongol commander was wounded, and the sailors aboard the invading ships were wary of an incoming storm that threatened the fleet in its crowded anchorage.

On October 20, the wind shifted, and a number of Mongol ships dragged anchor, capsizing or driving ashore. In all, some three hundred ships and 13,500 men were lost. Battered and depleted, the surviving Mongols retreated to Koryo, leaving the Japanese to cheer their salvation thanks to the storm that had ended the invasion.

Knowing that the Mongols would be back, the bakufu ordered the construction of defenses at Hakata Bay. In a six-month period in 1276, laborers erected a 12 ½-mile, 5- to 9-foot high defensive stone wall set back from the beach. The samurai also organized their vassals into a compulsory defense force and requisitioned small fishing and trading vessels for a coastal navy.

Kublai Khan renewed his demand for Japan's surrender in June 1279, just as the last remnants of the Sung dynasty in China crumbled

An artist's rendition of a thirteenth-century Mongol ship wrecked at Takashima Island. Courtesy of Kyushu Okinawa Society for Underwater Archeology

before the Mongol onslaught. The bakufu cut off the heads of the Mongol envoys as they landed. Furious, Kublai Khan ordered Koryo to build a new fleet of nine hundred ships to carry ten thousand troops and seventeen thousand sailors; and in China, he ordered a fleet of nearly thirty-five hundred ships and an invasion force of a hundred thousand Chinese warriors to prepare for battle.

Kublai Khan directed the two fleets—the Koryo Eastern Route Division and the Chinese Chiang-nan Division—to rendezvous at Iki Island to co-ordinate their attack. The Eastern Route Division sailed first on May 3, 1281, retaking Iki on June 10. Without waiting for the arrival of the Chiang-nan Division, the impatient commanders of the Eastern Route Division sailed to Hakata Bay. Takezaki Suenaga's second scroll depicts the second invasion, showing him riding off to war, passing in front of the newly built stone wall at Hakata Bay as other samurai sit atop the wall and wait for the enemy. The stone walls thwarted the Mongols, who pulled back to occupy an island in the middle of the bay. The Japanese used their small navy to cut into the Mongol fleet, with armed samurai springing onto the enemy ships and killing the crews and soldiers. The second scroll also shows Suenaga in a small boat, running up alongside larger Mongol ships and fighting his way forward to cut the throats of the crew in deadly hand-to-hand combat. The brushstrokes of the artist convey the ferocity of the fighting, with blood spurting as sharp blades and arrows cut down men. The paintings are a graphic testimony as to why the badly mauled Eastern Route Division retreated to Iki Island with the Japanese in pursuit.

The Chiang-nan Division finally sailed in June and met up with the Eastern Route Division at the small island of Takashima, 30 miles south of Hakata. The Japanese fought the combined Chinese and Mongol forces in a running two-week battle throughout the rugged countryside. The crews of the invading ships chained their vessels together and constructed a plank walkway, forming a massive floating fortress in preparation for the inevitable waterborne assault by the small defense craft of the Japanese.

The Japanese ships, some of them filled with straw and set on fire, attacked the Mongol fleet but were unable to do much harm. As the story was later told, the Japanese beseeched the Goddess of the Ise Shrine for another storm to help them, and their prayers were answered. The legend states that "A green dragon had raised its head from the waves" and "sulfurous flames filled the firmament." Driving rain, high winds and storm-lashed waves smashed into the Mongol fleet. Thousands of ships sank, drowning nearly a hundred thousand men. Mongol troops stranded on the beach, demoralized and cut off from escape, were rounded up and executed. The shores were strewn with debris and bodies; according to a modern Japanese history, "a person could walk across from one point of land to another on a mass of wreckage" at the entrance to Imari Bay. Kublai Khan abandoned his dreams of a Japanese conquest in 1286 when he abruptly cancelled the preparations for a third invasion.

Interestingly, Suenaga's scrolls and the handful of Japanese documents from the 1281 invasion do not depict or mention a storm. Critics of the scrolls deride them as the work of a "self-aggrandizer," while others point to persistent myth-building by Japan's military and political leaders that glorified the emperor as a god and celebrated Japan's divine protection and status. (Eventually, this led to a series of wars of conquest that greatly expanded the Japanese empire from the 1870s through the early 1940s.) But the Venetian adventurer Marco Polo, who allegedly spent several years in Kublai Khan's court, wrote an account of the Mongol invasion in which he mentioned the storm that destroyed it:

> And it came to pass that there arose a north wind, which blew with great fury, and caused great damage along the coasts of that Island, for its harbors were few. It blew so hard that the Great Kaan's fleet could not stand against it. And when the chiefs saw that, they came to the conclusion that if the ships remained where they were, the whole navy would perish. So they all got on board and made sail to leave the country. But when they had gone about four miles they came to a small Island, on which they were driven ashore in spite of all they could do, and a great part of the fleet was wrecked and a great multitude of the force perished.

Given the prominent place of the story of the kamikaze in Japanese history, who knows where the truth lies? For a handful of young archeologists, the truth lies in the remains of the events, which now lie beneath the waters of Japan's coast.

RELICS OF THE *KAMIKAZE*

The beautiful views of Hakata and Imari bays and their gentle waves belie the violence of the storms that are said to have twice destroyed the Mongol fleet, as well as the tremendous battles waged on their shores in 1274 and 1281. Apart from memorials and monuments, few physical traces of the invasion remain on the land other than a handful of reconstructed sections of the stone wall in the heart of modern Fukuoka. Some scholars do not believe that the stone anchor weight at Hakozaki Shrine comes from the Mongol invasion; they think that it is one of many similar anchors lost on the bay bottom during the centuries Hakata Bay was an active port, because no other evidence—such as weapons or broken hulls—has ever emerged. But the waters off Takashima Island in Imari Bay have yielded traces of the Mongol fleet and its destruction.

Fishermen are usually the first to discover shipwrecks, and for years, Japanese trawlers operating in the waters of Imari Bay had been dredging up pottery and other artifacts from the lost Mongol fleet of 1281. Then, in 1980, Torao Mozai, a professor of engineering at Tokyo University, used a sonoprobe—a sound-wave device that geologists use to discover rocks buried in ocean sediment—to survey the seabed off Takashima Island. He discovered that buried artifacts appeared as different colors on his screen.

A year later, Professor Mozai's team pinpointed many objects that divers then recovered. The artifacts attest to the diversity of the invading force and its weapons, as well as its need for provisions. In addition to spearheads, war helmets, stone balls for catapults and a cavalry officer's sword discovered sticking upright in the mud—exactly where it had been dropped seven hundred years earlier—the divers found stone handmills for grinding gunpowder, iron ingots, stone anchor stocks and mortars for pounding rice or corn. The discoveries made international headlines (and a *National Geographic* magazine article) in 1981, the seven hundredth anniversary of the second Mongol invasion, and sparked the creation of a new museum on Takashima Island. The opening of the museum inspired a number of local fishermen to donate their own discoveries, including a bronze statue of Buddha dating to the twelfth century and a bronze seal of authority that had belonged to a Mongol commander of a thousand-man group.

Since 1991, the Kyushu Okinawa Society for Underwater Archeology (KOSUWA), under the leadership of Dr. Kenzo Hayashida, has been conducting surveys and excavations off Takashima's shores. In 1994, they discovered three wood and stone anchors from the Mongol invasion fleet, buried in the mud 400 feet offshore and in 40 feet of water. One of the anchors is 21 feet long and weighs one ton. Analysis of the wood used in the anchor showed it was red oak dating to within a few years of the Mongol invasion. Analysis of the stone used in the anchor showed that it was granite from China's Fujian province, from which most of Kublai Khan's invasion fleet sailed to the shores of Japan. Of even greater interest were the remains of the anchor cable, which lay stretched out straight from the anchor to the shore, indicating the possible presence of a wreck. Excavations recovered 135 scattered artifacts, but the wreck itself remained elusive.

In October 2001, KOSUWA's hard work paid off with the exciting discovery of a ship from Kublai Khan's fleet. The wreck lay in Kozaki harbor, a small indentation on Takashima's southern coast on the shore of Imari Bay. In all the years of work at Takashima, never before had the remains of one of the ships been discovered. In fact, only two other Asian shipwrecks of this age ever have been found, one at Shinan in Korea and the other at Guangzhou in China. Finding another ship from the thirteenth century, a time when Chinese ships were the best examples of shipbuilding in the world, made the wreck at Takashima a very significant discovery in the world of maritime archeology. What the excavation of the site revealed in 2002, however, made it one of the greatest underwater archeological discoveries of the century.

The catch was that the archeologists had to work fast, as construction of a new fishing harbor at the site meant that they had to completely remove the wreck before October 2002. They met the deadline and recovered nearly eight hundred artifacts, ranging in size from a small tortoiseshell comb to what may be part of the ship's large keel or back-bone. Now their work continues in the laboratory.

DIVING INTO THE THIRTEENTH CENTURY

When *The Sea Hunters* team arrives, only half of the wreck has been cleared. Each morning begins with a briefing for all divers, and then the first Japanese team gears up to get to work. They wear masks that cover their faces, and they are connected to shore by air hoses and an underwater communications system. They are continuously fed air

KUBLAI KHAN'S LOST FLEET   111

and report on what they are doing to the dive supervisor and the super-
vising archeologist in the control room. We gear up to go in with them,
donning wetsuits, heavy tanks and our survey equipment. Stepping up
to the edge of the concrete dock, I check my air, make sure all my straps
are tight, then step off the edge, falling feet first into the water.

As the froth and bubbles from my jump clear, I check to ensure
all my equipment is in place. A single line leads down the slope to the
wreck, which rests in 43 feet of water. I swim in the gray haze of the warm
sea, visibility only 5 feet, until I hear a loud humming sound. To my left,
I see the air hoses of the first team and a thick, flexible tube that vibrates
when I place my hand on it. This is the outtake for a large underwater
suction dredge that the crew is using to uncover the wreck. I follow the
tube to a cloud of silt and the excavation.

The seabed is covered with a thick, viscous, almost gelatinous ooze
that the archeologists have to dig through to reach the wreck. The task of
moving all that mud is immense, as the area of the site covers about two
city blocks. The archeologists carefully sweep the handheld underwater
suction dredge over the bottom, lying down alongside the thick corru-
gated hose and gently fanning the mud into the dredge with their hands.

The divers work in shifts, slowly cutting through 5 feet of mud to
uncover the wreck, which lies on what was the seabed in 1281. This
historic level is hard-packed, coarse gray sand mixed with shell. When the
dredge exposes an artifact, a diver carefully fans away the silt and mud to
clean it off while reporting his find back to the surface over his communications system. The dive supervisor and archeologist in the control
room make notes on what has been found and assign a number to the
discovery; the diver then sticks a large numbered tag into the seabed next
to it. A team of diving archeologists will carefully map, photograph and
draw the object before another team removes it to shore for analysis.

Swimming over the site, I pass through a maze of metal pins with
tags—nearly a hundred of them—marking artifacts. A grid of metal legs
and twine covers the entire site, dividing it into square units. I swim up
to one unit and see scattered broken pots and dishes, timbers and a
round object. The round object is only 5 ½ inches in diameter, but it is

Some tetsuhau, *hollow ceramic shells packed with gunpowder and metal shrapnel. They are the world's oldest exploding projectiles and were found in the wreck of a Mongol ship off Japan. Courtesy of Kyushu Okinawa Society for Underwater Archeology*

one of the most significant discoveries made to date. It is a *tetsuhau,* or an exploding shell. Chinese alchemists invented gunpowder around A.D. 300, and by the year 1100, huge bombs, much like giant firecrackers, were being used in battle. The first reference to exploding projectiles thrown by catapults appears around 1221, when Chinese sources describe hollow shells packed with gunpowder. Some historians have doubted that such shells were made this early, and even recently suggested, in a new book on the Mongol invasion, that the scene in Suenaga's scroll, in which the wounded samurai is falling from his horse as a bomb explodes above him, was painted long after the fact because bombs did not exist then.

    The discovery of not one but six tetsuhau proves that the old samurai was right. While four of them are broken, two are intact. X-ray analysis of the two intact bombs shows that one is packed just with gunpowder, while the other is filled with gunpowder and more than a dozen half-inch thick pieces of iron—shrapnel—to cut down the enemy. They are the world's oldest exploding projectiles. They date to a century before Europeans first used guns at sea, and centuries before Europeans replaced solid stone and iron cannonballs with shells that exploded. Just a week before our arrival, the discovery of these tetsuhau made national news in Japan, though almost no one in the West has heard about the discovery. And here I am, hovering over this unique, technologically advanced and deadly weapon from more than 720 years ago.

Nearby lies a bunch of what looks like rust-colored twigs stuck together. It is a bundle of iron arrows. Japanese accounts of the invasion mention showers of Mongol arrows falling from the skies, impaling men and horses. Mongol soldiers used powerful laminated bows and could fire them rapidly—and from horseback. They were the undisputed master archers of their age. In 1245, a papal envoy, Friar John of Plano Carpini, visited the Mongols and described their bows and arrows: "They are required to have these weapons: two long bows or one good one at least, three quivers full of arrows . . . the heads of their arrows are exceedingly sharp, cutting both ways like a two-edged sword, and they always carry a file in their quivers to sharpen their arrowheads." Interestingly, the rusted mass I am floating over is the third bundle of arrows found at the site, and I wonder about the "three quivers" comment of the old priest. Could these be the arms of a single Mongol soldier?

Each of the seventy arrows in the bundle could easily penetrate the armor of a samurai. According to Father John, this was because of the Mongol technique of dipping forged iron arrows "red-hot into salt water, that they may be strong enough to pierce the enemy's armor." Some of the Mongol arrows were dipped in poison to weaken their opponents, and looking at the bundle of arrows, which rust has melded into a nearly shapeless mass, it is ironic to see how the salt water that once hardened them to make them more deadly has now taken the sting from them.

Another exciting find, resting upright on the seabed, is a Mongol war helmet. Close beside it are small fragments of red leather from a suit of Mongol armor, originally made of laminated strips of leather bound with brass. The mud has preserved these fragile traces by bury-ing them out of the reach of the water. Along with the armor, the dredge gently uncovers a small tortoiseshell comb, a fragment of red leather still clinging to one side. I think about another discovery nearby—the bones of a drowned member of the ship's complement, perhaps a Mongol warrior. The proximity of bones, helmet, armor and arrows raises the question of whether or not they all belong to one victim of the wreck. In the laboratory, just before the dive, I had looked at a broken skull that was found lying face down in the mud, and wondered what stories this victim of an ancient shipwreck could tell.

Some artifacts do tell tales. A small bowl, broken and found upside down, is painted with the name of its owner and his rank. One of my dive partners, Mitsu Ogawa, later tells me that the man's name was Weng and that he commanded a hundred troops. I wonder if it is Weng's armor, helmet, weapons and bones that lie together in the mud. Other artifacts tell us that the preparations for the invasion were hasty. Many of the ceramic jars are sloppily made, misshapen and badly fired, rushed into production for the war. The ship's massive anchor may also be proof of haste. Unlike the one-piece stone weight for the anchor at Hakozaki Shrine, this anchor's stones—and others found nearby at Takashima— are made of two crudely shaped pieces. The anchor for the ship now being excavated dragged in the mud and broke apart where the two stone weights were joined by wood and lashings—a fatal shortcut.

After our dive ends, we get into a discussion on the dock with Kenzo Hayashida. What sank this ship? The anchor is set tight, as if the ship dragged in heavy waves and then broke up. A storm might have sent the ship into the shallows and smashed it into the many pieces the Japanese are recovering. "The question is whether there was one storm," says Hayashida, or "several centuries of storms." I get his point. The periodic typhoons that lash this coast sweep into Imari Bay and churn up the seabed. The breakup and scatter of the huge wooden wreck being mapped by the archeologists may be the result of generations of storms, not a single catastrophic kamikaze sent by the gods. The timbers of the vessel also show evidence of burning. Did this ship go to the bottom as a result of a Japanese attack with a straw-filled "fire ship?" The fragmented remains may never reveal all their secrets, but they have already enabled archeologists to refute a few stories. Hayashida, who bases his opinion of just how many wrecks should be on the bottom of the bay from 1281 on years of surveys and the information they provide, firmly believes that the figure of four thousand is a gross exaggeration. "How many ships?" I ask him. "Maybe four hundred," he answers with a smile.

Over the next week, we make more dives and watch as more artifacts slowly emerge from the mud. Broken timbers from the ship, including the sockets where a mast would have fit into the bottom of the hull; shattered planks; ceramic bowls and pots once filled with provisions; weapons and armor; and personal possessions, like a small delicately cast bronze mirror, are reminders of the individuals behind the myths and the big sweep of history. The personal items and bones are all that remain of the forgotten warriors who came here, on the orders of Kublai Khan, to expand an empire and an emperor's prestige, and instead met their deaths far from home. I think of all the dead of 1281. And I think of the millions who died later in the 1930s and '40s, victims of what was, if not a false legend about the kamikaze, then a distorted and exaggerated one that was used to justify the militaristic expansion of a "divine empire" and a brutal war.

— CHAPTER NINE —

BURIED *in the* HEART *of* SAN FRANCISCO

FIRE IN THE CITY: MAY 4, 1851

S tanding on the Clay Street wharf in San Francisco, Etting Mickle stared
at the advancing wall of smoke. Since late the previous evening, he
had listened nervously to the roar of flames. The bright glow in the sky,
the flying sparks and the hoarse shouts had seemed distant, but now,
well into the new day, the wind shifted. With terrifying speed, fire raced
across the waterfront.

One block west of where Mickle stood, the ship *Niantic* began to
smolder, then suddenly exploded into flame. Embers carried by the wind
swept across the wharf and landed at his feet. "Get out the pump!" he
shouted to the crew of his ship, *General Harrison*. Mickle's fortune was
invested in that ship, now ringed by fire. Inside her hold lay a wealth of
merchandise: imported wines and liquor, tools, hardware, rolls of
fabric and fancy foods. The men pumped frantically, but it was too late.
General Harrison began to burn fiercely. Mickle and the men with him
turned and ran for the safety of the open water at the end of the pier.
Stopping just beyond the reach of the flames, they hacked away at the
wooden wharf, ripping up planks and chopping at the pilings. This last-
ditch effort succeeded in cutting off the advancing fire and saved many
other ships that sat in thick clusters in the deeper waters of the city's

anchorage. Standing on the truncated end of the Clay Street wharf, choking in the thick smoke, Mickle stared as *General Harrison* went up in a sheet of flame. A year of hard work and investment was gone.

UNDER CITY STREETS

Deep inside the excavation, the backhoe carefully pulls back layers of sand. When the scrape of the huge bucket exposes a dark-stained layer, I raise my hand to stop the huge machine and pick up the high-pressure hose. As water washes over the area, sand streams away to reveal ashes, burned wood, melted glass and twisted metal. Tips of charred pilings become visible alongside the fire-scarred planks of *General Harrison*. Over the past week, archeologists and construction workers have labored to uncover the ship from her tomb of mud and sand. Now *General Harrison*'s charred hull is exposed where she burned and sank in that long-ago fire on May 4, 1851.

Today, the ship lies 24 feet beneath street level. Lining the construction fence on the streets above are hundreds of spectators drawn to the incongruous spectacle of a ship lying deep in the heart of San Francisco's financial district. Whether you approach San Francisco by air or sea, or by car across the Bay Bridge, the view is dominated by the high rises of the financial district as they march up from the Embarcadero to the slopes of Telegraph, Nob and Russian hills. The distinctive profile of the Transamerica Pyramid rises above some of the city's few standing survivors of its youth. The relatively low two- and three-story brick buildings of Jackson Square are the last visible remnants of San Francisco's infamous "Barbary Coast," survivors of the 1906 earthquake, fires and urban renewal. They are survivors from another era, perched in the midst of a modern city.

Directly beneath the financial district lies an immense archeological deposit that dates back to the origins of San Francisco during the gold rush. Six major fires and innumerable smaller conflagrations have devastated the city. After the destruction wrought by the fires, entire burnt districts were filled over. The debris of those fires lies buried beneath the modern city. The astonishing collection of items that came to be buried beneath San Francisco attracted comment even during the gold rush. The *San Francisco Evening Picayune,* on September 30, 1850, remarked: "At some future period, when the site of San Francisco may be explored by a generation ignorant of its history, it will take its place by the side of Herculaneum and Pompeii, and furnish many valuable relics to perplex the prying Antiquarian. Buried in the streets, from six to ten feet beneath the surface, there is already a stratum of artificial productions which the entombed cities of Italy cannot exhibit. Knives, forks, spoons, chisels, files, and hardware of every description, gathered from the places of several conflagrations. Masses of nails exhibiting volcanic indications, stove plates and tin ware, empty bottles by the cartload and hundreds of other miscellanies, lie quietly and deeply interred in Sacramento Street, and perhaps will be carefully exhumed in days to come, and be distributed over the world as precious relics!" The *Evening Picayune*'s smug prophecy did not take long to come true. As early as the 1870s, excavation for construction unearthed relics of the gold rush period. The transient nature of San Francisco ensured that most residents were ignorant of the particulars of its past—and the "discoveries" that arose from beneath the streets and sidewalks delighted them.

Now, I stand watching the high-pressure hose strip away the shroud of mud and sand as history emerges from the buried ashes of a long-ago fire. The oak planks of the ship's hull are solid, and the wood is bright and fresh. Even more amazing is the stench of burned wood and sour wine rising from the charred debris. A century and a half ago mud, water and sand sealed the wreckage of the ship so perfectly that time has stood still.

GENERAL HARRISON AND GOLD RUSH DAYS

The product of the venerable New England seafaring town of Newburyport, Massachusetts, *General Harrison* was launched from the banks of the Merrimack River in the spring of 1840. Built for a group of local merchants, *General Harrison* worked as a coastal packet out of Boston

San Francisco in the gold-rush days, 1851. In the background are the masts of crowds of ships along the waterfront and the store ships Niantic *and* General Harrison *(circled). San Francisco Maritime National Historic Park, Smithsonian Institution Collection All.781.2n1*

and New York, running south to New Orleans with passengers and cargo, then returning north with southern cotton. In 1846, the ship's owners sold her to a consortium of well-known and moneyed Charlestown residents who had mercantile links to Pacific Coast ports from Chile to Alaska as well as Hawaii and China. The new owners sent *General Harrison* on a sixteen-month voyage around the world. After trading at Valparaiso, Tahiti, Hawaii and Hong Kong, she returned to New York in 1847. A new owner, Thomas H. Perkins, Jr., son of America's richest man of the day, kept the ship in his fleet until 1849, the year of the exciting news that gold had been discovered in California.

The gold discovery sparked a "rush" for California's riches. The editors of the *New York Herald* remarked in early January that the "spirit of emigration which is carrying off thousands to California . . . increases and expands every day. All classes of our citizens seem to be under the influence of this extraordinary mania . . . Poets, philosophers, lawyers, brokers, bankers, merchants, farmers, clergymen—all are feeling the impulse and are preparing to go and dig for gold and swell the number of adventurers to the new El Dorado."

Most gold-seekers chose to travel to California by ship, and between December 1848 and December 1849, 762 vessels sailed from American ports for San Francisco. One of them was *General Harrison*. Sailing from Boston on August 3, 1849, the ship rounded Cape Horn to reach the Chilean port of Valparaiso. There, the ship's agents, Mickle y Compañia, loaded merchandise from Chile's farms, wineries and shops to sell in San Francisco. On February 3, 1850, the ship reached San Francisco. With her passengers off to the gold fields and her cargo sold, *General Harrison* would have been ready for another voyage. But the lure of gold was too much for her crew, who deserted and headed for the mines, leaving *General Harrison*, along with hundreds of other ships, idle on the San Francisco docks.

The waterfront was then a constantly growing, hectic center of activity. Every day, more ships arrived, workers landed cargoes, and thousands of men crowded the sandy streets seeking passage up the bay and its tributaries to the heart of the gold country. Crowded beyond its capacity, San Francisco was boxed in on all sides by massive, shifting sand dunes and a shallow cove that was by turns either a stagnant pond or an expanse of thick foul mud at low tide. The city's entrepreneurs solved the problem of lack of space by building on top of the shallows of the cove. Thousands of pilings, shipped south from the forests of British Columbia and Puget Sound, were pounded into the shallows, enabling long wharves to march across the mud flats to the anchorage. Alongside the wharves, buildings were perched atop piles, and ships were hauled up onto the mud to serve the needs of the booming frontier town.

By the time of *General Harrison*'s arrival, a Chilean visitor to San Francisco described the city as "a Venice built of pine instead of marble. It is a city of ships, piers, and tides. Large ships with railings, a good distance from the shore, served as residences, stores, and restaurants . . . The whole central part of the city swayed noticeably because it was built on piles the size of ship's masts driven down into the mud."

The frequent fires that ravaged San Francisco exacerbated the city's need for buildings. Etting Mickle, who was in charge of the local branch of Mickle y Compañia, bought *General Harrison* to serve as the company's "store ship," or floating warehouse. Just a block west lay the *Niantic*, beached in August 1849 and converted into a store ship by friends of Mickle's. Workers removed *General Harrison*'s masts and hauled her up onto the mud flats alongside the Clay Street wharf. Nestled in the mud, her hull still washed by the tide, the ship was quickly converted into a warehouse. Carpenters built a large "barn" on the deck and cut doors into the hull, while laborers cleaned out the hold to store crates, barrels and boxes of merchandise. Mickle advertised, on May 30, 1850, that "this fine and commodious vessel being now permanently stationed at the corner of Clay and Battery streets was in readiness to receive stores of any description, and offers a rare inducement to holders of goods."

The new venture prospered. Mickle's neighbors on *Niantic* reported, in a private letter in July 1850, that their store ship, thanks to the inflated real estate values of the gold rush, was worth what in today's money would be $2.72 million and was raking in nearly $80,000 per month renting out space for storage and offices. Mickle doubtless was doing nearly as well. Commission merchants like him handled cargoes that arrived from around the world, storing them and arranging for their sale at auction. For his services, Mickle would collect a 10 per cent commission on the sale of merchandise, 5 per cent for procuring freight and flat fees for other services. He would also collect rent for storing merchandise inside *General Harrison*. In short, from the time a vessel arrived and Mickle's firm cleared it with customs officials, landed the goods, stowed them in *General Harrison* for a month or two, sold and then delivered the goods to buyers, each crate or barrel had earned more than a few dollars.

From May 1850 to May 1851, *General Harrison* was a thriving business in the midst of a rapidly changing and expanding city. Continued construction on the waterfront pushed out well past *Niantic* and *General Harrison*, surrounding them with streets and two- or three-story wooden buildings perched atop pilings. In April 1851, one San Francisco newspaper, the *Daily Alta California*, commented: "It looks very curious in passing along some of the streets bordering on the water to see the stern of a ship with her name and the place from which she hails painted upon it, and her stern posts staring at you directly on the street. These ships, now high and dry, were hauled in about a year since as store ships, before the building was carried on in that section of the city in so rapid a manner, and now find themselves out of their natural element and a part of the streets of a great city."

These new surroundings doomed *General Harrison* and *Niantic*. San Francisco had burned several times during the gold rush, but the worst disaster was the fire of May 4, 1851. The blaze began on the west side of Portsmouth Square just after 11 p.m. on May 3 and spread throughout the city. By early morning, the fire was still burning: "We do not know how great is the destruction, for the smoke is so dense and the fire intervening, it is impossible to tell." When the smoke cleared, San Francisco had lost nearly two thousand buildings, a number of lives and $7 million in destroyed property and merchandise. Among the losses were *Niantic*, *General Harrison* and another store ship, *Apollo*.

In the aftermath of the fire, the *Daily Alta California* reported that the "portion of the burned district which was built out into the bay and upon piles will have to be rebuilt in a very different manner. The piles generally are entirely ruined or so badly injured that they will not serve the purpose of foundations for houses. They cannot be replaced from the fact that there is not now sufficient water in that portion of the city to enable the pile driver to be used. It will therefore be necessary generally, to fill it up, and thus give future improvements the solid earth for a foundation." Over the next few years, sand from the dunes that hemmed the harbor was loaded by steam shovels and sent rocketing into the shallows on rail-mounted dump cars, burying the old waterfront beneath 16 feet of fill.

In the summer of 1851, before the burned area was completely filled in, Charles Hare, a "ship breaker," reportedly "broke up" the charred remains of *General Harrison* and sold them off "piecemeal." After that, as a progression of buildings arose on the corner of Clay and Battery, the story of *General Harrison* gradually faded from people's memory. In April 1906, the great earthquake and fire destroyed San Francisco and leveled the block. Rebuilding was slow, so it was not until 1912 that workers cleared the ruins and dug down into the sand to pour the foundations for a new building. Their steam shovels hit the buried remains of *General Harrison,* but no one remembered the ship's name, and newspaper reports suggested the wreck was that of a Spanish ship lost on the old waterfront in 1849. The workers tried to chop away the thick timbers of the ship, but the venerable old hulk resisted their axes and saws. A few pilings were hammered through the ship to support the foundations of the new building, and *General Harrison* was reburied. By the mid-1990s, that rediscovery had also been forgotten, and no one was sure of what lay beneath the street and the buildings at Clay and Battery. But one archeologist suspected that *General Harrison* was still there.

UNEARTHING A FORGOTTEN SHIP

Thanks to various laws, developers in San Francisco must conduct an archeological reconnaissance before any construction proceeds. In 1999, archeologist Allen Pastron began negotiations with the New York firm that was planning to build a new hotel at the corner of Clay and Battery streets. Pastron, a veteran of many digs in downtown San Francisco, believed that the remains of *General Harrison* were buried there. He used a powerful auger to bore a series of holes into the site. At one hole, the drill spit out a chunk of oak covered with copper. It was a section of the ship's wooden keel, or backbone, still sheathed with the copper that once protected the hull from marine organisms.

Just how much of the ship had survived was unknown. In early September 2001, construction crews cleared away the concrete floor of the basement of the recently demolished building on the site and dug into the wet sand beneath it. Within a few hours, the outline of a ship began to emerge. About two thirds, or 81 feet of the 126-foot hull, was exposed. The other end of the ship lay beneath an adjacent building.

The hull of General Harrison *buried in the heart of San Francisco. James P. Delgado*

Pastron had uncovered the long-forgotten *General Harrison*. He needed a maritime archeologist to help with the project and phoned me. I flew out right away to "get my hands dirty" on the dig.

On September 9, I arrive at the site and am struck by how this small hole in the midst of all the high rises is a portal to the past. After a steep climb down a construction ladder, then a walk over loose sand and slippery mud, I reach the wreck. *General Harrison* burned down to her waterline, so only the bottom third of the ship's once massive hull remains. The hold is largely empty, as it was cleaned out after the fire by salvager Charles Hare and his crew of local Chinese laborers. They pumped out the flooded lower part of the ship and mucked out the sodden, charred cargo. Hare's crew, working in toxic, awful conditions after the fire, did more than clean out the ship. They also wrenched out hundreds of solid copper and brass fasteners that held together the timbers and peeled off the copper sheathing on the outside of the hull, which meant diving into the surrounding fetid shallows.

Inside *General Harrison* is more evidence of the Chinese ship breakers. A thick iron pry-bar for removing the thick copper bolts lies in one area. Nearby is a pile of iron bolts, stacked ready for removal. We find a broken rice bowl, a shattered bottle and several pairs of worn-out boots. It is as if the workers have just gone home. They left the job unfinished, though. The ship is only partially broken down—nearly every bit of valuable copper is gone, but the work stopped short of cutting apart the wooden hull. That might mean that the scrapping ended in October 1851, when newspapers reported that the work of filling in the shallows had at last reached the burned-out *General Harrison*. When carts began dumping sand just outside the hull, Hare's crew simply dropped what they were doing and left. As I look at the half-cut planks, at sections of timber lying where laborers were chopping them up—the axe marks still fresh— and the discarded boots, bowl and bottle, I feel that I have truly stepped into the past.

Then time seemingly stops again, just before seven on the morning of September 11. As I walk to the site, my cell phone rings. It is my wife, Ann, at home in Vancouver, telling me that a jet has just crashed into the World Trade Center in New York. The crew gathers at the *General Harrison* dig, and down in our hole in the heart of San Francisco, we listen to a small radio as the terrible news comes in from back east. The second jet, the grounding of flights across the country and the rumors— we hear that the State Department has been hit, that the Capitol is in flames, that the White House has been evacuated, and that downtown San Francisco is also being evacuated. I look up at the Transamerica Pyramid and the towers of the nearby Embarcadero Center, and all this history beneath me seems insignificant, and the evidence of this long-ago disaster inconsequential. We are hustled off the site by security guards, and I make my way back to my hotel, with no place to go and nothing to do but wait as new history unfolds.

The next day, we return to work on *General Harrison*. Somber, and now stuck in San Francisco with no easy way to get home since all flights are grounded for an indefinite time, I turn to work and immerse myself in the past. It is cathartic and strangely reassuring. After all, we are exposing a layer of a once-devastated San Francisco that lies beneath yet another layer of destruction, atop which rests the modern city which now, on September 12, is beginning to reassert a semblance of normalcy. Life goes on, and the history we are exposing is a reminder of the great cycle of existence, not only for our crew but also for the crowds that again gather to watch. Local author Rebecca Solnit, writing in the *San Francisco Chronicle* a year after our dig, remarks that all those onlookers, "somehow drawn out of themselves in this place," in a social climate where few people even make eye contact, nonetheless "feel part of something, and that the place was somehow enlarged—not only in its sense of time as the ship hull made visible the ruined city of 1851, but in its sense of community."

The sense of timelessness and intimate contact with a lost community, the San Francisco that ended dramatically on May 4, 1851, certainly comes through as we continue to dig. As the backhoe starts to scratch out a rectangular trench close to the port, or left side, of the exposed hull, I hear the telltale crunch of breaking glass and stop the work. Over the next hour, with the backhoe operator delicately working the huge hoe like a surgeon's tool, we pull back the sand to expose the top of a thick mass of blackened, melted glass and cinders. This mass, glued together by mud and creosote from the burnt wood, is part of the onetime store of *General Harrison*.

The fire that destroyed *General Harrison* was intense, flashing over the ship so quickly that some items fell into the flooded hold and the tidal shallows next to the ship, landing in the mud practically unharmed. Using hoses, we slowly wash away layers of ash, cinders and mud to reveal a door with its brass pull-ring still bright and shiny—and with traces of paint on the wood. A broken box bears the partial trademark and name of a company that we cannot decipher, but which appears to say "Frères," indicating a French origin. It is a reminder that California's gold attracted the goods of a world market.

Then, as the water washes away more of the thick black sediment, I spot the corner of a small pine box. Carefully, and yet eagerly, we work for the next two hours to slowly free it from beneath fallen timbers and piles of broken glass. It is an intact crate. Finally, once the box is clear of debris and cleaned, we photograph and measure it, and survey its location on our site map. Only then do I carefully open the lid. Inside are twelve bottles, packed in straw. Soggy and stuck to the bottles, the straw easily yields as I pick up one bottle. The cork in it is covered with a silver foil cap. The label has disintegrated, but as I wipe the bottle clean and hold it up, the sun illuminates the wine inside. It is now red from oxidation, but the style of the bottle and the cap indicate that it is a German white wine, perhaps some of the "Rhine wine" that Mickle advertised for sale just months before the fire.

Even more bottles—of Madeira, brandy, sherry and Champagne—some still full of liquid, emerge from the mud. The fancy foods inside the store ship were probably all destroyed, I think, but we find what might be samples of pâté. Then I reach down and pick up a perfectly preserved peanut, still in its shell and only slightly singed. Other surprises include rolls and bolts of charred cloth, lying next to melted and fused kegs of nails and tacks. A glint of bright red reveals a bag of small red glass beads, and bits of hardware provide a hint of what was once nice furniture.

Our work reminds me of earlier digs in San Francisco—the store ship *Niantic,* destroyed in the same May 1851 fire and discovered in 1978, yielded a variety of well-preserved objects from linoleum rolls to a leather jacket folded by its owner and placed atop a crate. Faber pencils from London, sausage and truffle pâté and French Champagne from Rheims, mixed in with crockery and hardware, made the *Niantic* site a gold-rush Pompeii. Later, in 1986, Pastron and his crew, myself included, excavated an entire half block of buildings that had fallen, still on fire, into the bay's shallows during the May 1851 fire, and were encapsulated in cold, thick blue mud. We gently washed away the mud to reveal crocks filled with butter, bags of coffee, chests packed with tea leaves, bottled preserves—a jar of cherries was still bright red—and crates of army surplus rifles and ammunition: debris now made priceless by the passing of time and their near-perfect condition, thanks to their being sealed beyond the reach of air and light.

My career as an archeologist immersed me in the gold rush so fully that those times seem alive to me. When I walk the streets of downtown San Francisco, in my mind's eye I see the wharves, tent buildings and crowds of strangers from all lands as ships daily discharge more men and goods into this great and grand bazaar on the Pacific frontier. This sense of the past is reinforced by reading the letters, diaries and newspapers of the time, and from looking at faded photographs of the city as it was. Thanks to archeology, I feel privileged to have walked in the same mud as the 49ers, to have smelled the reeking aftermath of the May 1851 fire as its remains emerged. I have trod the decks and hulls of ships sepulchered in the mud as San Francisco filled in the old waterfront. I have sipped Champagne and brandy destined for a gold-rush saloon, when we unpacked it in the laboratory, and I have sorted through the detritus of the past to scientifically catalog what we have excavated. The smallest and humblest items add to the picture. Carbonized beans from *General Harrison* appear to be the small white beans common to Chile, and carbonized grains of barley, again probably Chilean, are proof of how that South American country served as the gold rush's principal larder until farming took hold on the California frontier.

Two weeks after the project began, it is time for me to leave. Very soon, *General Harrison* will return to the darkness when construction workers rebury her to make way for the new hotel on the site. Rather than destroy her, the developer has decided to put *General Harrison* back into her time capsule. Displays inside the new hotel will remind San Franciscans and visitors of a city born of the sea, as well as the romance of a buried waterfront that still holds the bones of the ships that helped to settle this town in the days of the gold rush. For me, the mental map of the waterfront of May 1851 is more complete, more detailed than before, and this foray is a powerful reminder of why I love what I do. This dig, in its unlikely downtown locale, is also a reminder that my work as a maritime archeologist does not always mean slipping beneath the waves.

KING PHILIP: OCEAN BEACH, SAN FRANCISCO

The uncovering of *General Harrison* reminded me of an earlier exploration of another buried shipwreck, this one covered over by the sands of a beach. That ship was wrecked in 1878 on San Francisco's Ocean Beach, a long expanse of sand that is exposed to the full fury of the open sea. Dozens of ships have come to grief in the surf there, though no trace of them is usually visible. The writer Bret Harte once likened that surf to ravenous wolves of the sea, racing up to meet the dunes.

The winter of 1982–83 hit the California coast with ferocious rain and driving winds. During one storm, high tides and heavy seas ripped up the shoreline, and at Ocean Beach, the sand receded 63 feet and dropped 9 feet, exposing the first hints of a long-forgotten shipwreck. When a local resident called to report that an old ship's timbers were sticking out of the surf, I rushed out to Ocean Beach and saw the tip of the bow rising out of the sand as the tide receded. Over the next year, more of the ship rose out of its grave, and by spring 1984, the entire outline of the wreck lay exposed.

We helped nature along by using fire hoses and a pumper truck, provided by a very helpful San Francisco Fire Department crew, to cut through the sand. We also pushed down a high-pressure water probe to find what lay buried inside the wreck and discovered that just a little less than half the hull, from the lower deck to the keel, lay beneath us. After washing away the sand at the stern, I put on dive gear and dropped into a maelstrom of swirling grit and water, trying to see what the outside of the hull looked like. As each wave crashed into the hull, I was flipped, twisted and bashed into the ship, but the dive was worth a few bruises and cuts. I could see that the entire outside of the lower hull was still sheathed in a bright yellow composition metal known as Muntz metal. The burnished hull looked like it was covered in hammered gold.

Much to the dismay of the crowd of curious onlookers, and despite the glittering "false gold" that covered the hull, the wreck yielded no tangible treasure. The hull, filled with gravel, was empty. We were able to establish that this was the wreck of a medium clipper named *King Philip*. But as the sand continued to erode, we were faced with a mystery. Strands of wire rope festooned the exposed hull, and chunks of Douglas fir timbers appeared. Then one morning we found ourselves looking at a tangle of iron chain with two wooden deadeyes. I recognized it as a bobstay, part of the rigging that attaches beneath the bowsprit of a sailing vessel, but it was too small for *King Philip*. What was all this? The mystery began to unravel as we mapped out our finds. The wire rope was ship's rigging, caught in the ribs of *King Philip*. The Douglas fir timbers were from a different hull—a ship built of that Pacific coast softwood and not the oak of our medium clipper. The bobstays were also from that other ship. Clearly, another vessel had come to grief on the same spot after the wreck of *King Philip*. But what ship?

We found the answer after a search in the archives. On March 13, 1902, the three-masted Pacific coast lumber schooner *Reporter* was heading in towards the Golden Gate with a load of pilings, milled lumber and shingles from Gray's Harbor, Washington. Her captain, Adolph Hansen, lost his way in the darkness after mistaking the lights of the Cliff House for the Point Bonita lighthouse that marks the northern approach to the harbor and sailed into the breakers of Ocean

James Delgado, at the stern, adjusts the baseline to map the wreck of King Philip *on Ocean Beach, San Francisco, in 1986. Photo by Edward de St. Maurice/National Park Service.*

Beach. Caught by the waves, *Reporter* hit the beach right next to where *King Philip* had gone ashore in 1878. The crew took to the rigging to save themselves after one of the masts fell and were rescued from their perch above the waves. But by the morning, according to the *San Francisco Examiner*, "There is no hope for the *Reporter*... the schooner can only fight until her tendons give. Her ribs and sheathing, masts and rails will wash ashore, to be carried away by thrifty seaside dwellers and be used as firewood." A few days later, the newspaper noted that *Reporter*, broken and scattered, was "fast digging her own grave along-side the bones of the *King Philip*, whose ribs are still seen."

Mystery solved, we turned back to learning more about our medium clipper. Then, out of the blue, I received a phone call from Nuna Cass. She had found the letter book of *King Philip*'s first captain, Charles Rollins, who was one of her ancestors. The letter book's detailed accounts of both Captain Rollins's experiences as well as that of the ship had sparked her interest. She offered to help reconstruct the ship's history. We learned that *King Philip* began life in November 1856 as the largest vessel ever launched from the shipyard of Dennett Weymouth in Alna, Maine. Nearly twice the tonnage of any other vessel built there, the 182-foot *King Philip* was also the last full-rigged ship built by Weymouth, who died in 1875, just three years before *King Philip* met her end.

I flew to Maine and, with the help of Peter Throckmorton, a good friend who was one of the fathers of underwater archaeology, I drove out to visit the "Old Weymouth place." A manicured lawn sloped down to the riverbank, and as we walked to the water, Peter pointed out the logs and timbers that marked the old shipyard's ways. More than a century after Dennett Weymouth's death, the remains of his shipyard were still there, preserved by the cold fresh waters of the Sheepscot River. This was the first time in my career that I'd made the journey, through space and time, from the grave of a ship that I was studying back to her cradle.

Peter, fired up by the moment, went up to the house and knocked on the door. The lady who answered was not a descendant, but she told us that there some old Weymouth family papers in the attic. She rummaged around and came downstairs with a faded drawing. While it was not labeled, we knew immediately what it was. Weymouth had carefully drawn the outline of *King Philip* and, with the sail maker, had laid out the sail plan for the ship. I don't know what stunned us more—finding the plan or that generous woman succumbing to Peter's entreaties to donate it to the maritime museum back in San Francisco.

We ended the day by driving to nearby Newcastle to visit the home of the Glidden family, one of *King Philip*'s first owners. Glidden & Williams operated the principal clipper ship line between New England and California from 1850 until well after the Civil War. *King Philip,* built after the heyday of the extreme clippers with their knife-like hulls and lofty spars filled with sail, was a more full-bodied "medium" clipper and a predecessor to the boxier "down-easters" that were the last generation of American wooden-hulled full-rigged sailing ships. To make money with these ships, they had to carry cargoes quickly. The fast clippers of the late 1840s and early 1850s made record time on their voyages, but their narrow hulls could not carry much cargo. The medium clippers were a compromise, sacrificing some of the form that made the ships fast for more capacity. Just the same, *King Philip* was said by historian William Fairburn to have been a good sailer with good (that is, fast) passages. "She was," commented Fairburn, "undoubtedly hard driven."

"Hard driven" applied not only to the ship but her crew. To get a slow ship to make good passages meant pushing both ship and men to their limits, if not beyond. And *King Philip*'s crew mutinied on more than one occasion, setting the vessel on fire on two occasions. In 1874, a U.S. naval officer, who sent an armed force aboard *King Philip* in Rio de Janeiro to quell an uprising, during which "the ship's steward had been killed and most of the crew had deserted," sympathetically commented that "perhaps they had good reason." Intrigued by the harsh reality of life before the mast, I spent more time digging into the ship's history than into the sand that shrouded her bones.

Instead of running to California like other Glidden & Williams ships, *King Philip* entered the "general carrying trade," loading all types of merchandise and delivering them to ports around the world. Captain Rollins's letter book spans the time between June 1857 and May 1860. Those early letters did far more to flesh out those water-stained oak bones than all of the archeology I could ever practice on the hulk, an invaluable lesson for me. Beyond the science and the study of the "object," in this case the half-intact hulk I was enthusing over, the significance of any find lies in the connections to real people.

Rollins's first letters recorded a voyage from Gravesend, England, around the tip of Cape of Good Hope to the Indian Ocean and then to Melbourne, Australia. He reported that "the ship sails fair" with all sail set but went on to say that "my crew have mostly left the ship," leaving him with two officers and seven men. "The cook is away today and it is doubtful if I see him again. They leave about £120 wages behind them. I do not think the ship shall lose anything by these men as I shall take but two mates from here and the Steward shipped in Boston was totally unfit for his place. He had no idea of cooking or of saving provisions and besides was abominably filthy." From Melbourne, *King Philip* sailed to the coast of Peru to load guano—the accumulated droppings of sea birds—being mined in the Chincha Islands as fertilizer. The reeking cargo stunk to high heaven but was literally worth its weight in gold.

After discharging the guano at Rotterdam in September 1858, Rollins took on four hundred casks of gin and headed for England, and from there to San Francisco with a cargo of lumber, sugar, pig iron, livestock and coal. His letter to Glidden & Williams from San Francisco is full of complaints, particularly about a "patent reefing gear" installed in the rigging to handle some of the work that the sailors usually did aloft. The gear should have acted like a rolling window shade to retract a sail in heavy wind so as to keep the wind from bursting it or breaking the yards or mast. Rollins raged that the gear was too tightly installed, slipped off its rollers and cut into the wooden spars, and jammed frequently. In a fierce gale, the gear stuck, leaving the sail exposed to the full fury of the wind instead of "reefing" or rolling up. The main topgallant mast bent and nearly broke, then the sail burst, ripping away in the storm.

I was amused by Rollins's comments on this Victorian-era invention to cut costs by replacing people with a machine. Reading his letter was a revelation, and one that I would not find in the cold dead hulk of a wrecked ship, about how frustrated people felt when confronted by technology that promised to help but did not.

Rollins left *King Philip* in early 1860, but under other captains and other crews, the ship carried a variety of cargoes around the world. In 1869, at a stop in Honolulu, the crew mutinied and set *King Philip* on fire. The damage was bad—so bad that the ship was condemned and sold at a "fire sale." Puget Sound lumber merchants Pope & Talbot bought and repaired *King Philip*, but the bad luck that had dogged the ship since the beginning continued.

On an 1874 voyage out of Baltimore, the crew mutinied and set fire to the ship. After the fire was put out, the crew still refused to sail. An armed force of U.S. Marines from the nearby United States Naval Academy at Annapolis finally had to go aboard to re-establish order. After that, Pope & Talbot never sent *King Philip* on another protracted voyage. They rerigged the ship as a bark for better maneuverability on the Pacific coast. Later that year, the press reported that "*King Philip* had just completed her tenth trip to Puget Sound and back since January 1st, 1876, and has still some days to spare. She has brought to port in that time nearly ten million feet in lumber." The regular run to and from Puget Sound occupied the ship's days.

But bad luck continued to trouble *King Philip*. On January 25, 1878, she was leaving empty, or in ballast, from San Francisco. Cast off on the bar by her tug without any wind to fill her sails, the ship drifted in the current and into the breakers. Both anchors failed to hold, and at five that evening, *King Philip* went ashore. At low tide, the hull was high and dry; sightseers were able to walk right up and touch the stranded hulk. By the next day, the ship was "immovable" according to press accounts, and the insurance company sold the wreck to John Molloy, a local grocer who also speculated on scrap and salvage. He blasted the hulk apart with black powder to salvage what he could, but the lower hull, set firmly in the sand, remained in place. Periodically uncovered by the shifting sands of Ocean Beach, *King Philip* finally disappeared from view in the 1920s, when sand was dumped there to build the Great Highway. Six decades later, thanks to the winter storms of 1982–83, I was introduced to the beached wreck whose story we fleshed out from the archives.

CAPE COD AND THE BARK *FRANCES*

My fascination with beached shipwrecks like that of *King Philip* continued through several years and other projects, but my last serious foray with them came in September 1987, as part of a team consisting of the National Park Service's Submerged Cultural Resources Unit (SCRU) and the U.S. Navy's Mobile Diving and Salvage Unit One, documenting wreck sites at Cape Cod National Seashore.

More than a thousand ships have come to grief off Cape Cod's shores, and local shipwreck historian Bill Quinn showed us dozens of photos of wooden wrecks in eroding dunes and washed up on beaches.

But the only skeleton we spent any time on was an iron ship that lay just offshore on a sandbar in rolling surf. That shipwreck, sitting off Head of the Meadow Beach in Truro, Massachusetts, was all that was left of the 120-foot German bark *Frances*. *Frances*, bound for Boston with a cargo of sugar and tin ingots, came to grief on the night of December 26, 1872. The fourteen-man crew took to the rigging and was slowly freezing to death as the salt spray coated them with ice.

Fortunately for them, Cape Cod's reputation as a ships' graveyard had inspired the government to erect lifesaving stations. Because of an average of two wrecks each winter month, the Commonwealth of Massachusetts had built huts to shelter shipwrecked mariners in 1797. But it was not until 1871, the year before *Frances*'s wreck, that the U.S. government had assumed responsibility for lifesaving with the creation of the United States Life-Saving Service (USLSS). Stations were built on dangerous sections of coast, manned around the clock, and lifesavers walked the beaches on patrol to spot ships in trouble and sound the alarm.

A crew of volunteers from Truro, led by Captain Edwin Worthen, keeper of the USLSS's new Highland Lifesaving Station, came to the aid of *Frances*'s crew. Dragging a whaleboat through the dunes and onto the beach, the lifesavers braved the surf and being crushed against the wallowing steel hull to pluck the freezing men from the rigging. Every soul aboard was saved, but the ordeal proved too much for Captain Wilhelm Kortling, *Frances*'s master. He died from the effects of his exposure to the cold, three days later. When the surf quieted down, some of the cargo was salvaged, and then *Frances* was left to the sea. But the wreck never broke up. Buried periodically by an offshore sandbar, the hulk, as the National Seashore's visitor guide explains, "pokes up occasionally above the Atlantic waves and serves as a memorial to the more than 1,000 shipwrecks that have occurred along the outer Cape over the past three and a half centuries."

To get to *Frances*, we had to walk carefully backwards through the surf, then turn around quickly to dive under the waves and swim fast to avoid becoming a scuba-clad surfer instead of a diver. I joined my friend and colleague, National Park Service (NPS) archaeologist Larry

Murphy, on a reconnaissance dive. Murphy is a tall, solidly built man whose nickname at the time was "Mongo," in recognition of his size and strength. As we swam up to *Frances,* I was amazed to see that most of the ship was there—not just a skeleton. Half buried in the sandbar was the entire iron hull, rising up out of the seabed to the decks. We took measurements of the bow and drifted up to the intact wooden deck. Holes bashed through the planking showed an open space below, which we thought was the forecastle where the crew had bunked. Neither Murphy nor I could fit through the holes, so we swam back down and headed aft to an open hatch in the deck. The main deck was half gone, battered away by the sea or nineteenth-century salvagers who were after the cargo of tin ingots. We easily dropped into the hold and were rewarded by the sight of a small scatter of ingots. Beyond them was a hole in the iron bulkhead that led directly into the forecastle. The light that came in through the holes in the deck above us illuminated the scene as the pounding of the surf boomed through the iron hull. We both realized that few if any had been in this compartment since that night just after Christmas 1872.

The wooden bunks of the German sailors had collapsed, but, as we surveyed the room, we spotted a wooden box, half buried in the sand, with a hole in the lid. We thought that it might be a sailor's sea chest, filled with his personal belongings, preserved by the sand and ready to reveal its secrets to us. Murphy cautiously stuck his hand into the hole to feel around, and suddenly yanked his hand back, bellowing through the regulator clenched in his teeth. As he waved his right hand frantically, I saw a large crab, its claw firmly holding on for the ride. I nearly drowned as I burst out laughing, holding my regulator in with my teeth. Larry managed to pull the crab off and, nursing his sore but not injured hand, beckoned that it was time to go.

Back on the beach, we were debriefing with the Navy divers, who had also been mapping the wreck and who had anchored a small inflatable boat over the bow. They had a strange tale to report. As they were swimming over the bow, a sudden burst of air bubbles had poured out from inside the wreck, and they could swear they heard, muffled through the water, alternating screams and shrieks of laughter that had convinced some of them that the wreck was haunted.

The state of preservation of *Frances*, like that of *King Philip*, was mirrored by what we found on other shipwrecks buried in the sand on other beaches. The fact that ships lost on storm-tossed coasts in violent surf conditions did not break up into matchsticks was not widely recognized by maritime archaeologists. Murphy and I had presented a paper on that topic in 1984, to our colleagues at an annual conference in Williamsburg, Virginia, though it was ignored in favor of more exciting deep-water discoveries. But the evidence we gathered, as well as some of the interesting real-life stories behind some of these ships, ultimately showed that you never know where a fascinating shipwreck is going to show up, be it buried below high rises in a modern city or in a sand dune on a long stretch of coastline.

CHAPTER TEN

HEROES UNDER FIRE

THE COAST OF CUBA

The long swell of the sea rolls in from the open Caribbean and breaks against the steep rocks of the promontory known as El Morro. The coast of Cuba, rocky and steep, stretches to the east and the west, defining the narrow gap that is the entrance to Santiago Harbor. Rising above the gap and the stone-lined terraces carved out of the cliff is the masonry mass of Castillo del Morro San Pedro de la Roca, also known, like the promontory it dominates, as El Morro. The ancient fortification, first built in the early seventeenth century and subsequently rebuilt numerous times to defend Santiago from the attacks of pirates and privateers, no longer bristles with guns. Fluttering atop its parapets is the flag of Cuba, which has flown here for a scant one hundred years in the five centuries since Christopher Columbus first circumnavigated the island's shores and planted a colony. For much of Cuba's history, the banner of Spain flew atop El Morro, though the rich harbor and island it claimed were contested by other powers and internal rebellions. It was supplanted in 1898, albeit briefly, by the flag of a newly awakened imperial power, the United States.

THE LAST MISSION OF USS *MERRIMAC*: JUNE 3, 1898

In February 1898, Cuba's three-year struggle for independence from Spain and fears for American lives and property in Cuba convinced President William McKinley to send the battleship *Maine* to "show the flag." American interest in Cuba—including demands from various quarters for the outright takeover of the island—dated back half a century, and Spanish officials were highly suspicious of the United States government's motives in sending the *Maine* to Havana. When *Maine* mysteriously exploded in Havana Harbor on the evening of February 15, suspicions of Spanish "treachery," fanned by the U.S. press, swelled public outrage and led Congress to declare war on April 11. Volunteers enlisted around the country, and soon camps were filled with troops training and assembling to sail to Cuba with the slogan: "Remember the *Maine* and to hell with Spain!"

The U.S. Navy dispatched a squadron of ships to hit Spain's fleet in the Philippines, and another to both blockade Cuba and counter the Spanish naval forces assembled there. But the Americans arrived off Cuba to find an enemy who would not come out to fight. The Spanish fleet lay out of reach of the American ships inside the harbor of Santiago de Cuba, protected by a series of seventeenth- and eighteenth-century forts that Spanish marines and sailors had hastily fortified with more modern breech-loading weapons. They also had protected the narrow entrance to the harbor with "torpedoes," or mines. The Cape Verde Fleet of the Spanish Navy, under the command of Admiral Pascual Cervera y Topete, consisted of four battle cruisers and two torpedo boat destroyers. The U.S. Navy's North Atlantic Squadron was a force of two battleships, five cruisers and more than a dozen other vessels, commanded by Rear Admiral William T. Sampson. Sampson's forces were augmented by a second group of ships, the Flying Squadron (so-called because it was intended to be a fast-response group of ships that would "fly" to wherever needed), commanded by Commodore Winfield Scott Schley. Schley's squadron of two battleships, three cruisers and the collier *Merrimac* (laden with coal to fuel the other ships) further stacked the odds against Cervera.

The Spanish admiral, a highly respected veteran, knew all too well that he was in a hopeless situation. Cervera had already resigned as Spain's Minister of the Marine when his inspections found the Spanish Navy was in poor condition, ill-equipped to fight, and ravaged by political machinations and corruption. When Spain prepared for war against the United States, he returned to uniform out of a sense of duty, but his correspondence with his superiors minced no words when he was ordered to sail to Cuba to try and break the American naval blockade. "It is impossible for me to give you an idea of the surprise and consternation experienced by all on the receipt of the order to sail. Indeed, that surprise is well justified, for nothing can be expected of this expedition except the total destruction of the fleet or its hasty and demoralized return." His concerns rebuffed, Cervera wrote back: "With a clear conscience I go to the sacrifice."

To forestall that sacrifice, Cervera kept his fleet in the protected anchorage of Santiago Harbor, his guns pointing at the entrance, because the large American force was too powerful to confront. The guns protecting Cervera and the threat of mines kept the Americans out, but to prevent the Spanish fleet from slipping away under cover of darkness, Sampson decided to "bottle them up" in the harbor. To do that, he turned to a young and eager engineering officer and to the most untrustworthy ship in his fleet, the collier *Merrimac*.

Merrimac, a four-year-old, British-built collier, was one of Schley's Flying Squadron, though the 333-foot vessel had slowed the fleet to a slow crawl across the ocean. Plagued with engine and steering problems, *Merrimac* probably would have been sent home had it not been loaded with coal. *Merrimac*'s crew fueled Schley's ships by filling bags with coal, hoisting them on deck and then slinging them over to whatever warship was moored alongside. It was hard, dirty work, not only for the stokers in *Merrimac*'s holds but also the receiving ship, as the thick black coal dust clung to everyone and everything.

Sampson picked the unreliable *Merrimac* to trap the Spanish fleet in the harbor by sinking herself to block the narrow entrance. On May 30, as the American fleet assembled off Santiago, Sampson ordered

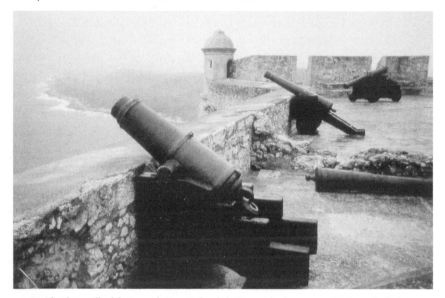

Inside El Castillo del Morro de San Pedro de la Roca, also known as El Morro, built in the early seventeenth century to defend Santiago de Cuba. Below these ramparts steamed the collier Merrimac *in a brave but failed attempt to block the harbor entrance. James P. Delgado*

Commodore Schley to prepare *Merrimac* for the mission. Schley disagreed with Sampson. He argued that if the Spanish were trapped inside Santiago Harbor, their guns would help to defend the city against the American troops preparing to march overland to seize Santiago. Schley thought it would be better to lure Cervera out of the protected harbor and destroy him, but Sampson reiterated his orders to use "the promptest and most efficient use of every means" and sent a bright but untested twenty-seven-year-old lieutenant, naval constructor Richmond Pearson Hobson, to ready *Merrimac* for the suicide mission.

Hobson, who was attached to Sampson's staff to make observations on how well the ships performed after recent work in the Navy Yard (that's what a naval constructor did), was vain, stubborn and eager to prove himself. He was also very unpopular with his fellow officers.

But he was brilliant, and his enthusiasm made him a perfect choice for Sampson. Hobson's plan was to strip *Merrimac* of "useful gear" and to rig her to sink quickly with charges once she was in position immediately inside the harbor entrance. There, if the charts were accurate, the 333-foot length of the ship would block much of the narrow channel.

Hobson set ten charges along *Merrimac*'s hull and connected them to electric batteries linked by wire to a central station on the bridge. Crews worked in the hot Cuban sun to grease the seacocks (valves in the engine room) so that they would open quickly to help flood the ship, and "all openings, hatches, manhole covers, etc. were opened." Hobson had the anchors rigged at the bow and stern, near the waterline, to swing the ship hard to starboard at the last moment to position her across the channel. As Hobson later explained: "The general plan contemplated a minimum crew of volunteers . . . with the simplest form of duty for each . . . The anchors were to be slung over the sides and held by simple lashings, ready to be cut with an ax, a man stationed at each anchor." Only two men were to stay below, one in the engine room and one in the boiler room. One man was to take the wheel and one was to assist with the torpedoes, making in all a crew of six. That was not enough, and another man was added.

Hobson selected his crew from hundreds of volunteers from the fleet. Seven men—Randolph Clausen, George Charette, Osborn Deignan, Francis Kelly, Daniel Montague, John Murphy and George Phillips—joined *Merrimac* as final preparations were made for an early morning run into the harbor on June 3, 1898.

Merrimac's last trip started at 3 a.m. Fortunately for Hobson, darkness cloaked the collier and the Spanish sentries at El Morro did not spot the ship until she was just 2,000 yards from the harbor entrance. The forts and batteries opened fire. Associated Press reporter "Chappie" Goode, watching from USS *New York*, reported: "In a few seconds the mouth of Santiago Harbor was livid with flames that shot viciously from both banks . . . the dull sound of the carronade and its fiery light were unmistakable evidences of the fierce attack that was being waged on Hobson's gallant crew." Captain Robley "Fighting Bob"

Evans, observing from the bridge of the battleship *Iowa*, said, "It looks like Hell with the lid off!"

Hobson and his crew, stripped to their underwear to make it easier to swim away when the ship sank, crouched down as shell after shell hit *Merrimac*. Hobson later wrote: "The striking of projectiles and flying fragments produced a grinding sound, with the fine ring in it of steel on steel. The deck vibrated heavily, and we felt the full effect, lying, as it were, full-length on our faces. At each instant it seemed that certainly the next would bring a projectile among us . . . I looked for my own body to be cut in two diagonally, from the hip upward, and wondered for a moment what the sensation would be."

As *Merrimac* entered the channel, Hobson found that he could not steer the ship. "Our steering gear was gone, shot away at the last moment, and we were charging straight down the channel." Then, as they neared their planned position to scuttle the ship, most of the explosive charges failed to detonate. Only two out of the ten exploded. Damaged but still afloat, and now ablaze, *Merrimac* drifted deeper into the harbor and directly into the line of fire of Cervera's ships and a gun battery on the shore. More shells tore into the collier's hull. Then came "a blasting shock, a lift, a pull, a series of vibrations, and a mine exploded directly beneath."

The last blast stopped the ship, and she began "steadily sinking two thirds athwart." *Merrimac,* stuck at one side of the channel, burned fiercely as the wind whipped through the torn hull and decks to fan the coal in the hold into a blast furnace. The steel decks began to soften and twist in the heat. "The *Merrimac* gave a premonitory lurch, then staggered to port in a death-throe," said Hobson. "The bow almost fell, it sank so rapidly . . . the stricken vessel now reeled to port . . . and plunged forward. The stern rose and heeled heavily; it stood for a moment, shuddering, and then started downward, righting as it went."

Incredibly, not one member of Hobson's crew was killed or even seriously injured. Two men were cut by shrapnel, but not badly. As *Merrimac* slipped away beneath them, the eight Americans found themselves in the water. A raft from the wreck washed by, and they grabbed its ropes and clung alongside, hiding from the bullets of Spanish soldiers and marines until the gunfire died away. At daybreak, a steam launch approached, searching for survivors. It was the personal craft of Admiral Cervera, who had insisted on an inspection of the sunken ship. Hobson and his seven men were pulled from the water at Cervera's order. The Spanish admiral turned to Hobson and spoke one word: *"Valiente!"*

It was a valiant but a failed mission. Hobson was disheartened, admitting *Merrimac* "did not completely block the channel," because at the end the current had swung the ship from its sideways position and straightened her out. Ships could steam past the wreck. But while Hobson and his crew had not succeeded, their bravery inspired more than Admiral Cervera. That afternoon, Cervera sent a launch out to the American fleet, under a flag of truce, to inform Sampson that his men had survived. The news cheered the American sailors, while correspondents filed reports for the papers back home praising the "gallant Hobson" and *Merrimac's* crew.

The eight Americans, meanwhile, remained prisoners of Spain, lodged in cells in the imposing fortress of El Morro. From his cell, Hobson could look out each day and see the masts of *Merrimac* sticking up in the water. He and the crew also watched from their cells when the U.S. fleet bombarded El Morro to weaken Spanish defenses while American troops waded ashore several miles south at Daiquiri and Siboney. Since the Spanish Navy had not been neutralized or defeated, the key to American victory was to seize Santiago by land. Troops pushed inland, joining Cuban rebels as they advanced towards the old city. Tropical disease, heat and tough Spanish resistance slowed the American advance, but finally, the outer defenses of Santiago were breached.

The breakthrough occurred on the city's outskirts at two small forts atop Kettle Hill and San Juan Hill, where the volunteer regiment of Rough Riders fought their way to victory. They were led into battle by Colonel Theodore Roosevelt after the regiment's commanding officer, Leonard Wood, was wounded. This was the beginning of a new phase of Roosevelt's life that would catapult him into the White House within a few years. It was also the death knell for Spain's empire in the Americas, which had been whittled down to just Cuba and Puerto Rico.

That death knell also resounded on the sea. On July 3, Cervera ordered his fleet to leave Santiago and make for the high seas. He hoped to outrun the Americans, whom he could not outgun, but the waiting U.S. fleet opened fire. Over the next few hours, one by one, the Spanish ships died. All were sunk, some dying in massive explosions as their magazines erupted, while others, torn by shot and shell and on fire, steamed for the rocky shore where their crews beached them rather than go down in deeper water where the sailors had less of a chance of surviving. Cuban rebels on the shore fired on Spanish sailors struggling in the surf, as sharks circled and ripped into the wounded men.

The victorious Americans treated the Spanish wounded, including Admiral Cervera, and accorded them the same chivalry that the Spaniards had granted to Hobson and his men. The war ended with the Spanish surrender outside of Santiago. Surprisingly, the victorious Americans did not invite their Cuban allies—in a war ostensibly fought for Cuban independence—to attend the negotiations or the surrender. Instead, the United States assumed control of Cuba, governing the island until 1903 and leaving only after writing a Cuban constitution that granted the U.S. the right to militarily intervene in Cuban affairs and a perpetual lease to Guantanamo Bay for a naval base. The seeds of Cuban discontent and a future revolution were thus sown.

With the war over, many of its combatants were acclaimed as heroes, among them Theodore Roosevelt, Admiral William Sampson, Richmond Hobson and the crew of *Merrimac*. Hobson gained fame for his exploits and his good looks, earning the sobriquet of the "most kissable officer in the Navy." He, like Roosevelt, rode his fame into political office. His crew also fared well. On November 2, 1899, the seven sailors of *Merrimac* were awarded the Congressional Medal of Honor. Hobson did not receive the medal because of a provision barring its award to naval and marine officers. It was not until April 29, 1933, that then Congressman Richmond Hobson finally received his Medal of Honor from President Franklin D. Roosevelt.

THE LOST WARSHIPS OF THE BATTLE OF SANTIAGO

Our plane drops from the clouds and banks along the line of cliffs that define the shores of Cuba's southeast coast. As we approach Santiago, I look out the window and see the walls of El Morro flash below me, then the lighthouse, and then we're down, bouncing on the airstrip that stretches out next to the ancient fortress. *The Sea Hunters* team is here to explore waters rarely dived in search of a doomed fleet and one forgotten American collier that a century ago had been the talk of a nation.

We're in Fidel Castro's Cuba, with his permission, to dive all of the wrecks from the Spanish-Cuban-American War of 1898. We have toured Havana and the site of the destruction of USS *Maine,* visited the U.S. memorial monument to *Maine's* dead on the city's oceanfront drive, the Malecon, and interviewed Cuba's top historians and curators about that war. Now *The Sea Hunters* team heads to Santiago to see the sites: Daiquiri and Siboney, where the American troops landed; San Juan Hill, where the Rough Riders stormed up to victory; Santa Iphigenia Cemetery, where the dead of the battles are buried, and El Morro. Standing on its parapets with Mike Fletcher and John Davis, I look down into the narrow harbor mouth at the scene of *Merrimac's* last mission. The collier would have steamed just a few yards away from El Morro's closest guns and into the mouth of more guns that doubtless rained fire into *Merrimac's* hull. "It's a miracle the ship made it through with no one killed," Mike says, and John and I nod in agreement. "It will be a miracle if anything has survived in that channel," John says. Looking out at the active shipping, we agree.

After touring the battlefields and memorials on land, with their manicured lawns, statues and bronze plaques offering a distant, cleaned-up and sanctified image of that hundred-year-old war, we head out to sea to search for Cervera's sunken fleet. Mike and his son Warren start by diving to find the wrecks of the torpedo boat destroyers *Pluton* and *Furor.* Their shattered and scattered remains litter the steep slope of the seabed, 100 to 120 feet down. From there, we head to the cruiser *Almirante Oquendo.* Dozens of shells ripped through the cruiser during

The wreck of the Spanish cruiser Almirante Oquendo, *a turret and gun sticking up out of the water. She was sunk off Cuba during the Spanish-American-Cuban War at the Battle of Santiago in 1898. James P. Delgado*

her final flight and fight, and at the end, burning fiercely with more than half of the crew dead, the wounded ship hit the rocks near shore and broke in two. Very few men made it off *Oquendo.* Today, the cruiser's grave is marked by one of its large 11-inch guns sticking up out of the sea. We follow it down into a broken field of debris that only after a careful survey reveals the outlines of the ship.

We travel farther down the coast to look at *Oquendo*'s sister ship, the cruiser *Vizcaya.* Running flat out, *Vizcaya* slugged it out at near point-blank range with Schley's flagship, USS *Brooklyn.* The fight ended when *Vizcaya*'s bow exploded as she lined up to either ram *Brooklyn* or fire a torpedo from the tube set into its bow. An American shell detonated the torpedo before the Spaniards could fire it. Sinking and ablaze, *Vizcaya* could no longer fight. Wounded and "faint from the loss of blood," the cruiser's commander, Captain Juan Antonio Eulate, was in the sick bay where he met one of his junior officers, Ensign Luis Fajardo. An American shell had torn off one of Fajardo's arms, but he told his captain "he still had one left for his country."

Captain Eulate, in his official report of the battle, said: "I immediately convened the officers who were nearest . . . and asked them whether there was anyone among them who thought we could do anything more in the defense of our country and our honor, and the unanimous reply was that nothing more could be done." As Spaniards, some with their uniforms ablaze, leapt screaming from their burning ship into the sea, some men on *Texas* started to cheer their victory until Captain John Philip yelled out, "Don't cheer, boys! These poor devils are dying!" USS *Iowa*, commanded by Robley Evans, approached next. Evans, incensed that Cuban sharpshooters were gunning down Spanish survivors struggling in the surf, sent a boat ashore and told the Cubans to stop firing or he would shell them.

With Mike Fletcher and his son Warren, I drop down into the sea, swimming past twisted armor plate and the broken engines of *Vizcaya*. We swim along the hull, punctured here and there by shellfire and the rocks where the burning hulk settled. Looming up in the milky sea, washed by the surging of the surf that breaks overhead, is the bulk of one of the cruiser's turrets, its 11-inch Hontoria cannon still in place but resting on its side in the sand. With Mike, I drop down to the narrow gap that the gun passes through. The men at these guns died at their posts, heavy shells raining down and setting off the powder inside as they raced to load and fire. *Oquendo's* survivors said that a 350-pound charge of powder exploded from a hit on a turret and flashed through it, killing the gun crew laboring inside before erupting in a sheet of flame that ripped off the head of a nearby officer. Similar scenes of horror played out on *Vizcaya*.

I shrug out of my dive vest and tank, and shove them through a narrow gap in the armor. Then, kicking and squeezing, I work my body into the turret. It is still and dark, as it should be— this is a tomb. Mike follows, and we strap our gear back on and carefully float in the enclosed space, filming it. We're probably the first living people to be in here in more than a hundred years, and we quietly and respectfully document the turret, disturbing its peace only with our lights and air bubbles in order to share the story of what happened here with the world.

Our last dive on Cervera's fleet is the cruiser *Cristobal Colon,* scuttled at the end of the battle by its crew. After opening the seacocks, they ran *Colon* up on the beach and abandoned ship as the Americans approached. Eager to salvage the newly built warship, the U.S. Navy tried to tow *Colon* off the rocks but, flooded and open to the sea, the cruiser sank in 100 feet of water. The sea is clear and calm, and as we descend down into the deep, the wreck of *Colon* is laid out before us, with gear on the decks and railings on ladders leading into the darkness of the cruiser's hull. Flicking on our lights, we cannot resist the siren call of the secrets within the hull. We drift into a magazine half filled with mud and open to the seabed outside thanks to a large hole blasted through the side. Sticking out of the mud are rows of shells, still live and deadly a century after *Colon*'s demise. Passing out of the hole, we follow the hull, now festooned with marine life and growth that make the steel hulk a beautiful artificial reef, a haven to countless fish. The warm, sunlit waters have granted new life to *Cristobal Colon* and helped lay to rest some of her ghosts. As we surface, we agree that the time has come to find the elusive wreck of *Merrimac.*

SEARCHING FOR USS *MERRIMAC*

Our boat pushes past the fortress of El Morro, following the track of *Merrimac*'s final run. Richmond Hobson published a book about the mission in 1899, and with it in hand, we're following the course he plotted in its pages to where the wreck should lie. Discussions with our Cuban hosts have given us hope. There is indeed a wreck near the spot, but it is a battered hulk that harbor authorities blasted around 1976 to clear the shipping channel. Now it may just be a pile of debris that we will have a difficult time proving was the famous collier. Getting permission to dive in this forbidden zone has also proved challenging, but the Cuban authorities, interested in learning just what lies there, and wanting all of the story told, have given their okay.

With five Cuban divers, we suit up—myself, Mike and Warren— and drop into the dark green water at slack tide. Even so, the current is

strong, and we hang on to the weighted line we dropped earlier and follow it down. The water is dirty with silt, and we cannot see our hands in front of our faces. It gets darker, closing in, grayer, verging on black . . . and then suddenly, 30 feet from the bottom, the water clears dramatically. Below us is the mangled stern of a large steel ship. We trace the stern and find the rudder, knocked free of its mounts and resting against the hull. We follow it to the bottom and find the propeller. Mike shines the light on it, pointing out that one of its blades is missing—and it looks like it was shot away.

We continue on, under the overhang of the hull, past steel plating that dangles from the hull, and up onto the deck. I swim back to the stern and look into a tangle of debris. Lying in there is the ship's steering gear, and it, too, looks as if it was hit by gunfire. Gouges and broken steel castings provide evidence of a tremendous blow, and I'm reminded, floating and kicking against the current, of Hobson's account of how *Merrimac*'s stern was hit by gunfire and lost her ability to steer.

My excitement grows as we drift with the current along the deck, moving towards the bow. The decks of the wreck are laid out exactly as on *Merrimac*'s plans, with large coal holds, scuttles and ventilators, and the mounts for the ship's two masts each lying between pairs of coal holds. This has to be *Merrimac*. I grin with my regulator clenched in my teeth and turn to Mike with a "high five" sign. The centrally located superstructure is badly mangled, the bridge smashed and gone, but, lying in the debris, I see a broken Champagne bottle. It's too perfect, I think. We know that just before they headed in, Hobson and his crew drank a toast in a melodramatic moment, and I wonder if this is their bottle. It could have been tossed in years later from a passing ship, but just the same, I wonder.

Nearby are pairs of the ship's davits used to launch *Merrimac*'s boats, again situated exactly where the plans indicate they should be. Shell holes in the decks are graphic evidence of heavy fire. One shell hole penetrates the deck on the starboard side of No. 3 hold, at an angle that suggests it was fired from an elevation off the ship's starboard quarter, so presumably from El Morro just after *Merrimac* cleared the harbor entrance and was proceeding in.

Swimming forward, we find that the charges lowered into the water by the Cubans in 1976 have torn the hull down to below the waterline at the bow, scattering steel fragments along the seabed. And yet, buried in the mud, is the forward anchor. Concealed by silt with only one shank exposed, it is connected to the mangled stem by thick anchor chain. Later, Warren Fletcher finds the stern anchor above the silt off the ship's starboard side, tightly held by chain, suggesting that instead of being shot away, as Hobson suspected, it had jammed and remained suspended alongside the hull when *Merrimac* sank. We also find two rows of anchor chain, partially buried in the buckled plating and sediment that covers the deck, running from the bow to the stern, exactly the way that Hobson described how his crew had rigged it.

We can find no definitive evidence of damage from the scuttling charges, though a hole and damage to the port quarter conceivably could be related to the charge that Hobson placed there. The hull is set into the silt of the harbor bottom to a level above the waterline, and our limited time on each dive does not allow for a comprehensive survey of the side of the hull to see if there is blasting damage. But we do see other damage that testifies to *Merrimac*'s end—and that demonstrates dramatically why *Merrimac*'s crew, like the men in the Spanish ships who fought through flame and shot—deserve the honor of being called heroes. The decks are warped and twisted from the intense heat of the fires that burned through *Merrimac*'s coal for an hour. Reaching into the torn hull, I pull out chunks of coal that laboratory analysis later shows are "coked" as a result of the fire.

There is nothing pretty about war, and when the pomp and ceremony and the glamour are stripped away, what is left, so visibly on this wreck and on the shattered hulks of Cervera's sunken fleet, is harsh evidence of the intensity of battle, the costs of war, and the strength of character and love of country that inspires people to sail into harm's way to fight for a cause or to defend what they hold dear. As we surface from the muddy grave of *Merrimac*, I think of how raw and untouched this undersea battlefield is compared to the museum-like setting of San Juan Hill and its cleaned-up, memorialized and glorified view of war.

HITLER'S ROCKETS

NEAR NEUSTADT, GERMANY

More than 400 feet beneath the Harz Mountains of Germany, we trudge through darkness, climbing over fallen rock and twisted metal, splashing through pools of stagnant scummy water. The darkness is as thick and oppressive as the silence that fills the tunnel. We interrupt both with flashes of light and the sound of our footsteps as we work our way deeper into the mountain. The chamber stretches on into blackness, and we can't help feeling some dread as we continue into what we know once was literally the depths of hell itself.

Ahead of us lie 12 miles of tunnels and subterranean galleries, hewn from the rock by slave laborers. Hastily constructed by the Third Reich in the wake of the unrelenting Allied air war against Hitler's Germany, this underground complex was once part of the Nazi concentration camp system. Buried deep within the mountain was a factory where inmates built jet engines and assembled v-1 and v-2 rockets. Abandoned by the Germans in April 1945, the complex was sealed shut in 1948 and disappeared behind the Iron Curtain, because it was in the Russian occupation zone.

Since 1964, the area above the former KZ (*Konzentrationslager*—concentration camp) Mittelbau-Dora has been the site of a memorial, and in 1974 a museum was built on the grounds. The barracks, guard towers and barbed wire are gone—only broken concrete foundations, cracked and rutted streets, and the crematorium on the hill that rises above the camp are grim reminders of what happened here. But below the surface, inside the mountain, lies a moment trapped in time. To access that stark, unmitigated evidence of evil and suffering, a reunified Germany completed a new 500-foot tunnel that cut into Kohnstein Mountain in order to reopen some of the underground complex for visitors. Only 5 per cent of the tunnels are open to the public because when the Russians blasted it closed in 1948, they brought down rock and portions of the concrete and metal that divided the tunnels into a multilevel factory. Postwar quarrying of the mountain above also cracked and loosened the rock, so the tunnels are dangerous. Large rocks fall without warning, and some galleries, once open, are now choked shut. To move deeper into the mountain, and back into the untouched past, we are wearing the rig of hard-rock miners as we climb, slip and slide over huge boulders, gravel and mud. Even so, at least a third of the complex lies sealed beneath cold water that has seeped in and flooded the tunnels, along with their assembly lines, workshops and offices.

It's December, and outside, the temperature is well below freezing, with snowflakes dancing in the wind. Inside the mountain, the temperature hovers just above freezing. Our breath fogs as we haul our dive equipment deep into the heart of the mountain. We will be among the first to slip beneath the water and explore the flooded depths of Mittelbau-Dora. Our goal is to venture into some of its forgotten rooms and bring back film footage to share with the world.

Our *Sea Hunters* team is now a close-knit band of brothers in the field, underwater, underground, on the decks of ships and in the studio. Producer and team leader John Davis, chief diver Mike Fletcher, his son Warren, our second underwater cameraman, Marc Pike and soundman John Rosborough make up the core team. Guided by our colleagues Dr. Willi Kramer, Torsten Hess (curator of KZ Mittelbau-Dora) and a mine safety engineer, we find ourselves in a unique situation, diving into the depths of a flooded underground concentration camp to see what untouched evidence remains of Nazi crimes against humanity. Dr. Kramer, who is with Germany's Department of Monuments and Culture, is the chief underwater archeologist for Northern Germany and the government's only underwater archeologist to work with Germany's hydrographic office and the military. That assignment has included diving to explore sunken warships and U-boats, downed aircraft and subterranean chambers. Willi was the first to dive here, and now he leads us into the darkness.

I turn to John Davis and say, "This looks like one of the rings of hell." He replies, "Dante couldn't have imagined this." He's right. The dark, the cold, the silence and the overwhelming sense of the horrors that took place here engulf us as we travel deeper into the tunnels.

ROCKETS FOR THE REICH

The achievement of the age-old dream of human flight in the early twentieth century spawned a new dream of flight into space. Scientists in various countries experimented to perfect rocket designs through the 1920s and '30s, with varying levels of success. In 1932, the new Nazi government set up a rocket program. Among the scientists who joined that program was Wernher von Braun, who, with full funding and Wermacht (Army) support, developed a series of rockets: the A1, A2 and A3. The Germans built and tested these first rockets at an artillery range outside Berlin. By 1935, they needed a new facility.

The island of Usedom, on the Baltic coast at the mouth of the Peene River, proved to be the ideal locale. Known as Peenemünde, this new test center, developed by both the Wermacht and the Luftwaffe (Air Force), opened in May 1937. There, in isolation, von Braun and his team began the design and testing of a new rocket, the A4. That weapon, designed to be a long-distance combat rocket, would later become notorious as the feared v-2. But the testing of the A4 was plagued by problems, because its twenty thousand individual parts required meticulous assembly. As the Germans worked to improve the range and targeting of the A4, they also took steps to simplify its construction on an assembly line.

The first successful launch of an A4 rocket came only after Germany lost the Battle of Britain and at Hitler's urging, as he wanted results after years of costly development and tests. On October 3, 1942, an A4 roared off the pad. The space age had begun, but with a deadly purpose. Hitler demanded that five thousand rockets be built for a mass attack on London. At the same time, the rocket scientists had designed a smaller but also deadly weapon, the Fi 103, later designated the v-1, to attack Britain. These small winged rockets were the world's first cruise missiles.

The "V" designation came from Nazi propaganda minister Joseph Goebbels, who called the rockets *Vergeltungwaffe* (vengeance weapons). The v-2, a single-stage rocket, was 46 feet long, weighed 14 tons, carried a one-ton payload (two-thirds of which was the explosive charge) and traveled at a maximum velocity of 3,600 miles per hour, with a range of 200 miles. Facilities for constructing the rockets were built at Peenemünde, using prisoners from concentration camps as workers. The first assembly lines to build v-1 rockets started up in July 1943, and in early August, a new line was added to build v-2s. First fired at Paris in early September 1944, v-2s were also fired at London and Antwerp. In all, out of 4,600 v-2s built, the Nazis fired about 3,200 in anger, most of them, despite popular belief, not at London but at Antwerp. The v-1 and v-2 rocket barrage against the Allies killed about five thousand people. Ironically, four times as many—nearly twenty thousand—died in slave labor camps constructing the rocket facilities and making the weapons themselves.

Located in the middle of Germany near the town of Nordhausen, about 35 miles from the infamous Buchenwald concentration camp, the Dora labor camp (later Mittelbau-Dora) became the primary center for the manufacture of v-1 and v-2 rockets after Allied bombing raids struck Peenemünde in August 1943. The bombers did not cause extensive damage, but Peenemünde's work was not a secret and it was vulnerable to further attack. Production and assembly of the rockets was taken over by the dreaded SS, which decided to relocate rocket production to underground factories built and manned by slave laborers from concentration camps. In late August 1943, the SS established a sub-camp of Buchenwald in an underground fuel storage facility at Kohnstein. A series of tunnels, originally excavated in the mountain for a gypsum mine, became the basis for a massive underground factory known as the Mittelwerk.

While scientific research and testing continued under von Braun at Peenemünde, the underground camp and complex were being hacked out of rock to serve as the primary production facilities for both the v-1 and v-2 rockets. From late August 1943 through to the end of the year, prisoners from Buchenwald lived in the tunnels, drilling, blasting and hauling rock in grueling twelve-hour shifts in the midst of incessant noise, dark and damp conditions that killed thousands. Jean Michel, a French resistance leader arrested by the Gestapo, who arrived at the Dora complex on October 14, 1943, described his first day as "terrifying":

> The Kapos [prisoner bosses] and ss drive us on at an infernal speed, shouting and raining blows down on us, threatening us with execution, the demons! The noise bores into the brain and shears the nerves. The demented rhythm lasts for fifteen hours. Arriving at the dormitory [in the tunnels]...we do not even try to reach the bunks. Drunk with exhaustion, we collapse onto the rocks, onto the ground. Behind, the Kapos press us on. Those behind trample over their comrades. Soon, over a thousand despairing men, at the limit of their existence and racked with thirst, lie there hoping for sleep which never comes; for the shouts of the guards, the noise of the machines, and explosions and the ringing of the bell reach them even there.

The prisoners worked twenty-four hours a day in alternating twelve-hour shifts. Tiers of wooden bunks in the dripping wet chambers served as their sleeping quarters, with oil drums cut in two serving as toilets. Very little water was available, save that which wept from the rocks and soaked everyone. Disease broke out and added to the death toll caused by overwork, falling rock and exhaustion. In such hellish conditions, the casualties were high. French historian André Sellier, himself a former inmate of the complex, documented the arrival of 17,535 inmates between August 1943 and April 1944. In that period, 5,882 either died and were cremated in the ovens at the complex or Buchenwald, or were "transported." Those prisoners too ill or too injured to work were shipped to Bergen-Belsen and the Majdanek camps in "liquidation transports." As new inmates kept arriving, the death toll grew higher. In all, some 26,500 died at Dora, according to Sellier's research: 15,500 in the camp or on "transports," and 11,000 at the end of the war, when the SS marched many survivors out of the camp and most of those unfortunates were killed.

The prisoners at Dora were for the most part prisoners of war— Russians and Poles—as well as French resistance fighters, German prisoners of conscience, political prisoners and, later in the war, Jews and Gypsies, who were singled out for particularly brutal treatment by the ss. Other nationalities also joined the ranks of Dora's inmates. After Italy's withdrawal from the Axis, the Germans turned on their former allies with a vengeance. A group of Italian officers, sent to Dora to work as slave laborers, balked at entering the tunnels, so the Germans shot them all. A Greek inmate, Anton Luzidis, spoke for all the prisoners at the end of the war when he testified: "The meaning of Dora was fright. I cannot find the proper words to characterize the conditions there. If often happened to me that I asked myself whether I was still alive in the world, or whether I was brought into this hell after my decease."

Production of Dora's first rockets began in January 1944 when the prisoners started work on v-2s. That same month, 679 prisoners died in the camp. By August 1944, work had started on the first v-1 rockets in the tunnels and the death toll of prisoners mounted. The v-1 factory was set up by the ss and their industrial partners in the manufacture of the weapon, Volkswagen. By March 1945, reacting against what they termed "sabotage," which could be something as simple as using a piece of scrap leather to make a belt to hold up a pair of pants that had grown too large because of starvation, the SS began rounding up inmates and hanging them in groups from the cranes in the underground factory. The executions increased in the last month of the camp's operation. When American forces began closing in, the ss evacuated the civilian support workers and the last remaining rocket scientists. Most of the inmates were shipped out to other camps for liquidation, while thousands were "death-marched" in the snow. At a barn in nearby Gardelegen, the ss locked 1,050 prisoners in a barn, set it on fire and machine-gunned those who made it out of the burning building. Only thirty-four men made it out alive.

The ss abandoned the camp on April 4, 1945, and the U.S. Army liberated Dora and its tunnels seven days later. Several hundred starving, dying inmates, all that remained of the approximately sixty thousand slave laborers who had filled the camp and built the rockets, greeted them. The Americans, well aware of the scientific and military value of the German rocket program, removed the parts of about a hundred v-2 rockets from the tunnels before the Russians arrived in July, because the camp and complex were within the recently established Russian zone of occupation. In October 1946, the Russians, too, removed rocket parts and equipment and shipped them to the Soviet Union. The Russians tried to destroy the tunnels with explosives but could not complete the job. In the summer of 1948, they blasted the entrances to the tunnels to seal them, supposedly forever.

PEENEMÜNDE

The Sea Hunters visit to Germany starts with a visit to Peenemünde, which, like Dora, was once locked away behind the Iron Curtain and was inaccessible, due to its use as a Soviet and East German fighter base. Peenemünde sits on the Baltic coast, at the end of long, low, sandy peninsula, surrounded by shallow marshes on one side and the open Baltic on the other. The cold wind blowing off the sea chills us to the bone as we drive through the largely intact base. Decades of harsh life under communist rule meant that little changed here, and as we pass fences and grim brick and concrete buildings, it is easy to imagine Peenemünde "in its prime" as a top-level Nazi base. It is a surreal moment made all the more so when we visit the former Luftwaffe airfield on our way to the rocket-launching sites.

As locked gates swing open, we drive past rows of bunkers, their huge blast doors hanging open, and rows of deteriorating East German MiG-21 and MiG-23 jets. Until 1989, this was part of the vast Soviet bloc, a potential foe that we were prepared to fight, and these aircraft were here to shoot down our planes in the event of war. The fall of the Berlin Wall, the end of the German Democratic Republic, the reunification of Germany and the unraveling of the Soviet Union are such recent events that I shake my head in wonder as our vehicle speeds through the abandoned air base. Not too many years ago, my presence here with a camera would have resulted in a death sentence, just as it would have sixty years earlier when this was the heart of Hitler's rocket program.

We stop first at the buckled concrete rails of the v-1 test firing range. Blasted and ruined by the Soviets in 1945, the collapsed bunkers and broken concrete look innocuous, and at the same time simple. Yet the weapon perfected here, and manufactured in the thousands at Dora, wrought enormous devastation and terrorized the skies of free Europe and England. Before I left Vancouver on this trip, my museum's board chair told me about his childhood just outside London. The memory of "doodlebugs" or "buzz bombs" as the British called the v-1, were still a source of both terror and anger to him. "You could here them coming," he told me, "and as long as you could hear them, it was alright." Only when the rocket motor cut off would the v-1 plummet to earth and explode. That's when you ran and hoped you were outside the blast zone. I think of him and the memories he still carries of these missiles as I gaze out at the now peaceful Baltic from the lip of the v-1 launch track.

From here, we drive into a forest and park next to a mound of broken brick, glass and twisted steel that was once the assembly building for v-2s at Prüfstande (test stand) 7. Blasted flat by the Soviets after the war, it towered above the plain to house an upright rocket before it was rolled out on rails to its launch platform and the actual test stand. Nestled inside an earthwork that still rings the launch site, the firing position is now a forested glade pockmarked by bombs and designated by a small granite marker. Here, humans first reached beyond the skies into space, but any thrill connected to standing at this monument to the beginnings of the space age is tempered by the grim reality of the evil that drove the invention of these rockets and the horrific human cost of their development and use. We pick our way carefully through the site, closed to public for the very good reason that many unexploded bombs still lie here.

Our next stop is a lagoon. Frozen by the winter's cold, it grips the protruding remains of a Lancaster bomber. As we slowly trek out across the ice, pulling our dive gear in a sled behind us, we talk about the raid that blasted Peenemünde and led to the creation of Dora. On the night of August 17–18, 1943, a force of 596 bombers set out to hit Peenemünde. In all, 560 bombers made it in, dropping 1,800 tons of bombs that hit the concentration camp and the scientists' housing project as well as the liquid oxygen plant and the rocket-launching facilities. A diversionary strike at Berlin drew off German fighters at first, but the Germans caught on and joined with antiaircraft crews on the ground to shoot down forty of the attacking bombers. Sam Hall, who was in one of the bombers, recalls that "after we'd bombed, the mid-upper gunner said, 'There's a fighter coming in! It's got a Lanc, it's got another, it's got another!' Three Lancasters were going down in flames. You didn't waste too much time thinking about it." Wilkie Wanless, in another bomber, remembered after the war that "They shot down a lot of aircraft from the Canadian Group in the last wave . . . Very few got out in the dark. At 4,000 or 5,000 feet your chances of getting out are slim."

No one got out of the Lancaster that we're approaching. One of our German guides tells us that this bomber came in burning, hit the shallow lagoon and cartwheeled as it exploded into pieces. Some of these pieces are sticking up out of the ice. Willi Kramer and I identify one as part of the tail of the Lancaster. Lying flat on the ice and wiping it with our gloved hands, we can make out the tail fins and the unmistakable outline of holes punched by cannon fire through the metal. John Davis and Mike

Fletcher, meanwhile, outline and then start cutting a hole through the ice as Warren Fletcher gears up and prepares the video cameras. The ice proves to be 6 inches thick. After John finishes cutting the hole, both Fletchers drop into the icy water but find themselves only chest deep. This is a shallow, muddy pond. Dropping down, wedged between mud and ice, they slowly survey the wrecked aircraft as we stand on the ice above their blurred outlines and the tracks of their bubbles that form beneath our feet.

Much of the plane is remarkably well preserved, albeit broken. The crew did not make it out, but the Germans recovered their bodies and buried them. What Mike and Warren find is battle-torn aluminum, original paint and what appears to be the barrels of the tail gunner's machine gun, stuck fast in the mud, as Warren squeezes inside the tail section. Cold, constricted and seemingly frozen in time as well as into the ice, the downed Lancaster is a shallow but difficult dive into the past. It is also a fitting introduction to the dives that await all of us at Dora.

DIVING INSIDE A MOUNTAIN

Our long trek into Dora's depths takes us to a side tunnel and to the half-flooded Gallery 44, where starving inmates built v-1 rockets. Not only is the gallery flooded, but its upper level, supported by steel beams and a concrete floor, has collapsed into the water. Our lights pick out the shapes of broken slabs and half-crushed rockets beneath the water, which lies one to nine feet deep over the mounded debris along the flooded, 30-foot wide, 500-foot-long gallery. The far end is sealed off, buried by a cascade of rock when the ceiling collapsed. The water is cold and has a sharp metallic smell. A faint scum of rust and oil slicks the surface.

I'm glad that I am sitting this dive out, watching Mike and Warren as they suit up to take an hour-long snorkel, floating along the surface to film what lies below them. The flooded gallery is so filled with silt and rust that we are keeping our presence in the water to a minimum to avoid stirring it up so the divers can capture the best images possible. The cameras record stacks of v-1 wings and rocket bodies and a

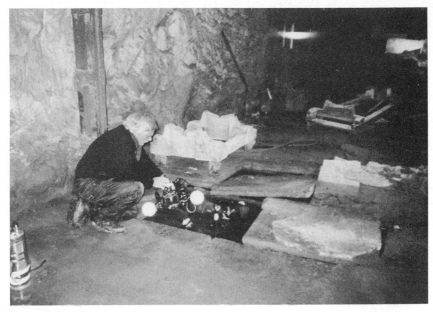

John Davis gives a hand to Mike Fletcher as he climbs out of one of the water-filled tunnels of Dora. James P. Delgado

stack of gyrocompasses that would have been assembled in the noses of rockets to guide them to their targets. Tumbled workbenches and tables, equipment, and signs painted on machines and walls—warnings to do not touch this and to go in that direction—show not only the assembly line but a little of what life was like here.

We have time for only one other dive, this one in a flooded chamber. It's my turn to join Mike and Warren, and I quickly dress in the half-darkness, pulling on a thick fleece undergarment and the dense shell of my dry suit. The rubber seals at my throat and wrists will close the suit off from the freezing water. I pull on my weight belt and tank, rigging my equipment tightly against my body to keep the hoses from dragging or catching once I'm inside the tight confines of the flooded room. A neoprene hood leaves only part of my face exposed, and my breath fogs and clouds the inside of my face mask. I'm already chilled as I gear up next to a black mold–covered, slimy piece of canvas that once curtained off this gallery as workers painted v-1 rocket bodies. My natural instinct is to not want to touch anything.

Mike and Warren go first, disappearing through a hole and into the darkness. I follow, feet first. The cold, even through the suit, is a shock. John Davis watches from above, and on my last glimpse of him through the oil-slicked surface of the hole, I see concern on his face. He should be worried. The three of us are entering a tight dark space that could collapse and bury us. Electric wires and lights still dangle from the ceiling, reaching out to snag us. Rust and silt, dislodged by our bubbles, filter down through the water and black out the light and our visibility. There's only one way out, through what now seems to be a tiny hole, and leaving it behind as we work our through the murky, dark water, takes resolve.

I'm spurred on by what I see. A coffee cup sits on the top of a desk, and a book rests nearby. Drawers, some half open, are filled with tools. Paint still covers the walls, and as I gaze up at the ceiling above me, the lights still hang from their wires, with unbroken bulbs inside the metal shades. As I swim forward through this dark, flooded room, I find Mike and Warren poised at a doorway that leads into another room. The door, on a sliding track, is half closed.

Mike gently reaches out and slides the door open. Slowly and carefully, we glide inside. The room is small and crowded. Tools and equipment lie exactly where they were left by the concentration camp inmates who worked in this hellhole. Like the coffee cup and the tools in the other room, the condition of this workshop is a reminder that we're the first to enter this space since April 1945. Due to the cold water, everything is preserved in a near deep freeze, and we feel the chill, not only of temperature but of the feeling that comes from the sense of encountering a tragic past. I can almost feel the presence of the ss and the inmates.

Our dives inside the mountain, into the flooded heart of Dora, provide a good understanding of what else may lie in other submerged chambers. The flooded rooms seem to be far better preserved than the dry portions of the tunnels, with a chance that even paper has survived—

A stack of v-1 rocket gyrocompasses lie on the floor of the tunnels of Dora, abandoned as Nazi Germany collapsed at the end of World War II. James P. Delgado.

as evidenced by our spotting a book. The flooding of Dora was sudden but not catastrophic. The loss of electrical power and the shutdown of the pumps allowed the seeping water to build up and engulf the lower sections, perhaps not too long after the last of the inmates and the ss abandoned the underground workshops and factories in April 1945. Some areas may have even escaped the notice of the teams of American and later Russian searchers who scoured this complex for the secrets of the Nazi rocket program.

The Dora museum, which manages the site of the camp, with its surviving barracks building and crematorium, ss bunker and numerous foundations, as well as the 5 per cent of the underground facilities open to visitors, preserves this place as a reminder of what happened here. The focus is not on the rockets but on the people who paid the price for those incredible yet terrible technological achievements. The museum's library is full of survivor accounts, interviews and archives about the Nazi system of camps as a means to eliminate people. After we exit the caves, we stand for a moment in the clear night air, gazing up at the swollen moon, breathing in the fresh air to cleanse the stench of Dora from our lungs and to savor the freedom of being out of those dark confined spaces.

Such is the power of a place like this, which is why we are visiting Dora to document its flooded and forgotten chambers. This place is more than a museum. It is a mirror that we must hold up to ourselves as a reminder of the worst that we as a species are capable of. As a child, I watched the astronauts with wonder when humanity first reached for the stars. I thrilled with countless others as men walked on the moon. But the roots of that triumph lie here, down in the darkness.

On our last night, I stroll through the nearby village of Neustadt with soundman John Rosborough. It's the Christmas festival, and we walk among booths filled with crafts and sample steaming hot mulled red wine. The stars glisten in the night sky, people are bundled up, buying presents and filled with delight. It seems too cheerful in the presence of the grim history we have seen today. And yet I know, from visiting Dora's museum, that every one of this village's schoolchildren has, since 1954, visited that camp, and since 1995, has ventured into the tunnels. They have encountered the relics of a horrific past, like many Germans who are facing their history. They, like the survivors of the camp—the Russian, Polish, French, Dutch, Jewish, Greek, Gypsy and German inmates who built the rockets in the depths of Mittelbau-Dora—live every day with the memory of those times.

A new generation of Germans is preserving the past in an effort to learn from it and to ensure that it is never repeated. I think about that as I sit in Neustadt's tiny church, surrounded by villagers raising their voices in song. As carols fill the air, I am reminded by those words of peace and love of the duality of the human heart. That gives me hope, even as I continue to be haunted by what I saw in the depths of the mountain.

CHAPTER TWELVE

THE LAST GERMAN CRUISER

MAS A TIERRA ISLAND OFF CHILE: MARCH 13, 1914

Kapitan zur See Fritz Emil von Lüdecke listened carefully as Leutnant Arnold Boker, standing rigidly at attention and breathless from his dash to the bridge, reported that he had sighted a British cruiser approaching their position. Turning his binoculars to the horizon, Lüdecke could make out the silhouette of the cruiser, black smoke from its funnels staining the morning sky. The enemy was heading straight for his position. The game was up after 21,000 nautical miles, two major sea battles and seven months of war. The German warship *Dresden* was trapped: her engines and boilers were worn out and her coal nearly gone, and the ship lay at anchor after three months of playing a game of hide-and-seek with the British.

Even as Lüdecke ordered the alarm to call the men to quarters, the smoke of another British ship appeared on the horizon, this one from the opposite direction. Then Lüdecke spotted the smoke of a third ship. Sharp whistle blasts ordered the crew to muster on the deck, but not at their battle stations. *Dresden* was, after all, off the coast of Chile in neutral waters, and was safe. The British could not take any hostile action against them.

Lüdecke watched in shock as a salvo of shells passed over *Dresden* and hit the steep cliffs off the starboard side. Another salvo screamed through the air, and this time the shells ripped into *Dresden*'s stern, mangling steel and men and sending a sheet of fire across the deck. *Dresden*'s gunners fired off three shots before British gunfire smashed the ship's guns at the stern, but Lüdecke's men were not at their stations. Most of them were piling into boats and leaping overboard, heading for shore on their captain's orders. With three British warships closing in, this was a fight Lüdecke knew he could not win.

The British cruisers circled the helpless German ship and kept pumping shells into the burning wreck. One witness later reported that the shells burst inside *Dresden* "with a sound like subterranean thunder." Flames were licking at two of the magazines, where what was left of the ammunition was stored, and Lüdecke knew he had to act. The enemy must not seize his ship. With what crew he had left, he had to open the ship's valves, set explosive charges and sink *Dresden*. That meant fighting through the fires and the smashed passageways to go below into the torn and broken hull. He also had to rescue the last men trapped in the burning hulk and take off the dead and wounded from the sinking ship.

To buy time, Lüdecke hoisted a signal calling for a cease-fire and surrender negotiations, and sent Oberleutnant zur See Wilhelm Canaris, in *Dresden*'s pinnace, over to HMS *Glasgow*. *Glasgow* ignored the signal, as did the cruiser HMS *Kent*. Captain Luce of *Glasgow* listened to the German officer's protests over the violation of Chilean sovereignty and replied that his orders were to sink *Dresden* and leave the rest to the diplomats. As the two men argued, *Glasgow* closed in and continued to pump shells into *Dresden*, raking the hull and sending debris flying.

Then, in a massive roar that shot out of the port side of the bow, *Dresden* shuddered as Lüdecke's scuttling charge detonated inside the No. 1 magazine. The forward casemate and its heavy guns blew out, and the bow was half torn off, leaving the rest of the hull open to the sea. It was 10:45 a.m.

At 11:15 a.m., *Dresden*'s bow slipped beneath the surface of Cumberland Bay. Striking the seabed, the bow twisted and tore free as

Dresden rolled to starboard. The ship was twice as long as the bay was deep, so instead of the stern rising dramatically into the air, the cruiser settled slowly by the stern. The shivering crew huddled on the beach and cheered a final explosion from a second scuttling charge deep within the engine room. Their ship, they felt, had died an honorable death, sunk by its crew rather than falling into enemy hands at the end of a long and eventful voyage. British sailors on *Glasgow* cheered, their ship's last shots insuring not just that the German cruiser sank but also exacting vengeance for the loss of British ships and sailors the last time their fleet had encountered *Dresden*.

THE LONG ODYSSEY OF *DRESDEN*

Built at the Hamburg yard of Blohm und Voss, which launched the half-completed hull in October 1907 and delivered it to the German Navy a year later, the 4,268-ton, 388-foot *Kleine Kreuzer* (small cruiser) *Dresden* was built to be a fast raider on the high seas rather than a rugged warrior built to slug it out with other warships. Modeled after the successful Confederate commerce raiders of the American Civil War, *Dresden*'s job was to range the oceans, seeking out the enemy's merchant fleet and sending its commerce to the bottom. *Dresden*'s steam turbines and four propellers drove the cruiser at speeds up to 25.2 knots. The cruiser carried ten 4-inch guns and eight smaller semiautomatic rapid-fire 2-inch guns, and could fire torpedoes from two tubes. If all else failed, or if they needed to save ammunition, the crew could ram and sink a ship with the huge cast-steel ram built into the bow

Troubles in the Caribbean, particularly a civil war in Mexico, where rebels fought to overthrow the despotic government of President Victoriano Huerta, sent *Dresden* there in December 1913. Remaining on station in the region through July, the cruiser spent considerable time in Veracruz protecting German citizens and commercial interests, particularly when the United States invaded it and seized the port and city to protect its interests. On July 20, when rebels toppled Huerta's government, *Dresden*'s captain took the Mexican president, his family

A 3-D model of the German cruiser Dresden. *Willi Kramer*

and staff aboard, then carried them to Jamaica, where the British government granted Huerta asylum.

   Dresden was due back in Germany for a much-needed refit, and on
July 26, rendezvoused with the new cruiser *Karlsruhe* to trade captains.
Dresden's new commander, Fritz Emil von Lüdecke, was to take the ship
back to Germany, but when war broke out in Europe a few days later, he
took *Dresden* to Brazil to attack British merchant ships. *Dresden* engaged
several British ships, sinking some but letting others go because they
carried cargo from countries not yet at war and, in one case, because the
ship was loaded with women and children, and Lüdecke was an officer
and gentleman of the old school with "incredible gallantry."

As British forces in the region mobilized to find and destroy *Dresden* and *Karlsruhe*, Lüdecke headed for the Pacific, steaming through the Straits of Magellan at the tip of South America in early September. There, at the Chilean port of Punta Arenas, Lüdecke received new orders to link up with Germany's East Asia Squadron.

The East Asia Squadron, under the command of Reichsgraf Maximilian von Spee, was Germany's only fleet in the Pacific. Based in Tsingtao, China, von Spee's ships included the armored cruisers *Scharnhorst* and *Gneisenau*, and the light cruisers *Emden*, *Leipzig* and *Nürnberg*. When the war began, von Spee ordered his squadron out to sea, realizing that the allied forces outnumbered and outgunned his ships, particularly after Japan entered the war on Britain's side.

Von Spee's squadron rendezvoused with *Dresden* at Easter Island in early October. Then they all then steamed for Chile and the island of Mas a Tierra. There, von Spee learned that a pursuing British squadron, under the command of Admiral Sir Christopher Cradock, had followed *Dresden* into the Pacific. Spee and his captains decided to head to the Chilean mainland port of Coronel, in the hope of finding and destroying HMS *Glasgow*, which was coaling there. Instead, they ran into most of the British squadron.

The two forces met in battle on the afternoon of November 1, 1914. The fight started with the Germans in a better position—the British were firing into the setting sun and could not see as well. Within a few hours, von Spee's ships had devastated Cradock's. Cradock's own ship, *Good Hope*, on fire and hit many times, exploded and sank with no survivors. HMS *Monmouth* also sank after a point-blank pounding from the German cruiser *Nürnberg*, which fired seventy-five rounds into the burning ship to finish it off; there were no survivors. The Battle of Coronel was the Royal Navy's first defeat at sea in over a century, and it filled the British with a strong desire for retribution.

After Coronel, von Spee kept his squadron in the Pacific to hunt the enemy, despite orders to return to Germany. When von Spee finally decided to move into the Atlantic, his procrastination had allowed the British enough time to create a new battle force, this one under the command of Vice-Admiral Frederick Sturdee. When von Spee and his ships arrived at the Falkland Islands to raid them, Sturdee and his fleet were waiting in ambush. The British cruisers could outrun and outgun the German ships, and in an unequal battle, Sturdee chased down and sank all but one of von Spee's fleet. The first to die was *Scharnhorst*, with von Spee aboard; there were no survivors. *Gneisenau* sank next after a hard fight; the British pulled only 190 of the 765 crew from the water, and many of the badly wounded Germans died after being rescued. The smaller cruisers—*Leipzig, Dresden* and *Nürnberg*—ran for it, but soon *Leipzig*, out of ammunition, her mainmast and two funnels shot away, and sinking, stopped dead in the water. There were only eighteen survivors. *Nürnberg* fought until two of her boilers exploded and British shells sank her, leaving only twelve survivors.

Of all of von Spee's squadron, only *Dresden* escaped the carnage, outrunning the pursuing British by sailing through bad weather that provided cover. The crew of *Dresden* ran with the bitter knowledge that they could do nothing to help the other German ships and that they had to try to escape to fight another day.

After returning to Punta Arenas for coal, *Dresden* steamed into the narrow channels of Tierra del Fuego, near Cape Horn, to hide from the British. For the next two months, British and other allied ships searched in vain for *Dresden*. But in early March, harassed by bad weather and with his crew restless, Lüdecke decided to return to the Pacific. He felt that they could not safely make it home by running across the Atlantic with so many ships hunting for them. His concerns were underscored on March 2, when the British cruisers *Kent* and *Glasgow* discovered *Dresden* in the channels of the Straits of Magellan and chased her at high speed for hours until Lüdecke outpaced them and escaped.

With only 80 tons of coal left, which was not enough to go anywhere, *Dresden* arrived at Mas a Tierra on March 8 with a rust-streaked hull and worn-out machinery. Lüdecke argued with Chilean authorities for more than the legal limit of twenty-four hours for a combatant to remain in a neutral port, claiming that his coal situation and the ship's condition required more time. He also radioed passing

Mike Fletcher geared up to dive on the German cruiser Dresden, *sunk off the coast of Chile. James P. Delgado*

ships in vain, seeking more coal to help them escape. But he also knew that as a last resort he could land his crew and intern them with the ship for the duration of the war.

The British intercepted one of *Dresden*'s radio calls for coal on March 13 and raced for Mas a Tierra. At 8:40 the next morning, *Kent* and *Glasgow*, along with the auxiliary cruiser *Orama*, sighted *Dresden* at anchor in Cumberland Bay and opened fire, despite the fact that they were violating Chile's neutrality and breaking international law. Less than three hours later, *Dresden*, shattered and burning, sank. Most of the crew had made it ashore and survived the final battle. They remained in Chile until 1919 as unwilling guests of the Chileans, interned in accord with the international agreements that the British had ignored. Some of the German officers escaped and made their way home to fight again in a war that would continue for three more years. But the sinking of *Dresden*, following the earlier destruction of *Emden* in the Indian Ocean, brought an end to the naval war in the Pacific. The last of the proud East Asia Squadron of the Reichsgraf von Spee lay rusting in the deep, a legacy for the future when explorers and archeologists would venture into the sea to reconstruct her final hours.

A FABLED ISLAND

The empty sea surrounds our ship for as far as the eye can see, nearly 500 miles off the coast of Chile. Our ship gently rolls in the swell as we drive west at 16 knots. The Armada de Chile (Chilean Navy) ship *Valdivia*, an amphibious landing ship, is a day out from Valparaiso, en route to the Archipelago de Juan Fernandez and an island with a romantic name and a famous history, Isla Robinson Crusoe (also known as Mas a Tierra). The island is one of the world's most inaccessible and remote places, home to some five hundred people and host to only a few hundred more each year. The tourists are mainly Chileans who come to visit the island's unique ecosystem or who are drawn, like others before them, by one of literature's most famous castaways, Daniel Defoe's Robinson Crusoe.

In addition to her other duties, *Valdivia* makes two trips to Isla Robinson Crusoe each year. The ship carries 177 passengers, as well as their baggage and other items and equipment that have no other way of reaching this isolated Chilean colony. Our *Sea Hunters* crew of eleven hauls tons of dive equipment, cameras and other gear into the large tank bay below the main deck and into our berths. Our team has come to dive and film an episode about the Imperial German Navy's small cruiser *Dresden,* eighty-eight years after she sank. We will be the first to dive down and return with detailed images and extensive footage of the wrecked warship in her grave 180 feet below the surface.

Our team includes Dr. Willi Kramer, the first German official to visit the wreck and the graves of some of *Dresden*'s sailors, who are buried ashore. Willi's professional expertise is Viking and medieval sites, but he now finds himself drawn around the world to document the legacy of the First World War.

After twenty-eight hours at sea, we catch our first glimpse of Isla Robinson Crusoe, rising faintly out of the mist on the horizon. As we approach the island, the ship rolling in the swell, we're struck by how small it is. Only 36 square miles in area and 2,800 feet above sea level at its highest peak, this island has, for all its isolation, long been a part of the world's consciousness. It is a storied island that features in tales of explorers, pirates and privateers, buried treasure, shipwrecks, castaways and sea battles. One nineteenth-century visitor, the writer Richard Henry Dana, called it "the most romantic spot of earth" because of its unique history and its association with the fabled Crusoe.

If this is an island of dreams and romance, it is because of the three-hundred-year-old tale of Robinson Crusoe and his real-life inspiration, Alexander Selkirk. A native of Largo, which is north of Edinburgh on the rugged Fife coast, Selkirk was a troubled lad who ran away from the censure of his village and found a haven in a life at sea. He fared well, advancing in rank from ship's boy to officer over the next several years. The lure of adventure and riches led him in 1703 to join a privateering venture into the Pacific led by William Dampier.

One man's privateer is another man's pirate, and Dampier's ships and crews faced the wrath of Spain, which controlled the Pacific to the extent that the ocean was known as a "Spanish lake." Thanks to Dampier's incompetence, the venture ended badly, with very little gained and a number of men lost. One of Dampier's ships, the privateer *Cinque Ports*, anchored at Mas a Tierra in October 1704, leaking and in bad condition. Her captain, Thomas Stradling, wanted to reprovision before heading south and trying for home. Selkirk, his sailing master (mate), was convinced that the ship would never reach a safe port and decided that he would rather stay on the island than take his chances at sea.

The captain was more than happy to leave the quarrelsome, headstrong Selkirk behind and so set him ashore with a few tools, his gun and bedding, and his Bible. As the ship's boat pulled away from the island, Selkirk regretted his decision and dashed into the surf, begging them to return. Stradling reportedly yelled back, "Stay where you are and may you starve!" Thus began a lonely exile that lasted four years and four months, until another English privateer, Woodes Rogers, landed for provisions. Rogers reported that "Immediately our pinnace return'd from the shore, and brought abundance of Craw-fish, with a man Cloth'd in Goat Skins, who look'd wilder than the first owners of them."

Selkirk sailed with Rogers and returned to a life of privateering in the Pacific before reaching London in 1711, eight years after he left England. He also brought home a small fortune from his years with Rogers. Selkirk's adventures were first recounted in Rogers's account of *A Cruzing Voyage Round the World* in 1712, and then again in 1713 in a short article by journalist Richard Steele in a magazine called *The Englishman*. But the story took on even greater fame in 1719, when author Daniel Defoe published *Robinson Crusoe*, based in part on Selkirk's adventures. The book was an immediate success; three hundred years later, it remains the second-most published book in the world, next only to the Bible, translated into most languages and available in nearly every country. Robinson Crusoe and the real-life Selkirk have also been the inspiration for other literary endeavors, paintings and movies—

and, in time, for the decision by the Chilean government, in the 1960s, to change the name Mas a Tierra to Isla Robinson Crusoe.

DIVING *DRESDEN*

Dresden rests beneath the waters of Cumberland Bay off Isla Robinson Crusoe. Every day, we load up one of *Valdivia*'s launches with dive gear and position ourselves over the wreck. Working with Willi Kramer and me, master diver Mike Fletcher breathes a complex mix of gases and descends to make the first survey the warship, relaying what he sees by video camera to the surface as we guide him through the ruined ship in the deep blue twilight below. It is far more difficult than this simple explanation—Mike is working hard, pulling 330 feet of heavy hose and electrical lines, clearing himself when they snag or catch on wreckage, and all the while using his eyes and experience along with ours to find and identify important areas of the ship, searching for clues about what happened in the final hours.

The dives are limited to 30 minutes, and then Mike has to decompress for more than twice that time to eliminate the deadly gas bubbles in his blood caused by the depth. In a series of later dives, Willi and I join Mike in surveying the wreck, slowly investigating the cruiser from bow to stern. Mike's son Warren is also diving, filming the scene from a distance to capture as much of the wreck and the survey action as he can. *Dresden* lies as she sank, pointing almost due north and towards the beach, resting on the starboard (right) side. The funnels and masts have fallen away and lie on the seabed. Some of the guns have ripped free of the deck and also lie on the bottom.

The bow is heavily damaged, and the severed end of it rests upright on the seabed. One of our first conclusions is that *Dresden* sank heavily by the bow, hitting the bottom of the bay with enough force to break off the huge steel ram at the bow. As the ship twisted and sank, the hull cracked and the decks opened up. But the damage is so severe that we wonder if hitting the bottom was responsible for all of it. Gradually, it becomes clear that the split decks and the ripped-out hull near the bow are the result of the massive internal explosions when the Germans' scuttling charges detonated. Despite the damage, one anchor remains on the deck, at the ready. A long string of anchor chain trails off the bow and heads off into the gloom of deeper water, where the anchor that held *Dresden* in place when the cruiser sank remains set in the sand.

The bridge is gone but the wood decking remains in place under the debris of broken steel, torn wiring, machinery and loose fittings. The stub of the aft mast rises up out of the deck, and the broken main-mast, lying in two pieces, rests on the deck at an angle. We see three empty cartridge shells, and I am tempted by the thought that they might just be from those three shots that *Dresden*'s crew managed to fire before the ship sank. But an even more interesting discovery awaits us. Nearby, still in place, is the cruiser's auxiliary steering station, a paired set of steering wheels that stops Mike in his tracks as we all admire them.

A 4-inch gun, possibly hit by British shellfire, angles inward and points at *Dresden*'s deck. I count three perfectly spaced shell holes, one after the other, along the ship's hull towards the casemate, which is partially collapsed. At least it is still here. Its partner, the forward case-mate on the port side, is gone—gun, thick armor and all—disintegrated by the scuttling explosions. The level of damage is greater than we had expected. Accounts of the battle emphasize that after a few hits on the stern and on the deck guns, *Dresden* sank intact when the crew set off a scuttling charge deep in the hull. But what we are finding is evidence of a sustained shelling and at least two massive internal explosions. The entire aft section is heavily damaged, with the main deck gone, shell holes in the steel plates that lie inside the ship's exposed interior, and plates bent out near the aft port casemate from an internal explosion.

Lying amidst the wreckage is a German sailor's boot. Willi Kramer believes it to be the evidence of a dead man. Fifteen of *Dresden*'s crew died, thirteen in the battle and two who succumbed later from their wounds. Willi reminds us that as floating men die, their bodies relax and their boots fall off. Hundreds of boots lie around the Second

World War wreck of the German battleship *Bismarck* in the North Atlantic, grim testimony to the majority of the crew who perished while bobbing in the cold, oil-stained waters. This solitary shoe on the deck of *Dresden* is a reminder of the individual cost of war, just as the broken hulk of the cruiser is a reminder of the larger costs and waste of war.

Our survey of the wreck indicates that the history books have not told the complete story. It is evident that many shots went into *Dresden*, even as she sank. The British cruiser commanders had orders to sink *Dresden*, and they made sure they did just that. The extent of the damage makes us wonder just how close they came to the German cruiser. Historical accounts and maps of the battle show *Glasgow*, *Kent* and *Orama* outside of Cumberland Bay, firing at *Dresden* from a distance of 9,000 yards, but what we are seeing argues against that. Willi and I, with John Davis, decide to go ashore and search the cliffs for some of the shells fired during the battle and which, according to the locals, are still here.

Moving along the beach, outside of town and past the cemetery with its monument to three of *Dresden*'s dead crew, we find our first shell hole. It is nearly perfectly round and has bored 3 feet into the cliff. Buried inside, we find the steel base of an unexploded shell. We wonder if this is one of *Dresden*'s, so we measure it—at 6 inches it is too big to be from *Dresden*, whose largest guns fired a 4-inch projectile. This is a British 6-inch shell that missed. Imbedded in the cliff's soft volcanic rock and mud, it is more than a relic of the battle. It is a piece of forensic evidence that we are using to reconstruct what happened. Plotting the angle that the shell came from, we line it up with the cape at the entrance to the bay, just where a ship would turn to enter the anchorage. This could be one of the first shots fired at 8:40 on the morning of March 14, 1914, as the British sailed into range and opened up with their guns. We find five other hits, closely spaced as if from a salvo of rapidly fired shots. One hole retains its shell; the others are empty, shells tumbled out by erosion or pulled free by souvenir hunters not realizing what a deadly trophy they had in an unexploded live shell.

Back on board *Valdivia,* we work with the ship's officers to add the location of the shells to our survey map of the bay and the wreck. We also plot the range and bearing of the shellfire, based on the position and angle of the shell holes. The last five holes we found must have come from shells fired near the end of the battle, because our plots show that the British cruiser that fired them was very close to the sinking *Dresden*—in fact, just about where we are anchored in *Valdivia,* 800 feet off *Dresden*'s port side and just 2,500 feet away from the cliff. These last shell holes indicate that one of the cruisers sailed into the bay, broadside to *Dresden,* and opened up a final salvo or series of salvoes that ripped into the foundering German ship. The shots that missed drove deep into the cliff, where we found them.

The next day, we journey to the other side of the bay to search the cliffs there. We are rewarded with the discovery of more shell holes and unexploded shells, indicating that the British cruisers engaged in a deadly crossfire. In a brilliant but brutal tactical maneuver, *Glasgow* circled *Dresden* and pumped lethal rounds into the anchored German warship. Captain Luce of *Glasgow* had orders to sink *Dresden,* and he took no chances, firing at point-blank range even after the last Germans abandoned their ship.

Dresden is a ruin. Some of the destruction was caused by the shelling, some of it by the deep internal explosions caused by the scuttling charges but some of it appears to be from a much later attempt to blast open the sunken cruiser's stern. This damage puzzles us, because history records no attempt to salvage *Dresden.* Indeed, for many years, the cruiser's decks were beyond the reach of divers. What happened to the stern—which is intact in photographs of the sinking cruiser—remains a mystery. Later, Willi Kramer finds a formerly top-secret document in the German naval archives that suggests *Dresden* was carrying gold coin pulled out of Germany's Tsingtao bank accounts by von Spee. That would explain why we were not the first divers to explore the wreck. Someone has secretly blasted open the stern to get at the gold. We wonder when this was, and how the salvagers knew about the gold, given that the only record is a top-secret piece of paper.

One possibility, shades of *Raiders of the Lost Ark,* is that it was the Nazis, eager to recover some of Germany's lost riches to fund their preparations for war. We may never know.

But what is clear is that the sea has claimed *Dresden* after her final battle. Slumbering in the depths, the broken hulk is an undersea museum, a war grave and an evocative relic of the destruction of war. And yet, in the middle of the debris, Mike spots a small, unbroken flower vase. It is an unexpected find, this delicate survivor. It is also a reminder of the touches of home and life ashore that often accompany sailors on warships on their distant journeys, even into death.

— CHAPTER THIRTEEN —

ARCTIC *FOX*

THE HIGH ARCTIC: MAY 5, 1859

As the sledge bumped and slid across the frozen ground of the Arctic, Lieutenant William Hobson's eyes swept the surrounding area searching for signs of the lost expedition led by Sir John Franklin. Cakes and slabs of ice piled up along the shore separated the snow-covered land from the frozen sea. Hobson, however, kept his gaze fixed on a pile of rocks in the distance, close to the shore. No accident of nature, that rock pile was a cairn, and Hobson hoped that other explorers, perhaps even Sir John Franklin and his men, had deposited records or notes in it, the usual practice in the Arctic. For many days, Hobson had followed a faint trail of scattered relics and broken bones to this spot. Little did he realize that the quest to discover the fate of Franklin, upon which he and his captain, Francis Leopold McClintock, had embarked, was about to reach its climax.

Pulling apart the top of the cairn, Hobson found a small tin canister. He opened it and reached inside to pull out a rolled-up sheet of yellowed, rust-stained paper. As he read it, Hobson realized that these were words from beyond the grave and that in the sparest of sentences, they told what had happened to the lost Franklin expedition:

25th April 1848. H.M. Ships Terror and Erebus were deserted on the 22nd April, 5 leagues NNW of this, having been beset since 12th Sept. 1846. The officers & crew consisting of 105 souls under the command of Captain F.R.M. Crozier, landed here.

Sir John Franklin died on the 11th June, 1847 and the total loss by deaths in the expedition has been to this date 9 officers & 15 men.

F.R.M. Crozier
Captain & Senior Officer

And start on tomorrow 26th for Back's Fish River
James Fitzjames
Captain H.M.S. Erebus

THE SEARCH FOR FRANKLIN

In 1845, *Erebus* and *Terror,* commanded by F.R.M. Crozier and James Fitzjames, had sailed from Britain under the overall command of Captain Sir John Franklin, a veteran of three Arctic expeditions, to map the last unknown waters of the Canadian Arctic archipelago and to complete the transit of the elusive Northwest Passage, for which the English had been searching for nearly three centuries.

Most of the Northwest Passage had been mapped by the Royal Navy and explorers from the Hudson's Bay Company, but the last link— a blank spot on the map—remained. So what was envisioned by the British as the final Arctic expedition set sail under the experienced Franklin and his crew, many of them also veterans of Arctic forays, in two well-equipped ships, "to forge the last link." But after entering Lancaster Sound from Baffin Bay in the summer of 1845, *Erebus* and *Terror* were never seen or heard from again.

For more than a decade, thirty-one expeditions, both public and private, British and American, searched in vain for Franklin. Tantalizing

An engraving of Fox *trapped in the Arctic ice. Vancouver Maritime Museum.*

clues—three graves on a small Arctic beach, relics bought from the Inuit, and disturbing stories told by the Inuit of ships trapped in ice, of men struggling to march overland and dying along the way, and of cannibalism and murder—filled the years of searching, but no conclusive evidence—wrecked ships or records of the Franklin expedition—had been found. Lady Jane Franklin, wife of the missing explorer, pushed the British government to keep on looking, even after a large search expedition in 1854 ended with the loss of several ships: "The final and exhaustive search is all I seek on behalf of the first and only martyrs to Arctic discovery in modern times, and it is all I ever intend to ask."

But Britain had sacrificed much to search for Franklin, and now, in 1854, was caught up in an expensive war on Russia's Crimean Peninsula. *Blackwood's Edinburgh Magazine* summed up what Britain had gained, at great cost: "No; there are no more sunny continents—no more islands of the blessed—hidden under the far horizon, tempting the dreamer over the undiscovered sea; nothing but these weird and tragic shores, whose cliffs of everlasting ice and mainlands of frozen snow, which have never produced anything to us but a late and sad discovery of depths of human heroism, patience, and bravery, such as imagination could scarcely dream of."

In April 1857, the British government informed Lady Franklin that they had "come, with great regret, to the conclusion that there was no prospect of saving life, [and] would not be justified . . . in exposing the lives of officers and men to the risk inseparable from such an enterprise." But the determination of Lady Franklin and her years of urging on the search for her missing husband and his men touched many heartstrings. So, when the British government gave its final refusal, Lady Franklin made a public plea and raised nearly £3,000 to send out her own search expedition. She bought the steam yacht *Fox*, a 120-foot, Scottish-built vessel, from the estate of Sir Richard Sutton, a master of the traditional hunt who had named the ship for his favorite quarry.

Lady Franklin placed *Fox* under the command of Captain Francis Leopold McClintock, a veteran of two Arctic voyages in search of Franklin. At his direction, shipyard workers stripped off the fancy fittings of the yacht, strengthened the hull with extra layers of planking to protect it from the ice, enlarged the boiler, sheathed the bow in iron "until it resembled a ponderous chisel set up edgeways" and braced the hull to keep it from being crushed when frozen in for the winter in the pack ice. McClintock explained: "Internally she was fitted up with the strictest economy in every sense, and the officers were crammed into pigeon-holes, styled cabins, in order to make room for provisions and stores; our mess-room, for five persons, measured 8 feet square."

The *Illustrated London News* also described *Fox*: "There is very little ornament about her, but what she has is in wonderfully good condition. The *Fox* has three slender, rather raking masts, is of topsail schooner rig, and small poop aft. She is rather sharp forward and her bows are plated over with iron . . . She looks not unlike a bundle of heavy handspikes, iron pointed at each end, for fending off drift ice."

McClintock and his officers and crew all volunteered their services without pay. For two long years they would endure hardship, cold, near shipwreck and three deaths on their quest to find Franklin.

Fox steamed out of Scotland on June 30, 1857, but when she reached the Canadian Arctic, was stopped in Baffin Bay by the early onset of winter and was trapped in the ice. There was nothing to do but dig in and wait, drifting with the ice pack. It was an occasionally harrowing eight-month ordeal, in which the boredom of confinement gave way to the terror of moving ice. After drifting 1,194 miles, the chance to escape came at last in late April. As *Fox* fought for eighteen hours to be free, ice constantly struck the hull, causing "the vessel to shake violently, the bells to ring, and almost knocked us off our legs." McClintock commented, "I can understand how men's hairs have turned grey in a few hours." The ice, when it hit the stern, wrenched the rudder and stopped the propeller: "deprived of the one or the other, even for half an hour, I think our fate would have been sealed."

Once free of the ice, *Fox* headed to Greenland for more supplies. After sending letters home to explain why they would be gone longer than planned, McClintock and his crew turned west again for the Canadian Arctic. In the Arctic archipelago, McClintock explored the shores of Somerset Island and Bellot Strait before anchoring *Fox* near the eastern entrance to the narrow strait. With the ship frozen in for the winter, McClintock prepared to sledge west over the ice and land to reach King William Island, where a few years earlier, Hudson's Bay Company explorer Dr. John Rae had met some Inuit who told him about men whose ships, trapped in ice, had been abandoned. The men, trekking south, were starving and many had fallen on their march. Some had resorted to cannibalism. The Inuit had a number of items belonging to the dead men that Rae bought from them, including the personal effects of several of Franklin's officers and Franklin himself. The story, when it reached England along with the "relics," excited great interest and horror. Now McClintock, Lieutenant William Hobson and Sailing Master Allen Young would head off in three separate parties to search the region to see what they could find.

On his journey, McClintock learned from Inuit that two ships had been trapped by ice near King William Island, that one had sunk in deep water and that "all the white men went away to the large river, taking a boat or boats with them, and that in the following winter their bones were found there." The Inuit had salvaged steel and wood from the doomed expedition, and as McClintock pushed farther south, he found Inuit who had in their possession silver spoons and forks "bearing the crests or initials" of Franklin and some of his officers, as well as "uniform and other buttons" and wood from a ship. They told McClintock about a ship, pushed onto shore by the ice, where they had gathered their treasures.

McClintock continued on to King William Island, where he and his party found more relics, and finally, on May 25, "when slowly walking along a gravel ridge near the beach, which the winds kept partially bare of snow, I came upon a human skeleton, partly exposed, with here and there a few fragments of clothing appearing through the snow," McClintock also recovered a notebook that yielded up a few sentences about abandoning the ships and ended with a scrawled: "Oh death, whare [sic] is thy sting?" He found a hairbrush and comb, and from the fragments of the uniform, deduced that it was the skeleton of a steward or officer's servant from the Franklin expedition. As McClintock stood looking at the bones, he recalled the words of an old Inuit woman he had questioned: "They fell down and died as they walked along."

When McClintock headed north, back up King William Island to return to *Fox*, he made a last poignant discovery: a ship's boat, laden with equipment and spare clothing, and two more skeletons, one wrapped in clothing and furs. After loading up a small quantity of items—silverware and ship's instruments—McClintock continued his search for the wrecked ship. Instead, he found a pile of goods, stashed on the shore by the Franklin expedition. Plucking more relics from the pile, McClintock travelled back to *Fox*, arriving on June 19. When warm weather returned in July, McClintock reassembled the steam machinery laid up for the winter, and *Fox* set off for home.

McClintock, Hobson and the crew of *Fox* reached England in September 1859 with relics of the doomed expedition and the "last note." The tiny yacht, its commander and crew made headlines around the world. Parliament rewarded *Fox*'s crew with a payment of £5,000, and in 1860 the Queen knighted McClintock. Subsequently promoted to admiral, McClintock enjoyed a long career, serving as commander of the West Indies and the North American station for the Royal Navy and as an honored Fellow of the Royal Geographical Society before his death in 1907.

Fox outlived McClintock by five years, a surprising fact considering that most ships have short lives, particularly those that work in the Arctic. Sold to Danish owners in 1860, the tough little steamer carried supplies up and down the Greenland coast for the next fifty-two years. The end for Fox came when she went aground on the west Greenland coast in June 1912. After getting off and returning to Qeqertarsuaq (Disko Island), the damaged Fox was discovered by surveyors to be beyond repair. And so the famous ship, stripped of her fittings, was beached in a small cove near the harbor entrance. There, lying half submerged on the starboard side, the hulk slowly deteriorated.

Even in death, however, Fox attracted visitors drawn by the vessel's fame. Arctic explorer Donald MacMillan photographed the wreck in 1926, dismasted but still solid, though the local Inuit had been salvaging loose wood from the hull. Accounts of visitors to Qeqertarsuaq mentioned the wreck through the 1930s, but in 1931 and 1934, visiting naturalist Tom Longstaff boarded the hulk to find it breaking apart. He pulled two oak treenails from the hull as souvenirs. In 1940, Fox finally broke apart when a spring storm swept into the harbor and smashed up the deteriorated hull, leaving, one account reported, "only parts of the metal engine" behind.

FOX AT QEQERTARSUAQ

The cold spume of the sea sprays over the deck as the bow of Mary West buries itself in a wave. The wind whips around, chilling us to the bone, as we stand clustered on the small deck of the fishing boat. We're two hours out of Aasiaat, a mainland port, making our way to Qeqertarsuaq, sailing across the waters of Disko Bugt, a bay that cuts into the western coast of Greenland above the 69th parallel. Icebergs, large and small, fill the sea, most of them towering above our deck. It is the height of the brief Arctic summer, and yet the temperature hovers just above 30°F.

Qeqertarsuaq, a small port community of a thousand, is more than two hundred years old. Founded by Danish traders and whalers, it was named Gødhavn, or "good harbor," by them. Later known as Lievely, it became a major port of call for Danish, British and American whalers working in Arctic waters. Now known by its original name of Qeqertarsuaq, the settlement survives on fishing, hunting, tourism and the presence of the Arktisk Station—the Danish Polar Scientific Station of the University of Copenhagen. Founded in 1906, it remains a center for Arctic research, hosting two hundred visiting scientists a year. It will be our home for the next week as we venture out to find and dive on the wreck of *Fox*.

We've traveled to this remote spot in search of a famous ship-wreck for *The Sea Hunters*. This is our northernmost adventure. The team includes Mike Fletcher, his son Warren (our dive co-coordinator and underwater cameraman), land cameramen Marc Pike and camera and soundman John Rosborough. We rendezvoused in Iqaluit, the capital of Nunavut, where we took a small chartered plane across Baffin Bay to Aasiaat, where we boarded *Mary West* for the last leg of a thirty-six-hour trip.

Aasiaat, a small coastal settlement, allows the team to either famil iarize, or in some cases, like mine, to refamiliarize, ourselves with the Arctic. For me, that involves a walk to the harbor front where Inuit hunters and fishermen are busy butchering fish and seals. One of the great deli-cacies of the Arctic is raw fresh seal—or so I've been told, somehow having missed this treat on previous northern expeditions. But now, standing on the shores of Aasiaat, with John Rosborough pointing a running camera right at me, how can I refuse the bloody chunk of fresh seal liver that the cheerful hunter is offering me?

With a smile, I pop the oozing morsel into my mouth, slowly savor-ing each chewy bite. I must look like I really enjoy it, because my gracious host cuts off a bit of fresh seal blubber and hands it to me. It truly is an honor and a gift not to be refused, so I pop that in, too, finishing off my snack by smacking my lips and licking the blood and glistening fat off my fingertips. He offers me another bite, but I politely decline with "Thanks, I've already had a big lunch." We both laugh. Feeling fully reintegrated with the Arctic and like I've just swallowed a glass of oil in which sardines have been soaked, I rejoin the rest of the crew for the voyage across Disko Bay.

Qeqertarsuaq is a beautiful town, nestled against high cliffs that at present are carpeted with a summer bloom of grass and flowers. The tops of the cliffs are capped with snow, and in the distance, the solid mass of a glacier that covers the center of the island gleams in the sunlight. The houses, built on the crests of the rocks that line the coast and on the small bay that forms the harbor, are a well-kept array of brightly painted red, blue, green, orange and yellow buildings. Some of them, like the Qeqertarsuaq Museum, are old, dating to the nineteenth century. The museum, formerly the home of the *inspektor*, the government official in charge of this coast, was built in 1840. Solidly constructed of heavy beams atop a stone foundation, its red walls now contain displays that tell the history of the settlement's Inuit and Danish inhabitants.

Here, we meet the museum's director, Elisa Evaideen, and Karl Tobiassen, "an old Greenlander" who knows where all the wrecks on the coast are. Karl points across the harbor to a small cove, known to the locals as K'uigssarssuak, and says that that is where *Fox* ended her days. More surprisingly, he also tells us that, on the way in, we'd passed a small island, Qeqertaq, where a tall, red-painted metal stack stands as a navigational marker. It is the smokestack or funnel of *Fox*, taken off the wreck and recycled. Nothing goes to waste in the Arctic.

With the help of our host, the Arktisk Station, and its director, Bente Jessen Graae, we borrow an inflatable boat to reach the wreck site. We refill our dive tanks every day at the local fire hall (there are no dive shops north of 60 degrees). All this helps us to take advantage of the rare opportunity to dive down into history beneath the waters of the Arctic. Pulling into K'uigssarssuak's small cove, we realize we will not have to search for the wreck—the tip of *Fox*'s boiler rises out of the water at low tide. Wedged into the rocks, just where we've tied up our boat,

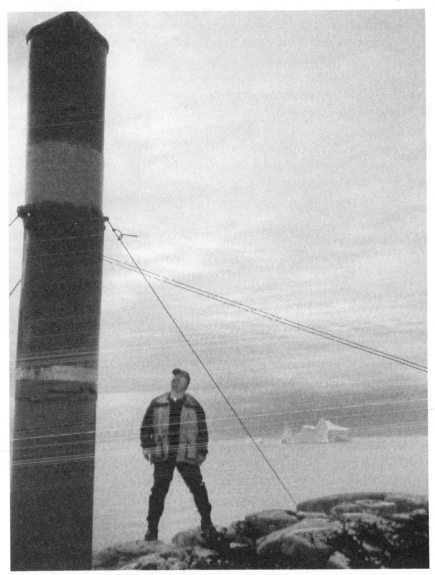

James Delgado beside the smokestack or funnel of Fox, now serving as a navigational marker in Qeqertarsuaq harbor in Greenland. Mike Fletcher.

are *Fox*'s hawse pipes, the iron sleeves that once protected the wooden hull from the anchor chain. Pulled free of the wreck after *Fox* broke up, they were probably left here for salvage and then abandoned, just like the boiler. Wooden hull planking lies on the beach, nearly perfectly preserved. Close by is a section of *Fox*'s wrought-iron propeller shaft. I'm worried that the hulk, which broke apart in 1940, has been picked away and that nothing but the boiler remains. There's only one way to find out, though. Pulling on our thick dry suits to keep out the freezing water and our heavy gear, Mike, Warren and I step off into the numbingly cold water and drop down to the bottom to see what remains of *Fox*.

The rocks that surround the resting place of *Fox* are worn and rounded by the ice, and covered with slippery seaweed. We follow the rocks down to the sand and gravel seabed, 16 feet below. The cold bites into me, right through the thick layers of the dry suit and the protective "woolies" beneath it. My lips and cheeks, the only bare skin exposed to the sea, throb with the cold, then quickly turn numb.

The water is relatively clear, and ahead we see the ship's boiler, completely submerged at high tide. Lying in the sand next to it are the shattered remains of the stern: broken timbers, twisted bronze bolts and a massive iron yoke that once reinforced the rudder. Nearby, a large iron pulley, part of the ship's steering apparatus, lies atop fallen timbers. We swim past the boiler as Warren films the scene. The boiler has been torn free of its mount in the hull and dragged here to the stern, probably by the ice that buries the wreck each winter. The thick iron is ripped and part of the boiler gapes open, exposing the fire tubes inside it. Coal-fired heat once flowed through those tubes to make the steam that powered *Fox*, but now they lie cold and dead in the shattered remains of the ship-wreck. Trailers of weed drape the boiler, and small fish dart into the protection of the dark boiler as we swim by.

The keel and keelson that formed the sturdy backbone of *Fox* lie before us, along with the collapsed starboard side of the hull, partially buried in the sand and the mats of algae that blanket the bottom of the cove. The current sweeps through the wreck, exposing brief glimpses of dark oak, rusted iron, and the shrouded shapes of frames (the "ribs" of the ship) and planks. As Mike and Warren videotape the wreck, I work quickly with a measuring tape and use a pencil to make notes and draw what I see on a sheet of frosted Mylar taped to a plastic clipboard. My notes, together with the video images and the photographs I am also taking, will help us to assemble a map of the broken-up ship, replicating on paper what we see in the gloom of the cove. I am particularly keen to capture as much information as possible because *Fox*'s plans vanished many years ago.

Astonishingly, half of *Fox* survives, pressed into the seabed by years of ice pushing into this small cove. It is an unexpected boon. The ice has flattened the curving side of the hull, shattering the thick layers of planks that formed it and wrenching the bolts out of the timber. And yet much survives, telling us a great deal about the ship. One of the keys to *Fox*'s survival in the Arctic was the original hull laid down in the Aberdeen shipyard of Alexander Hall & Company. From what remains, I can see that it was formed from diagonally laid planks of Scottish larch, fastened with thick bronze bolts to make a tightly sealed hull with the strength of an interwoven basket. Over these planks, McClintock had the shipyard fasten two layers of thick planks to sheath the hull against the ice. Splintered and torn, one layer of these planks remains in place, held on by the stubs of tough oak treenails that pegged them to the hull. The hull itself was formed from thick curved frames of oak, tightly spaced to make an almost solid wall of wood. Rows of iron stanchions were set into the hull at McClintock's suggestion to brace *Fox* against the crushing pressure of the ice.

But as I examine and document these sturdy features, Warren Fletcher finds a reminder of the exquisite handicraft of the yacht builders. Lying loose on a section of the hull is a small, beautifully lathed and decorated deadeye from the ship's rigging. Deceptively strong despite its delicate carving, it has that extra touch that befits a gentleman's yacht. Somehow, perhaps because its lignum vitae wooden heart was stout, the deadeye was kept when many other "decorations" were stripped off for the difficult Arctic voyage.

The steam engine's parts lie scattered nearby. As I swim over them, I think of the famous voyage of 1857–59. At the end of the expedition, as the crew prepared to leave their frozen berth and make their way home with the news of the fate of the Franklin expedition, the steam engine lay stowed in the hold, disassembled to keep it from cracking in the freezing months of winter. The ship's engineer had died, so McClintock had to put the engine back together and fire it up to escape the Arctic. Looking at the scattered pieces of machinery lying on the timbers of the hull like a three-dimensional jigsaw puzzle, I am reminded of what a talented and determined man Francis Leopold McClintock was.

Over the course of a week, we make more dives, sometimes surfacing in the bright twilight of the midnight sun as we work around the clock to gather as many images and as much information as we can. We may not only be the first but perhaps the only team of divers, and me the only archeologist, to visit *Fox* at the bottom of the sea. Even in the twenty-first century, this is a distant, hard to reach spot.

After surfacing on my final dive, I look out at the wind-whipped waters of Qeqertarsuaq's harbor. Ice is drifting in, in small chunks, and the sun has gone, replaced by gray skies. Snow dusts the cliffs above the settlement. Winter is on its way, and soon the wreck will again be covered by many feet of ice. Slowly, inexorably being ground away by the forces of winter, *Fox* is returning to the elements in the Arctic where she gained international fame and spent most of her working life. It is a perfect grave for this polar explorer, and as I float over it, I think of Sir John Franklin's epitaph, carved in marble over his empty crypt at Westminster Abbey:

> Not here: the white North has thy bones; and thou,
> Heroic Sailor-Soul,
> Art passing on thine happier voyage now
> Towards no earthly pole.

CHAPTER FOURTEEN

A CIVIL WAR SUBMARINE

A MYSTERY IN PANAMA

Standing on the hot sand beach of San Telmo, a small deserted island in the Bay of Panama, I look out at the water. Nothing. Not a thing to be seen, and yet here, according to the locals, lies the wreck of a "Japanese two-man submarine," sent in secret to attack the Pacific entrance to the Panama Canal. An unlikely tale, to be sure, but after a few years of sea hunting with Clive Cussler, I've come to realize that the truth is often stranger than fiction.

The tide starts to drop, and suddenly, I see a rusted bit of metal sticking up out of the surf. As the water continues to recede, the unmistakable form of a submarine emerges, dripping wet, stained red and orange with corrosion. But it looks nothing like a Japanese midget submarine of the Second World War. In fact, it looks nothing like most submarines I've ever seen, save one, a turn-of-the-century precursor to the sub *Holland I*. That 60-odd-foot submersible, the first of the Royal Navy's fleet of submarines, is preserved ashore at the Royal Navy Submarine Museum in Gosport, England, not far from where navy divers discovered the sunken *Holland I* and raised her for exhibition.

But while this looks a little like *Holland I* and its numerous early sister subs, the products of the genius of an eccentric Irish-American

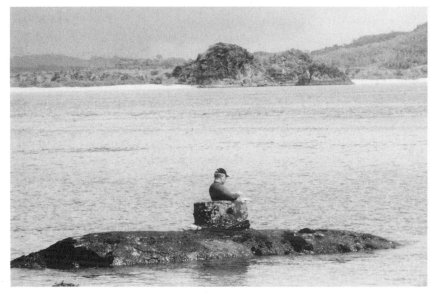

James Delgado in the hatch of Sub Marine Explorer *in Panama. Photo by Ann Goodhart*

inventor, John Holland, it's not one of his. It is simply too small. Football shaped, with a low conning tower, this riveted iron craft looks like something out of *20,000 Leagues Under the Sea*.

Wading out into the ocean, I splash in water up to my chest to reach the wreck. As the sea washes over and around the hull, I can see that it is firmly bedded down in the sand and that the sea has opened a hole in the iron plates that form the hull. Crawling inside, and ignoring the pain as the sharp metal bites deeply into a shin, I ponder the spider-web lattice of thick iron bars that brace the chamber. I've never seen anything like it. The hull form looks to be from around the year 1900, but these iron bars look like they've been forged with a heavy hammer, like something out of the 1850s. After crawling out and nicking myself again, I scramble up the slippery top of the submarine to reach the conning tower. It is small, barely big enough for me to fit, and as I look in, I hear the booming of the surf and feel a rush of cool salty air hit my face. There's more than one hole in this hull.

Balancing myself on my hands, I drop into the hatch. My feet catch on a lip—the seat for another, inner hatch, perhaps. But it is missing, and so, camera in one hand, I carefully line myself up and drop into what I hope will be chest-high water. It turns out to be only waist deep. My feet hit sand, and I'm suddenly in darkness as my eyes adjust. I grab my camera and hit the flash, and see that I'm in an iron cavern that's dripping with water and rust. I hit the flash again and look into the water. I wish I hadn't. This submarine, half filled with sand, looks like a perfect haven for the region's well known venomous sea snakes. At this moment, I know exactly how Indiana Jones felt in the Well of Souls. "Snakes. Why did it have to be snakes?" I jump up, catch the lip of the hatch and pull myself out of the hull just as my imagination pictures a tiny pair of fanged jaws reaching for my ankle. As I jump off the sub and wade to shore, I speculate about just what it is I've found on this deserted beach. Whose ancient submarine is it, and how did it end up here?

The truth is often stranger than fiction. A return trip to the beach in November 2002, this time armed with a tape measure and a pad for making notes, gives me more than a basic understanding of the submarine. I e-mail photographs of it around the world to colleagues who study old submarines. No one can figure it out, though one researcher, Gene Canfield, says it looks similar to *Intelligent Whale*, a submarine built for the Union Navy during the Civil War but never finished. Could it be that old? I wonder as I continue to send out my queries. Then, in mid-2003, I get an answer from Rich Wills, who thinks it looks more like another long-forgotten Civil War submarine, the *Sub Marine Explorer*. No one knows what happened to that sub, Rich explains. After the war, it ended up in Panama, working for the Pacific Pearl Company, harvesting pearls from deep-water oyster beds.

I sit up and take notice. After all, the wreck lies in the Bay of Panama, in an island group known as the Pearl Archipelago. But is it really a Civil War submarine that vanished from the pages of history after 1869? Could a submarine survive, half submerged on a tropical beach, for more than 130 years? Rich sends me a copy of a 1902 article on pioneer submarines of the nineteenth century. It reproduces a profile plan of *Sub*

Marine Explorer and gives its basic dimensions. As I look at it, I smile. The profile matches perfectly, down to the placement and size of the conning tower. The rounded chamber at the top of the submarine with the forged iron braces would be filled with air for buoyancy. And, as I compare the measurements with my notes, it all fits. The 36-foot *Sub Marine Explorer* is a perfect match.

But how does *Sub Marine Explorer* fit into the history of submarine development? Built in 1865, what role did it play, if any, in the Civil War? And how does it compare with another recent discovery, the Confederate Civil War submarine *H.L. Hunley?* Found after years of hard work by Clive Cussler's National Underwater and Marine Agency team and raised by the State of South Carolina, *Hunley* is one of the great archeological treasures of the Civil War, on a par with the ironclad USS *Monitor,* whose engine and turret have also been pulled from the depths. Even as I sit pondering the mysteries of *Sub Marine Explorer,* a team of archeologists is carefully excavating and dismantling *Hunley* to reveal its secrets. So for the answers on *Sub Marine Explorer,* I turn to *Hunley* project historian Mark Ragan. "There's no one better," Clive tells me as he reads Ragan's number to me over the phone.

Mark answers his phone with a laconic drawl that quickens with excitement as I tell him what I've found on a Panamanian beach. I e-mail him a handful of photos, and as he opens them on his computer 3,000 miles away, I hear the subtle but sharp intake of his breath. That's a good thing, because Clive is right. No one knows Civil War submarines better than Mark Ragan. He literally wrote the book on them, and he now turns his considerable energy and skill to dig deep into the archives to learn more about *Sub Marine Explorer* and its inventor, a forgotten American engineering genius named Julius H. Kroehl.

PIONEER SUBMARINES

War spurs terrible and magnificent inventions, often taking ideas and concepts developed in peacetime and testing them hurriedly in times of crisis. During the Civil War, technology played a significant role. Among other innovations, the war introduced new guns and more powerful cannon, ironclad warships with rotating turrets, undersea mines—and the submarine. There was nothing new about each of these inventions save their first practical and deadly use in combat. The pioneering naval accomplishments of the war started with the attack on the wooden fleet of the Union Navy at Hampton Roads, Virginia, by the Confederate ironclad CSS *Virginia*, demonstrating that this new type of warship doomed the "wooden walls" that had dominated naval warfare for centuries. The first clash between ironclads took place when the Union's USS *Monitor* interceded between *Virginia* and the Union wooden fleet the following day and fought the Confederate ship to a standstill.

Another innovation was the use of an electrically detonated "torpedo," or mine, one of which sent the Union's ironclad *Cairo* to the bottom of the Yazoo River, giving the ill-fated gunboat the dubious distinction of being the first warship in history to be sunk by a mine. Later, there was the brave but doomed sortie of the Confederate submarine *H.L. Hunley* into Charleston Harbor to sink the Union warship *Housatonic* with a spar-mounted "torpedo" projecting from her bow. Shortly after this victory, *Hunley* sank, taking her crew with her, just a few hundred yards from her victim. No one knows why *Hunley* sank, but the tiny craft gained fame as the first submarine to destroy an enemy vessel in combat. Quickly buried by silt, *Hunley*'s grave remained undiscovered for 150 years.

As for submarines, both sides embraced this new technology. Inventors proposed various underwater craft and built some that operated with various levels of success, killing their builders and crews on more than one occasion. A number of projects were launched, some in secrecy, others more publicly, leaving behind an unfortunately incomplete record of pioneer submarines and submariners. But the rediscovery of Julius Kroehl's *Sub Marine Explorer* and a slow unraveling of his wartime career, buried in the National Archives, suggests that at every step of the way, as the Confederates developed both their "torpedoes" and submarines, Kroehl was there to develop something to counter them for the Union side. It may well be one of the last great untold stories of the Civil War.

Julius Kroehl was a German-born immigrant who came to America in 1838. He studied to become an engineer, and in 1845 he won a U.S patent for a flange-bending machine for ironwork. In 1856, he was well enough established to win a contract from New York City to build a cast-iron "fire watch tower" in Manhattan's Mount Morris (now Marcus Garvey) Park. In an age before fire alarm boxes, volunteer fire fighters watched the city from towers, ringing a bell to sound the alarm.

But Kroehl's real interests lay underwater. At the same time that he was engaged in his fire tower project, Kroehl and his business partner, Peter Husted, were contracted by the City of New York to remove part of Diamond Reef, near Governor's Island in the East River, as it was a hazard to navigation. According to the *Scientific American* of August 5, 1856, "Messrs. Husted & Kroehl" were blasting to remove 6 feet of depth on the 300-foot reef. "Large tin canisters attached to the lower ends of strong pointed stakes, are sunk to rest on the face of the reef, and are discharged with a galvanic battery." It was on this job that Kroehl became interested in diving. In 1858, Husted and Kroehl hired a new partner, Van Buren Ryerson, who had just built a pressurized diving bell that he called Submarine Explorer. Eight years later, Kroehl used the basic principle of Ryerson's bell to build the world's most sophisticated submarine.

With the outbreak of Civil War in April 1861, Julius Kroehl was the first inventor to write to the U.S. Navy to offer a submarine that could be used to enter Southern ports and destroy "obstacles" from below. His "cigar-shaped" design was not adopted, as the Union Navy ended up with another submarine, courtesy of a daring demonstration by French inventor Brutus de Villeroi, who had built a 32-foot submersible and tested it on the Delaware River. Chased by the harbor police and captured when it ran aground, de Villeroi's submarine attracted the attention of the press and the Navy, which ended up buying it and commissioning it as USS *Alligator*. Never successful and plagued by problems, the tiny craft ended up being cast adrift off Cape Hatteras in a storm on April 2, 1863, and was lost.

Meanwhile, Julius Kroehl, his proposal for a submarine rejected, joined the war effort as an expert in underwater explosives. He worked to clear the way for the Union assault up the Mississippi River, which the Confederates had blocked. On the night of April 10, 1862, "Mr. Kroehl went with a party in two boats to make a close reconnaissance of the hulks, rafts and chains below the forts. On the strength of his report plans were made by Admiral Porter and him for the destruction of the obstructions." Unfortunately, the attempt, made with electrically detonated charges, was "not completely successful," but the Union fleet did successfully navigate the river.

In recognition of this and other efforts, the Navy promoted Kroehl to Acting Volunteer Lieutenant and in January 1863 assigned him to remove the Confederate rafts blocking the Yazoo and Red rivers. Just then, Kroehl heard that a Confederate "torpedo" had sunk the ironclad gunboat *Cairo* on the Yazoo. Ironically, the commander of *Cairo*, Thomas Oliver Selfridge, had served as captain of the ill-fated submarine *Alligator*. A colleague sarcastically noted that Selfridge "found two torpedoes and removed them by placing his vessel over them."

A month after the fall of Vicksburg on July 4, 1863, Kroehl was discharged with malaria. During his convalescence, he planned a submarine that could descend into the water and there, on the bottom, send out a diver to disarm torpedoes and set charges of his own, beyond the reach of Confederate guns. His submarine would be a perfect counter to the South's own program of underwater warfare. Kroehl needed backers and money to build his sub, knowing full well from experience that the Navy would not accept plans alone and authorize funds to build an experimental craft. He found his backers in the Pacific Pearl Company, which was interested in exploiting the pearl beds off Panama.

"Discovered" by Spanish conquistadors who seized examples from the natives of the isthmus in the early sixteenth century, Panama's pearls had been the source of many fortunes in the succeeding centuries. But as divers cleaned out the shallower beds, that left only the ones in deeper water. Using a submarine was one way to tap into the hitherto inaccessible riches in the sea off Panama. Kroehl appealed, doubtless, more to the profit motive of his employers than to their patriotism. If the

Navy wouldn't buy the submarine, they could always take it to Panama and use it to rake up pearls off the seabed.

Work on the submarine began in early 1864. On June 14, Kroehl wrote to the Navy's Chief of the Bureau of Yards and Docks to press his case: "I sent you last week a pamphlet issued by the Pacific Pearl Company, for whom I am now building a submarine boat... In the operations against some of the rebel forts and harbors I have no doubt the Navy Department will require submarine boats, and I think it would be advisable to bring this to the attention of the Honorable Gideon Wells, and have the plans examined by a proper board." The following day, he received a reply. The plans were interesting, and he should send them to the Secretary of the Navy. Kroehl did so, and on June 18, just four days later, was told by Secretary Welles to present his plans to W.W. Wood, the Chief Engineer of the United States Navy.

Sitting in a folder in the National Archives is Wood's meticulous eighteen-page report on Kroehl's submarine, written after he toured the vessel as it was being built in New York. Wood also drew up a large plan of the submarine—a sheet of paper that rolls out 3 feet—fully one-twelfth of the length of the actual craft. Reading the report and perusing the plan, it is obvious that the submarine on the beach at Isla San Telmo is the same vessel. The chamber on the top, according to Wood, was the "compressed air chamber... it has a semi-elliptic form and is built of two shells of best boiler iron ½ inch thick, the different pieces lapping 4 inches are double riveted with ¾ inch countersink rivets, and braced with ribs of 3 ½" × 3" × ½" angle iron and 1 inch braces." That kind of intricate detail is invaluable to an archeologist.

Wood's report goes on to explain how a compressor inside the submarine was used to build up sufficient pressure to not only clear the upper ballast chamber to enable the submarine to rise but also to pressurize the hull to allow the unbolting of bottom plates so that the crew could reach into the water and harvest pearls—or to serve the purposes of war. This self-propelled "lock out" dive chamber—which many historians think is an innovation of the twentieth century—was designed and built in 1865. Wood's report concluded by enthusing that "the uses

A *section drawing of* Sub Marine Explorer *from the* Journal of the American Society of Naval Engineers, 1902. *James P. Delgado.*

to which a boat...in Naval Warfare, would be the removal of submerged obstructions in the channels of rivers and harbors. Approaching hostile fleets at anchor and destroying them by attaching torpedoes to their bottoms and exploding such localities as are commanded and covered by the guns of an enemy. The importance of a successful application of the principles involved in such a vessel for such purposes are of much importance and can not be too highly estimated." Julius Kroehl couldn't have said it better himself. It is a glowing endorsement, and I wonder what happened. Why didn't the Navy buy the sub?

Part of the answer is that the submarine was not yet finished. Another is that the war was winding down. Most of the major ports of the South had fallen, the Mississippi was secured and the collapse of the Confederacy was just a few months away. With the end of the war imminent, the Navy Department probably viewed Kroehl's submarine, brilliant though it was, as coming a bit too late. A genius, yes, an engineering breakthrough, yes. But the time for such an invention to help "win the war" had passed.

And so the Union Navy, which had already invested much in the unfortunate sub *Alligator,* declined Kroehl's offer. But there were still pearls to harvest in Panama, and the Pacific Pearl Company used Wood's letter as an endorsement, publishing it in a promotional pamphlet to sell stocks in 1865. They mentioned it again in an article in the May 31, 1866, edition of the *New York Times:*

Yesterday afternoon there was a private trial of the Pacific Pearl Company's *Sub Marine Explorer*, in the dock foot of North third-street, Eastern District...Julius H. Kroehl, engineer, with Frederick Michaels, August Getz and John Tanner, entered the explorer through her man-hole, which being finally closed and the signal given the boat was submerged, and for an hour and a half she traversed the bed of the dock. During the submersion the friends of those onboard the boat exhibited considerable anxiety for their safety, but then at last when she rose to the surface...they gave vent to their feelings in repeated cheers. These were again and again repeated, when the engineer held up a pail of mud which he had gathered at the bottom of the dock, showing conclusively the success of the experiment.

But even if the end of the war had not ended the Navy's interest in submarines, then the failure of its own great wartime experiment, the submarine *Intelligent Whale*, decisively closed the door. After three years of work, the shipyard finally launched *Intelligent Whale* just a month before Kroehl's highly publicized demonstration of *Sub Marine Explorer*. Unlike Kroehl's boat, *Intelligent Whale* was not a success, reportedly killing dozens of crewmen in various trials and tests. Renamed "Disastrous Jonah" by wags, *Intelligent Whale* ended her days laid up, unused. Thirty-one years would pass before the U.S. Navy acquired another submarine, in 1897. Another seventeen years would pass until a submarine again sank an enemy vessel in wartime, when the German *U-21* sent HMS *Kent* to the bottom of the North Sea, an act that heralded the opening of a new and far deadlier campaign of submarine warfare and that changed the way war was fought at sea.

TO PANAMA AND OBLIVION

After the demonstrations of Kroehl's submarine, both he and his invention left New York. Sometime that fall, or early the following year, the Pacific Pearl Company shipped *Sub Marine Explorer* to the Pacific coast of Panama. There, it worked for a while, according to a report published in a company prospectus published in or around 1867, and a 1902 article reported that at Panama, *Sub Marine Explorer* "was successfully used, and Mr. Kroehl said, the divers employed in the boat enjoyed better health than the other divers ... The bottom of the boat could be opened or closed as desired. When exploring in considerable depths the bottom was closed, to save the crew from the heavy pressures." But at some stage the submarine was abandoned, perhaps as early as the fall of 1869. Kroehl was not around then. He had died of the "fever" in Panama two years earlier.

Why there and when? Just off the beach where *Explorer* now rests is a large pearl bed in about 100 feet of water, and it was there that the submarine was working in 1869 in the last known contemporary mention in print. Perhaps *Explorer* was left on the beach after something broke, or perhaps the pearl bed was fished out. Perhaps, without Julius Kroehl around to care for his invention, no one else could. We may never know. Someone did try to salvage the wreck at some distant time, because the conning tower is wrapped with wire cable, and the tower and the hull around it are slightly deformed from torquing from an offshore direction, as if someone had tried to pull it off the beach and failed. And some features are missing from the submarine—the propeller and the conning tower hatch are gone, stripped for salvage.

Julius Kroehl's *Sub Marine Explorer*, now abandoned on a little-known island off Panama, was the only successful "Union" Civil War submarine, the brainchild of an undersea pioneer whose service in the war was relegated, along with his magnificent invention, to the backwaters of history. History is often dominated by "what if?" What if Kroehl had invented his submarine earlier and sent it into combat against the Confederacy? What if, on one of those missions, *Sub Marine Explorer* had sunk, carrying vessel and crew into the honored halls of wartime sacrifice like *H.L. Hunley?* There would have been two Civil War submarines, forever linked in history. But events didn't work that way, and *Sub Marine Explorer* had a more peaceful career, far from home, where the memory of her location and identity faded with time, to be resurrected only by chance by a vacationing archeologist.

— CONCLUSION —

WHAT'S NEXT?

What's next? It's a big ocean full of wrecks, and as I write this, *The Sea Hunters* team is planning to return to Chile to dive on the flagship of the Chilean Navy, *Esmeralda*, sunk in combat during the War of the Pacific in 1879. That war, between Chile and Peru, was a bloody struggle largely forgotten by the English-speaking world. It is not forgotten in South America. The captain of *Esmeralda*, Arturo Prat, is buried in a place of honor on Valparaiso's harbor front, and his name lives on many buildings and streets. Prat died when his wooden warship was rammed by the Peruvian ironclad monitor *Huascar*. He leapt from the decks of his sinking ship onto the prow of *Huascar* to inspire his men to follow him and try to take the Peruvian ship. Instead, he was shot down and died, sword in hand, a hero honored by both sides. *Esmeralda*'s wooden hulk is still intact and holds the bones of many of her dead sailors more than a century after the battle.

We will also journey to the coast of Vietnam to explore the history-rich waters off the ancient city of Hoi An. Located at the silted mouth of a river, Hoi An was a port of the seafaring Cham empire. The Cham, an Indo-Asiatic people, were traders who built magnificent cities of brick, which rivaled nearby Angkor Wat, up the rivers in the heart of Southeast Asia. The Cham empire ultimately fell in the late fifteenth century as a result of warfare with the people of Angkor and the rising power of the Da Viet people of the North, but Hoi An lived on. In the sixteenth century, Hoi An served as Vietnam's major port. Centuries later, trade shifted to a nearby bay just off the port city of Danang.

As a result of the centuries of trade, storms and warfare, the waters off Hoi An and Danang are filled with shipwrecks. Medieval wrecks laden with trade goods—mostly pottery—have been discovered by fishermen. Unfortunately, some of the wrecks have been salvaged and their artifacts sold to feed the voracious international antiquities market. Our trip to Vietnam has more than one purpose. We will work on the wrecks of Hoi An to find a suitable site for scientific excavation so that its contents and story can form the basis of a new maritime museum there. Operated by the Vietnamese, the new museum, we hope, will become a centre for Vietnamese archeologists to work to study and recover their country's rich underwater heritage, and not let it be taken away and sold. Our partner in this new venture is George Belcher, the discoverer of the U.S. brig *Somers*, who has created the Asia Maritime Foundation to fund the museum and the training of Vietnamese archeologists.

Then we're off to the coast of Normandy, where, in June 1944, the greatest amphibious invasion in the history of warfare breached the walls of Hitler's Fortress Europa on D-Day. Colleagues from the U.S. Navy and Texas A&M University's Institute of Nautical Archeology have surveyed the wrecks of D-Day's Omaha beach, site of the American landings. We'll go there to complete the survey at Juno beach, where Canadian troops poured ashore under heavy fire on "the longest day." Earlier surveys have found sunken ships, landing craft and tanks just off shore, and we expect to find even more—fallen warriors who never made it to the beach sixty years ago, in a battle that literally changed the face of history. All the more significant is the fact that in the waters of the English Channel, those remnants of battle lie exactly where they fell, on a raw submerged landscape of war that is very different from the manicured lawns, memorials and museums that commemorate D-Day ashore.

In the years to come, there will be many more adventures and many more encounters with shipwrecks and the relics of the events that shaped the world we live in. But as I write, I think of one particular dive with *The Sea Hunters*. We were surveying the depths of Lake Ontario, on the Canadian side near Point Petre, a graveyard of ships. It is also the site of a 1950s Canadian missile range, where the rocket-launched Avro Arrow test models we were hunting for had been shot out over the lake. A sonar survey of the lake bed by Mike Fletcher's friend, Dave Gartshore, had discovered a rocket and a two-masted wreck.

The rocket turned out to be the remains of a Canadian-built missile used to test launch a Velvet Glove air-to-air missile, the weapon being considered for use in the Avro Arrow. This remnant of testing at the Picton range, while an indirect link to the Avro Arrow program, was not what we had come looking for. Them's the breaks in sea hunting. Sometimes you find what you seek, and sometimes you don't.

The unexpected treasure is the shipwreck, which turns out to be a completely intact two-masted schooner. She lies nearly upright and the masts rise out of the deck to reach for the surface, just like *Vrouw Maria*'s. Unlike that fabled Finnish shipwreck, however, this mystery schooner as yet has no name. But we can say, based on the equipment and the way it is built, that it seems to date to just around 1865, and may have sunk within twenty years of its launch. It may even be older, built around 1850 and updated, as some of its fittings are from that earlier time.

The quarterdeck at the stern served as the roof for a small cabin, probably the captain's. The sliding hatch that led below is gone, but looking inside, we see the top of a small iron stove and scattered furniture. Close by, the ship's wooden wheel sits waiting for a helmsman. The cargo hatches gape open, their wooden covers lying off to one side. The schooner was heavily loaded with coal, which indicates that she had loaded the cargo on the American side at Oswego, New York, the principal coal port on the lake in the mid-nineteenth century.

A forensic look at this intact wreck tells us even more. This ship sank suddenly, probably in a winter storm. Fresh water, driven by the wind, will quickly ice up decks, rigging and masts, weighing down a vessel. The position of the gaffs, boom and mast hoops suggests that the schooner was scudding along the lake on a storm-tossed crossing with very little sail set—"close reefed" in sailor parlance—and perhaps, in a gale or a snowstorm, with very little visibility. The location of the wreck, very close to shore, but turned away from it, suggests that the crew suddenly realized that they were driving onto shore. Not surprisingly, the rudder is angled sharply to starboard, literally stopped in time in the middle of an incomplete turn. Experienced mariners would turn about and head back out to deeper water, perhaps to drop anchor and ride out the storm. The anchors do look as if the crew was in the midst of trying to drop them when the ship sank. The davits for the ship's boat are empty at the stern, indicating the boat may have been launched; but, in heavy seas, it was probably carried away. Then schooner slipped beneath the waves, leaving the sailors suddenly alone in the cold dark water, struggling until their thick clothing and heavy boots pulled them under.

We don't know the name of this ship or when she sank. Perhaps, based on our discoveries, researchers will ultimately learn what it is we found and perhaps just what happened. This wreck and its story will not rewrite history or enlarge our understanding of the past, but they serve to remind us that when we go into tombs, dig in the ground or dive into the sea, what we are really seeking is a connection to everyday people whose experiences and lives make up the rich fabric of history. That's why we keep on exploring.

BIBLIOGRAPHY

BOOKS

Ahlström, Christian. *Looking for Leads: Shipwrecks of the Past Revealed by Contemporary Documents and the Archeological Record.* Helsinki: Finnish Academy of Science and Letters, 1997.

———. *Viestejä syvyyksien sylistä.* Hämeenlinna: Karisto Oy, 2000.

Ballard, Robert D. *The Discovery of the Titanic.* New York: Warner Books Inc., 1988.

———. *Graveyards of the Pacific: From Pearl Harbor to Bikini Atoll.* Washington, D.C.: National Geographic, 2001.

Barry, T.A., and B.A. Patten. *Men and Memories of San Francisco, in the "Spring of '50."* San Francisco: A.L. Bancroft, 1872.

Bass, George F., ed. *Ships and Shipwrecks of the Americas.* London and New York: Thames and Hudson, 1988.

Bassi, Maria Teresa Parker de. *Kreuzer Dresden: Odyssee ohne Wiederkehr.* Herford: Koehlers Verlagsgesellschaft mbH, 1993.

Bearss, Edwin C. *Hardluck Ironclad. The Sinking and Salvage of the Cairo.* Baton Rouge: Louisiana State University Press, 1980.

Beesley, Lawrence. *The Loss of the S.S. Titanic.* Boston: Houghton Mifflin Company, 1912.

Benemann, William, ed. *A Year of Mud & Gold: San Francisco in Letters and Diaries, 1849–1850.* Lincoln & London: University of Nebraska Press, 1999.

Bennett, Geoffrey. *Naval Battles of the First World War.* New York: Penguin, 2002.

Béon, Yves. *Planet Dora: A Memoir of the Holocaust and the Birth of the Space Age.* Boulder, Colorado: Westview Press, 1997.

Bound, Mensun, ed. *Excavating Ships of War.* Oswestry, Shropshire, England: Anthony Nelson Ltd., 1998.

Brown, John. *The North-West Passage and the Plans for the Search for Sir John Franklin, with sequel.* London: E. Stanford, 1860.

Carrell, Toni, ed. Submerged Cultural Resources Inventory: Portions of Point Reyes National Seashore and Point Reyes–Farallon Islands National Marine Sanctuary. Submerged Resources Center Professional Report No. 3. Santa Fe, NM: National Park Service, 1984.

Conlan, Thomas D., trans. *In Little Need of Divine Intervention: Takezaki Suenaga's Scrolls of the Mongol Invasions of Japan.* Ithaca, New York: Cornell University, 2001.

Cussler, Clive, and Craig Dirgo. *The Sea Hunters: True Adventures with Famous Shipwrecks.* New York: Simon and Schuster, 1996.

———. *The Sea Hunters II: More True Adventures with Famous Shipwrecks.* New York: G.P. Putnam, 2002.

Delgado, James P., ed. *The Log of Apollo: Joseph Perkins Beach's Journal of the Voyage of the Ship Apollo from New York to San Francisco, 1849.* San Francisco: Book Club of California, 1984.

———. *To California By Sea: A Maritime History of the California Gold Rush.* Columbia: University of South Carolina Press, 1990.

———, *Ghost Fleet: The Sunken Ships of Bikini Atoll.* Honolulu: University of Hawaii Press, 1996.

———, ed. *British Museum Encyclopaedia of Underwater and Maritime Archeology.* London: British Museum Press, 1997.

———. *Across the Top of the World: The Quest for the Northwest Passage.* Vancouver and Toronto: Douglas and McIntyre/New York: Checkmark Books, 1999.

———. *Lost Warships: An Archeological Tour of War at Sea.* Vancouver and Toronto: Douglas and McIntyre/New York: Facts on File/London: Conway Maritime Press, 2001.

Delgado, James P., and J. Candace Clifford. *Great American Ships.* Washington, D.C.: Preservation Press, 1991.

Delgado, James P., and Tom Freeman. *Pearl Harbor Recalled: New Images of the Day of Infamy.* Annapolis: Naval Institute Press, 1991.

Delgado, James P., and Stephen A. Haller. *Shipwrecks at the Golden Gate.* San Francisco: Lexikos, 1989.

Fairburn, William Armstrong. *Merchant Sail.* Center Lovell, Maine: Higginson Book Company, 1955.

Gilens, Alvin. *Discovery and Despair: Dimensions of Dora.* Berlin: Westkreuz-Verlag, 1995.

Gould, Richard A. *Archeology and the Social History of Ships.* New York: Cambridge University Press, 2000.

———, ed. *Shipwreck Anthropology*. Albuquerque, New Mexico: University of New Mexico Press/School of American Research, 1983.

Gracie, Archibald. *The Truth About the Titanic*. New York: Mitchell Kennerley, 1913.

Guttridge, Leonard F. *Mutiny: A History of Naval Insurrection*. Annapolis: Naval Institute Press, 1992.

Hayford, Harrison, ed. *The Somers Mutiny Affair: A Book of Primary Source Materials*. Englewood Cliffs, New Jersey: Prentice-Hall, 1960.

Hill, Richard. *War at Sea in the Ironclad Age*. London: Cassell & Co., 2000.

Hobson, Richmond Pearson. *The Sinking of the 'Merrimac': A Personal Narrative of the Adventure in the Harbor of Santiago de Cuba, June 3, 1898 and the Subsequent Imprisonment of the Survivors*. New York: The Century Company, 1899.

Howe, Octavius T., and Frederick C. Mathews. *American Clipper Ships, 1833–1858*. Salem, Massachusetts: Marine Research Society, 1926 and 1927.

Jasper, Joy, James P. Delgado and Jim Adams. *The USS Arizona*. New York: St. Martin's Press, 2001.

Kennedy, Hugh. *Mongols, Huns & Vikings*. London: Cassell & Co., 2002.

King, Benjamin, and Timothy Kutta. *Impact: The History of Germany's V-Weapons in World War II*. Rockville Center, New York: Howell Press, 1998.

Lenihan, Daniel. *Submerged: Adventures of America's Most Elite Underwater Archeology Team*. New York: Newmarket Press, 2002.

———, ed. *USS Arizona Memorial and Pearl Harbor National Historic Landmark: Submerged Cultural Resources Assessment*. Santa Fe, New Mexico: National Park Service, 1989.

Lightoller, Commander. *Titanic and Other Ships*. London: Ivor Nicholson and Watson, 1935.

Linenthal, Edward Tabor, and Robert M. Utley. *Sacred Ground: Americans and their Battlefields*. University of Illinois Press, 1991.

Lotchin, Roger W. *San Francisco, 1846–1856: From Hamlet to City*. Lincoln: University of Nebraska Press, 1974.

Lubbock, Basil. *The Down Easters, American Deep Water Sailing Ships, 1869–1929*. Glasgow: Brown, Son & Ferguson, Ltd., 1929.

McClintock, Sir F.L. *A Narrative of the Discovery of the Fate of Sir John Franklin and His Companions*. London: John Murray, 1859.

———. *The Voyage of the Fox into the Arctic Seas*. London: John Murray, 1860.

McFarland, Philip. *Sea Dangers: The Affair of the Somers*. New York: Schocken, 1987.

Matthews, Frederick C. *American Merchant Ships, 1850–1900: Series 1*. Salem, Massachusetts: Marine Research Society, 1931.

Melton, Buckner F., Jr. *A Hanging Offense: The Strange Affair of the Warship Somers*. New York: The Free Press, 2003.

Michel, Jean. *Dora,* trans. by Jennifer Kidd. New York: Holt, Rinehart & Winston, 1980.

Morris, Paul C. *American Sailing Coasters of the North Atlantic.* New York: Bonanza Books, 1979.

Murphy, Larry F., ed. *Dry Tortugas National Park Submerged Cultural Resources Assessment.* Submerged Resources Center Professional Report No. 13. Santa Fe, NM: National Park Service, 1993.

————, ed. *Submerged Cultural Resources Survey: Portions of Point Reyes National Seashore and Point Reyes-Farallon Islands National Marine Sanctuary.* Submerged Resources Center Professional Report No. 2. Santa Fe, NM: National Park Service, 1984.

Neatby, Leslie H. *Search for Franklin,* New York: Walker, 1970.

Neufeld, Michael. *The Rocket and the Reich: Peenemünde and the Coming of the Ballistic Missile Era.* Cambridge, Massachusetts: Harvard University Press, 1995.

Nicolle, David. *The Mongol Warlords.* London: Firebird Books, 1990.

Pastron, Allen G., and Eugene M. Hattori, eds. *The Hoff Store Site and Gold Rush Merchandise from San Francisco, California.* Society for Historical Archeology Special Publication Series, Number 7. Ann Arbor, Michigan: Society for Historical Archeology, 1990.

Pastron, Allen G., Jack Prichett and Marilyn Zeibarth, eds. *Behind the Seawall: Historical Archeology Along the San Francisco Waterfront,* three volumes. San Francisco: San Francisco Clean Water Program, 1980.

Ragan, Mark K. *Submarine Warfare in the Civil War.* Cambridge, Massachusetts: Da Capo, 2003.

Rossabi, Morris. *Khubilai Khan: His Life and Times.* Berkeley and Los Angeles: University of California Press, 1988.

Rosthon, Sir Arthur H *Home from the Sea.* New York. Macmillan Company, 1931.

Samuels, Peggy, and Harold Samuels. *Remembering the Maine.* Washington and London: Smithsonian Institution Press, 1995.

Sellier, André. *A History of the Dora Camp,* trans. by Stephen Wright and Susan Taponier. Chicago: Ivan R. Dee, 2003.

Semmes, Raphael. *Service Afloat and Ashore During the Mexican War.* Cincinnati: Wm. H. Moore Publishers, 1851.

Shurcliff, W.A. *Bombs at Bikini: The Official Report of Operation Crossroads.* New York: Wm. H. Wise & Co., 1947.

Souhami, Diane. *Selkirk's Island: The True and Strange Adventures of the Real Robinson Crusoe.* San Diego and New York: Harcourt, Inc., 2002.

Stick, David. *Graveyard of the Atlantic: Shipwrecks of the North Carolina Coast.* Chapel Hill: University of North Carolina Press, 1952.

Stillwell, Paul. *Battleship Arizona: An Illustrated History.* Annapolis, Maryland: Naval Institute Press, 1991)

Twitchett, Denis, and Franke, Herbert, eds., *The Cambridge History of China, Volume 6: Alien Regimes and Border States, 907–1368.* Cambridge: Cambridge University Press, 1994.

Van de Water, Frederick F. *The Captain Called It Mutiny.* New York: Ives Washburn, 1954.

Wagner, Jens-Christian. *Das KZ Mittelbau-Dora: Katalog zur historischen Ausstellung in der KZ-Gedenkstätte Mittelbau-Dora.* Göttingen: Wallstein Verlag, 2001.

Wallace, H.N. *The Navy, the Company, and Richard King: British Exploration in the Canadian Arctic, 1829–1860.* Montreal: McGill-Queen's University Press, 1980.

Weisgall, Jonathan M. *Operation Crossroads: The Atomic Tests at Bikini Atoll.* Annapolis: Naval Institute Press, 1994.

Wels, Susan. *Titanic: Legacy of the World's Greatest Ocean Liner.* New York: Time-Life Books, 1997.

Woodman, David C. *Strangers Among Us.* Montreal and Kingston: McGill-Queens University Press, 1995.

———. *Unravelling the Franklin Mystery: Inuit Testimony.* Montreal and Kingston: McGill-Queens University Press, 1997.

Woodward, Frances J. *Portrait of Jane: A Life of Lady Franklin.* London: Hodder and Stoughton, 1951.

Wright, Noel. *New Light on Franklin.* London: W.S. Cowell, 1949.

———. *Quest for Franklin.* London: Heinemann, 1959.

Yamada, Nakaba. *Ghenko: The Mongol Invasion of Japan.* London: Smith Elder, 1916.

Yamamura, Kozo. *The Cambridge History of Japan, Volume 3: Medieval Japan.* Cambridge: Cambridge University Press, 1990.

ARTICLES

Belcher, George. "The U.S. Brig *Somers.* A Shipwreck from the Mexican War," *Underwater Archaeology Proceedings from the Society for Historical Archaeology Conference, Reno, Nevada.* Ann Arbor, Michigan: Society for Historical Archaeology, 1988.

Delgado, James P. "No Longer a Buoyant Ship: Unearthing the Gold Rush Storeship *Niantic,*" *California History* 63:4 (winter 1979).

———. "What Becomes of the Old Ships? Dismantling the Gold Rush Fleet of San Francisco," *The Pacific Historian* 25:4 (winter 1981).

———. "A Gold Rush Enterprise: Samuel Ward, Charles Mersch, Adolphe Maillard and the *Niantic* Store ship," *The Huntington Library Quarterly* 44:4 (autumn 1983).

———. "Skeleton in the Sand: Documentation of the Environmentally Exposed 1856 Ship *King Philip*," in *Proceedings of the Sixteenth Annual Conference on Historical Archaeology*, ed. by Paul F. Johnston. Ann Arbor: Society for Historical Archaeology, 1985.

———. "Documentation and Identification of the Two-Masted Schooner *Neptune*," *Historical Archaeology* 20:1 (1986).

———. "Documenting the Sunken Remains of uss *Saratoga*," United States Naval Institute *Proceedings* 116:10 (October 1990).

———. "Recovering the Past of uss *Arizona*: Symbolism, Myth, and Reality," *Historical Archaeology* 26:4 (1992).

———. "Operation Crossroads," *American History Illustrated* 28:3 (May/June 1993).

———. "Rediscovering the *Somers*," *Naval History* 8:2 (March/April 1994).

———. "The Brig *Isabella*: A Hudson's Bay Company Shipwreck of 1830," *The American Neptune* 55:4 (fall 1995).

———. "The Lure of the Deep," *Archeology* 49:3 (May/June 1996).

———. "Bombshell at Bikini," *Naval History* 10:4 (July/August 1996).

———. "The Bermuda Brig *William and Ann*: Fur Trading Pioneer on the Northwest Coast of America," *Bermuda Journal of Archaeology and Maritime History* viii (1996).

———. "Arctic Ghost," *Equinox*, May 1997.

———. "Wreck Site of the U.S. Brig *Somers*," in Mensun Bound, ed. *Excavating of Ships of War*. Oswestry, Shropshire, International Maritime Archaeology Series, Anthony Nelson, 1998.

———. "Underwater Archaeology at the Dawn of the 21st Century." *Historical Archaeology* 34.4 (2000).

———. "Galvanic Ghosts," *Naval History* 14:1 (February 2000).

———. "Diving on the *Titanic*," *Archaeology* 54:1 (January/February 2001).

———. "The Gold-Rush Store Ship *Niantic*," *Maritime Life & Traditions* 13 (spring 2002).

———. "Relics of the Kamikaze," *Archaeology* 54:1 (January/February 2003).

Eliot, John E. "Bikini's Nuclear Graveyard," *National Geographic*, June 1992.

Erskine, Angus B., and Kjell-G. Kjaer. "The Arctic Ship *Fox*," *Polar Record* 33, 187 (1997).

Keenleyside, Anne, Margaret Bertulli and Henry C. Fricke. "The Final Days of the Franklin Expedition: New Skeletal Evidence," *Arctic* 50:1 (March 1997).

Lenihan, Daniel J. "The *Arizona* Revisited," *Natural History Magazine* 100:11 (November 1991).

———. "Bikini Beneath the Waves," *American History Illustrated* 28:3 (May/June 1993).

Murphy, Larry. "Preservation at Pearl Harbor," *APT Bulletin* 9:1 (1987).

Nordby, Larry V. "Modeling *Isabella:* Behavioral Linkages Between Submerged and Terrestrial Sites" in James P. Delgado, ed., *Underwater Archaeology Proceedings from the Society for Historical Archaeology.* Reno, Nevada: Society for Historical Archaeology, 1988.

Pastron, Allen G., and James P. Delgado. "Archaeological Investigations of a Mid-19th Century Shipbreaking Yard, San Francisco, California," *Historical Archaeology* 25:1 (1991).

Solnit, Rebecca. "The Rifts That Unite Us," San Francisco *Chronicle,* September 8, 2002.

ACKNOWLEDGEMENTS

My dad taught me about life and how to value people for who they are, not what they are.

Lynn Vermillion, the librarian at the California History Room at the San Jose Public Library, showed me the way to books and files from the first afternoon I asked my father to drop me off at the downtown library.

Constance "Connie" Perham, founder and curator of the New Almaden Museum, took me in as a fifty-cent-per-hour assistant at age fourteen and taught me that collecting the past meant nothing unless you could share it with others and make it relevant and exciting for them.

Ted Hinckley convinced my parents to send their precocious child not to the local community college but to university.

Tom Mulhern and Gordon Chappell of the Western Regional Office of the National Park Service, with help from Roger Kelly and Robert Cox, taught me about nominating historical resources to the National Register of Historic Places and about cultural resources management.

Allen Pastron let me join his crew at the bottom of a deep pit that had just reached the top of the hull of *William Gray*. That dig in 1979 lured me with the siren song of the sea, and the drama of a lost and buried ship now fills my archeologist's soul. My work with Allen continues and remains my touchstone.

Doug Nadeau, Golden Gate National Recreation Area's first chief of the Division of Resource Management and Planning, was the best boss that I've ever had the privilege to work for.

No-nonsense master diver Lawrence "Dutch" Bowen often said while training me, "There are bold divers, and there are old divers. There are no old bold divers." Through the years, whenever I make some mistake underwater and nearly kill myself, Dutch's basic training comes back to mind to save the day.

Dan Lenihan and Larry Murphy of the National Park Service's Submerged Resources Center Unit taught me how to dive wrecks and how to "do" underwater archeology. Their philosophical discussions over the role of anthropology in underwater and maritime archeology, as well as a strong preservationist approach to saving wrecks from the ravages of treasure hunters, also formed a solid core in my education.

William N. "Bill" Still and Gordon P. Watts, the founders of the Program in Maritime History and Underwater Research at East Carolina University.

Dave Burley, Chairman of the Department of Archeology at Simon Fraser University, picked up where Still and Watts left off to show me what else I lacked in the quest to finish school and get that Ph.D.

George Belcher introduced me to the infamous *Somers*, and later the beauty and history of Vietnam and its people. He exemplifies the concept of cool as an international man of mystery.

Edwin C. "Ed" Bearss, Chief Historian of the National Park Service, assigned me to be Project Historian on the USS *Monitor* and then hired me to head up the federal maritime preservation program as the first maritime historian for the National Park Service.

Val Casselton and Chris Rose, my editors at the *Vancouver Sun*, encourage and support my journalistic forays.

Tom Beasley and his successors as President of the Board of the Vancouver Maritime Museum took the risk in hiring a non-museum-trained bureaucrat. Through the years, they've helped me move along the path of museum manager and interpreter while giving me latitude to continue being an archeologist and sea hunter.

Werner Zehnder, Mike McDowell, Scott Fitzsimmons, Anatoly Sagalevitch and Evgeny Chernaiev introduced me to *Titanic*. Thanks to Werner and Scott, other great world adventures followed aboard Zegrahm's vessels.

Monte Markham taught me how to act on television.

John Davis, Clive Cussler, Mike Fletcher, Warren Fletcher, Marc Pike and John Rosborough, are my *Sea Hunters* family: we've shared many adventures and learned much in our quest for famous shipwrecks.

I'd also like to thank Jim Adams, Catherine "Kitty" Agegian, Christian Ahlström, David Aiken, the late Raymond Aker, Mike Anderson, Michele Aubry, Fabio Amaral, Santiago Analco, Marianne Babal, Dan Bailey, Ken Ballance, Robert D. Ballard, Carole Bartholemeaux, George Bass, the late Edward L. Beach, Judith Hudson Beattie, Owen Beattie, Lan Huang Belcher, Robert Bennett, Howard Bennink, Carlos Fitzgerald Bernal, J. Peter Bernhardt, Kathy Bequette, Nancy Binnie, Kathy Blackburn, Len Blix, Lisa Bower, Rowland T. Bowers, John Brooks, Greg Brown, John "Alan" Brown, Dave Buller, the late Charles Burdick, Burl Burlingame, Susan Buss, Stephen Canright, Nuna Cass, Bill Caswell, Robert J. Chandler, Patrick Christopher, J. Candace Clifford, Wendy Coble, Bob Cox, Todd Croteau, George Culley, Bill Curtsinger, Fran Day, Nick Dean, Nick Del Cioppo, Hugo Desch, Doug Devine, Bill Dudley, Manuel Cortés Dumas, Rob Edwards, Bill Ehorn, John Eliot, Pilar Luna Erreguereña, Angus Erskine, Richard Everett, Joe Featherston, Franklin Fisher, Leo Fonteyn, John Foster, Kevin Foster, Tom and Ann Freeman, Julie Gallo Lucero, Frank Geisel, Al Giddings, Richard Giles, Larry Gilmore, Gary Goodyear, Andrew Gottsfield, Dick Gould, Bente Jessen Graae, Rachel Grant, Lloyd Graybar, Bob Guertin, Stephen A. Haller, David Hansen, Rich Harned, Edward C. Harris, Thomas L. Hartman, Gene Hattori, Kevin Hay, Kenzo Hayashida, Bob Henderson, Gregg Herken, Torsten Hess, Kent Hiner, Eric Hiner, David Hull, Jack Hunter, Gillian Hutchinson, Steve James, Rick James, Kane Janer, Joy Waldron Jasper, Manami Ikeda, Bill Jardine, Roger Joel, Thompson Johnson, Carolyn Jones, Samuel Kahan, Gary Keep, Chester and Linda King, Kjell Kjaer, Greta Kleiner, Roger Knight, Minna Koivikko, Willi Kramer, John

Lachelt, Rebecca Lafontaine, Matias Laitenen, John Lajuan, Fernando Landeta, George Lang, Diego M. Lascano, Richard Lawrence, Thomas N. Layton, David C. Lee, Ben Levy, Santos H. Gomez Leyva, Bill Livingston, Jerry Livingston, Dave McCampbell, Michael McCaughan, Susan MacDonald, John Macdougall & family, Lee McEachern, Leonard McKay, Edward Maddison, Rebecca Magallanes, Jacques Marc, Mitch Marken, Mike Mair, Betty Marshall, Daniel Martinez, Guy Mathias, Cathy Maurer, Martin Mayer, Roger Meade, Tomas Mendizibal, Roy Mengot, Mike Messick, Bebe Midgette, Robert Mikesh, Mark Miller, Norman Y. Mineta, Mike Montieth, Greg Moore, Armando Morales, Elsy Yamina Zaldívar Morales, Torao Mozai, Ginger Muldoon, Larry E. Murphy, Mike Naab, Harry Nashon, Juan Enrique Suarez Peredo Navarette, Dave Nettell, Mark Newton, Johanna Nicholson, Jack Niedenthal, Tomoko Nishizaki, Larry Nordby, Stephen Notarianni, Mitsuhiko Ogawa, Brian O'Neill, Wayne Olival, Jerry Ostermiller, Lt. Commander Alejandro Peña, the late Ernest Peterkin, Maurice De La Pintiere, Linda Plauner, Peggy Puett, Margaret Purser, Yvonne Munro Pynisky & family, Bill Quinn, Mark Ragan, Fred Rainbow, Dave Rattay, Jeanne Rawlings, Monica Reed, John Reilly, Gil Resindez, Wilma Riklon, Juan Rique, Ash Roach, Rhonda Robichaud, Bill Robison, Omar Lopez Rodriguez, Phil Sceviour, Fred Schultz, the late Doug Scovill, Tamio Shibuta, Linda Shore, Robert Schwemmer, Clyde Smith, Leon Smith, Sheli O. Smith, Richard Stephenson, David Stick, David Stone, Robert Sumrall, Woodrow Swancutt, Hideyuki Tatsuguchi, the late Peter Throckmorton, Brian Ticehurst, Saalamaria Tikkanen, Harald Tresp, Joe Valencic, Carlos Velasquez, John Vandereedt, Alberto M. Vazquez de la Cerda, Christopher C. Wade, Jens-Christian Wagner, Mike Walker, Gary Ware, Jonathan Weisgall, William J. Whalen, James Seeley White, Mark Wilde-Ramsing, Rich Wills, Robert Woody, Wayne Yamaguchi.

I'd also like to acknowledge the following institutions and agencies: Archeo-Tec; Archives of the Russian Federation, Moscow; Armada de Chile; USS Arizona Memorial; Armada de Mexico; Bancroft Library, University of California, Berkeley; Bermuda Maritime Museum, Hamilton; Blohm + Voss Gmbh; British Museum, London; British Titanic Society;

Bundesarchiv Koblenz; California Historical Society; California Room, San Jose Public Library; Cape Cod National Seashore; Cape Hatteras National Seashore; Castillo del Morro San Pedro de la Roca, Santiago de Cuba; Central Military Archives, Poland; Channel Islands National Park; Columbia River Maritime Museum, Astoria, Oregon; Danish Arctic Station; Danish National Business Archives; Dansk Polarcenter; Deutsches Museum; KZ Dora-Mittelbau Museum; Eco Nova Productions, Ltd., Halifax; Fort Vancouver National Historical Site, Vancouver, Washington; German Naval Academy, Murwik; Glenbow Archives; Golden Gate National Recreational Area; Hakozaki Shrine, Fukuoka, Japan; Historical Archives of Hapag-Lloyd Ag., Hamburg, Germany; Honbutsuji Temple; Hudson's Bay Company Archives, Provincial Archives of Manitoba; *Illustrated London News;* Instituto Nacional de Antropologia y Historia, Mexico City; Instituto Nacional de Cultura, Panama; J. Porter Shaw Library, San Francisco Maritime National Historical Park; Knickle's Studio And Gallery, Lunenburg; Korean Heritage Library; Specialized Libraries & Archival Collections of the Archival Research Center; Kyushu Okinawa Society for Underwater Archeology; Library of Congress; Marine Base Kunitomi; Maritime Museum of the Atlantic, Halifax; Maritime Museum of British Columbia, Victoria; Maritime Museum of Finland; Mariner's Museum, Newport News, Virginia; Municipality of Juan Fernandez; Museum of Northern History; National Archives, Washington D.C.; National Archives of Canada; National Library of Canada; National Maritime Museum, Greenwich; National Museum of Greenland; National Museums & Galleries on Merseyside (Merseyside Maritime Museum); Naval Historical Center, Washington, D.C.; New Hampshire Historical Society; Norsk Sjofartsmuseum, Oslo, Norway; Oficina del Conservador de la Ciudad, Santiago de Cuba; Oficina de la Historiador de Santiago, Santiago, Cuba; Peabody Essex Museum; Peary-Macmillan Arctic Museum; Peenemünde Historical Technical Information Center; Perpetual Motion Films; Peter Tamm Collection; Private Collection Bornemann; Private Collection Schmalz; Public Archives of Nova Scotia, Macaskill Collection; Qeqertarsuaq Museum; Royal Canadian Mounted Police Archives; Royal

Naval Museum; Royal Navy Submarine Museum Photography Archive; Royal Air Force Museum, Hendon; Scott Polar Research Institute, Cambridge; Shipwreck Search Vessel *Ocean Venture;* Southampton City Cultural Services; Takashima Town Board of Education; TV Latina, Havana, Cuba; Titanic Historical Society; Ulster Folk and Transport Museum; Underwater Archeological Society of British Columbia; U.S. Coast Guard; National Motor Lifeboat School, Cape Disappointment, Washington; United States Holocaust Memorial Museum; U.S. Naval Institute; University of Liverpool Library; University of Southern California; W.B. and M.H. Chung Library of the Vancouver Maritime Museum; War in the Pacific National Historical Park; Wells Fargo Bank History Department, San Francisco; Wilmington Institute Library; Zegrahm Expeditions.

My wife, Ann Goodhart, encouraged and supported this book, as she always does. My friend and publisher Scott McIntyre agreed to do yet another work for me, bless his soul. This book benefited greatly from the skilled editorial hand of Saeko Usukawa, and the design and layout of Peter Cocking and Ingrid Paulson.

Any errors or omissions are my sole responsibility.

INDEX

References to captions and/or images are in *italic type*.